Postcard History Series

Around Middlebury

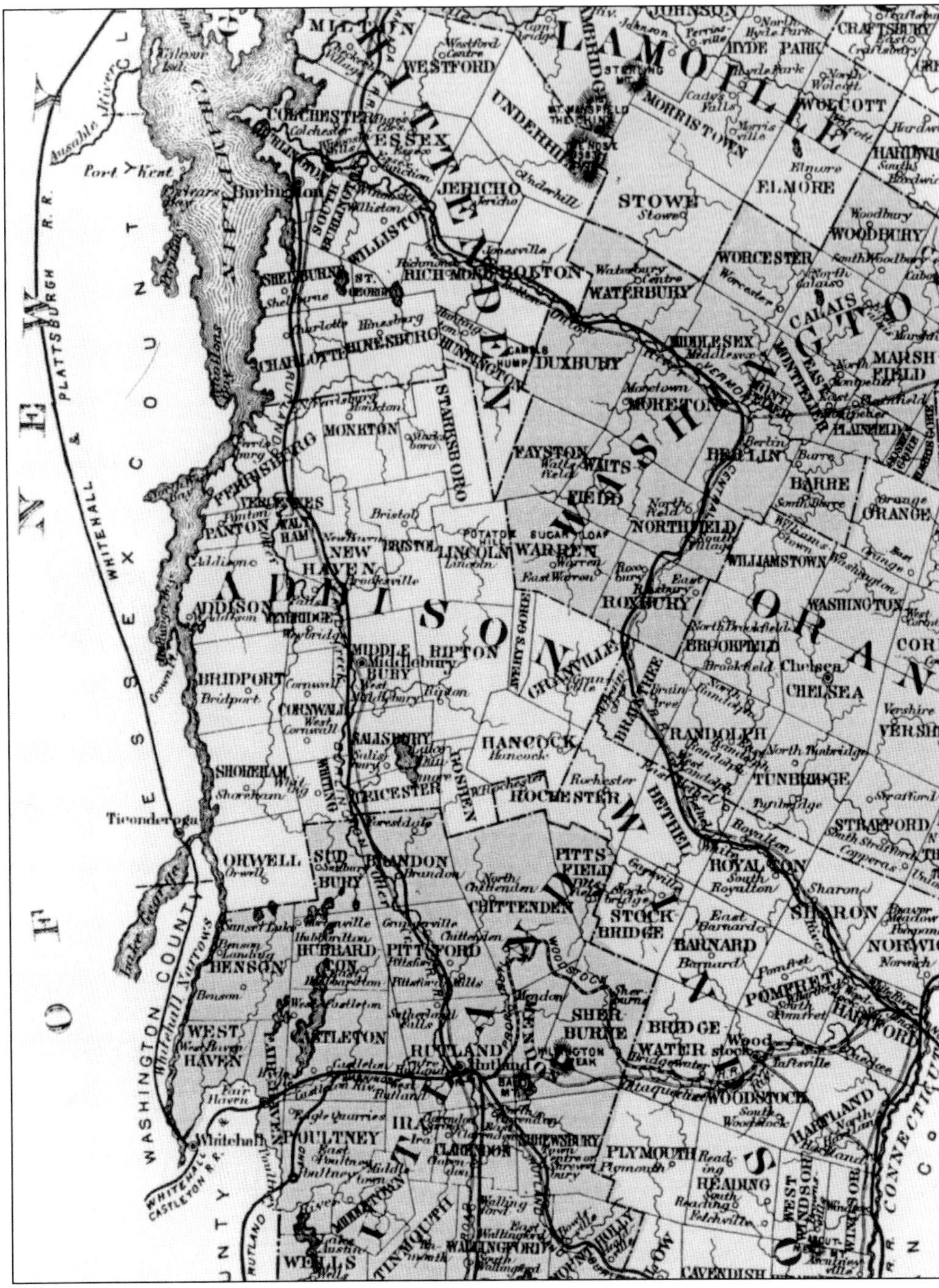

Addison County, shown here in a section of the 1871 *Beers Atlas of Addison County*, is located in the middle of western Vermont, stretching from Lake Champlain to the Green Mountains. Since 1790, Middlebury has been the county seat of Addison County. Settled soon after the Revolutionary War, Addison County has some of the most productive agricultural land in the Northeast and prospered with the expansion of the new nation. Each of the periods of development has left a lasting visual mark on the structures and institutions of the County.

POSTCARD HISTORY SERIES

Around Middlebury

Robert E. Zaremba and Danielle R. Jeanloz

ARCADIA PUBLISHING

ISBN 978-0-7385-0449-0

Published by Arcadia Publishing
Charleston, South Carolina

Printed in the United States of America

Library of Congress Control Number: 00104057

For all general information contact Arcadia Publishing at:
Telephone 843-853-2070
Fax 843-853-0044
E-mail sales@arcadiapublishing.com
For customer service and orders:
Toll-Free 1-888-313-2665

Visit us on the Internet at www.arcadiapublishing.com

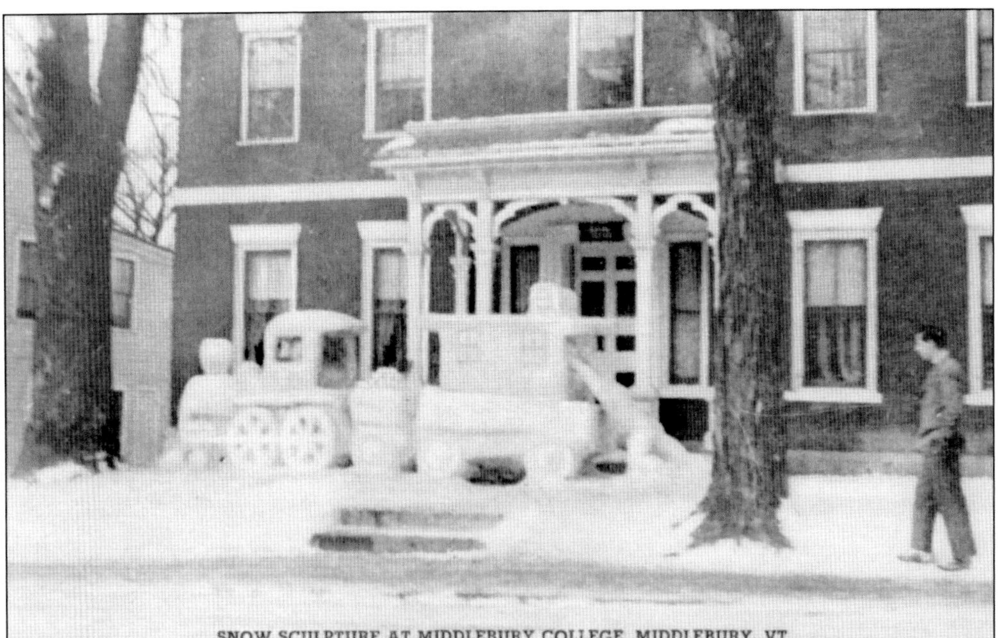

Middlebury College Winter Carnival is an energizing break near the end of the long, cold Vermont winter. The carnival is held in late February and includes intercollegiate sport events as well as an ice sculpture competition among fraternities. Many of the ice sculptures are detailed and elaborate, such as this train, shown in a postcard from the 1940s.

Contents

Introduction

In 1905, when postcards of Middlebury first began to appear, the town center had a new and modern look. Middlebury emerged from the 19th century with a very different appearance from 100 or even 25 years earlier. The streets were only recently paved. The second stage of the Battell Block was new, with the signature tower at its corner. The dignified stone bridge over Otter Creek was only 11 years old. Most of the brick and stone buildings along Main Street were in place, but there were still scattered wooden commercial buildings, some of them remnants of the town before the 1891 fire and some quickly erected to replace burned buildings. The Middlebury Inn was there and was called the Addison House. The Congregational and Episcopal churches and most of the significant homes in the center of town were already old. The Addison County Fairgrounds off Court Street was a thriving center of county social life. The courthouse, town hall, Methodist church, and Beckwith Block were all relatively new. However, the Baptist church, the Middlebury National Bank, the post office, the Ilsley Library, and several of the brick commercial buildings along Main Street were not yet constructed. In 1904, only a year earlier, the Academy Building had burned.

At the college, the women's campus had not been constructed. The Field House was years from taking its dominant position along South Main Street; the Chateau, Forest Hall, Pearsons, Hepburn, and Mead Chapel were not yet built. The nearby Catholic church, long under construction, was nearing completion.

At Lake Dunmore, the Lake Dunmore House and Spring Lake House were still popular hotels. The Lake Dunmore House burned the following year and was never rebuilt. On Silver Lake above Lake Dunmore, the Silver Lake House was in its last years as a remote and beautiful retreat. There were only a few cottages along the Dunmore shore; the road was not extended along the east shore for another eight years.

The railroad frequently ran through Middlebury. The spur to Bristol was reviving town industry, and the line from Leicester Junction to Ticonderoga crossed Lake Champlain at Larrabee's Point. The railroad service provided a critical link by bringing Addison County dairy products, apples, and the production of local industry to the prosperous Hudson Valley, New York City, and Canada. Barges regularly carried goods the length of the lake and to distant points through the canal system. Steamboats still cruised between the lakeshore ports. The valley towns had grown smaller in the last 50 years, with ambitious sons and daughters leaving for the Midwest and distant California. However, the towns remained vital and agriculture continued to prosper on the fertile soils of Addison County.

During the next 30 years, the character of Middlebury, the lower Champlain Valley, and Lake Champlain itself changed dramatically. The centers of population shifted to cities. The towns grew only slightly, if at all. The resort hotels lost their importance, and new forms of recreation and tourism developed as a result of the decline of the railroad and the emergence of travel by car. The barge traffic on the lake decreased, and the steamboats disappeared entirely.

Postcards were produced by the thousands, documenting these changes. Some postcards reflected the past history of Middlebury, the college, and the surrounding towns; others proudly announced new buildings and documented current events. Postcards were made first in Europe from itinerant photographers' images. Later, local merchants created their own cards, published in Chicago, Detroit, and Boston. Real photo postcards were also popular and were produced at local photograph shops and later from a kit purchased from Kodak. These often personal images were generally made in very small quantities and are now highly prized by collectors. Gove Studio in Middlebury was a major source of town and Lake Dunmore cards. There were also stock cards created with images used in any area, with space for a town or village name to be written onto the scene or into the social message.

There are certainly well over 1,000 different postcard scenes of Middlebury and the nearby towns. Together, they constitute a colorful record of the changing character and tastes of the area. Combined with reminiscences, personal photographs, newspaper articles, and the numerous scholarly reports related to the Middlebury vicinity, postcards document an important linkage between the past and the present. This is true of most areas, but particularly true of Middlebury, which has a good measure of pride in its past and respect for its new institutions. *Around Middlebury* includes nearly 200 postcard scenes and images from a broad range of topics that reflect the experiences of Vermont, as seen from a small town outside Middlebury. The images include Middlebury's Main Street and public buildings, the college, Bread Loaf and Lake Dunmore, the nearby larger villages, and the countryside extending from Middlebury to Lake Champlain and Fort Ticonderoga.

Middlebury was, from its earliest days, an important intellectual and cultural center, set at the western edge of the Green Mountains facing toward the Lake Champlain Valley and the distant Adirondacks. Postcards document the pride and beauty of the village and surrounding areas. They are an entertaining and stimulating view of history. These cards, however, fail to capture adequately the drama and vitality of the brilliant fall colors remembered by all who have been in Middlebury in October. They cannot show the blinding whiteness of the coldest winter days, the magical lights in the trees following a severe ice storm, and the seemingly endless decline of winter and weeks of sticky mud, followed by the great variety of green in the spring. Postcards do connect our past to the present and remind us of the depth of our community structure and the traditions in which we can find comfort and inspiration.

ACKNOWLEDGMENTS

This postcard history is the work of my parents and many others who have been a part of our connection to the Middlebury area over the years. I was born in Middlebury at Porter Hospital, the son of Ted and Bea Zaremba, who owned an apple farm in Shoreham. Until I was 17, my family lived on a ridge top with dramatic views of the Adirondack high peaks and the Green Mountains. Middlebury was our "city," where we went for groceries, doctors' appointments, and shoes. My parents were both from cities—Buffalo, New York, and Worcester, Massachusetts. They both graduated from Middlebury College in the 1930s and settled to raise a family. They first lived in Middlebury and worked at the college, but owned a small farm in Shoreham with a young apple orchard next to the farm of my father's college roommate, Sanford Witherell. By the war, the family had moved full time to Shoreham, where they lived until 1967.

My parents loved Middlebury and its neighboring towns as only outsiders could. There was never a sunset with any red or orange in it that we children did not have to watch with them. We saw our share of sunrises, too, and deep snowfalls and ice storms causing power failures, when car lights turned all the trees to jewels. The college was always in the background, but less prominent in their lives and mine because the years were passing. There were old college friends who came to visit and reminisce with stories of college days. There were hikes at Bread Loaf, to Texas Falls and Moosalamoo, visits to Red and Velma Walker at Lake Dunmore, and annual visits to Fort Ticonderoga and the Revolutionary War historic sites. I can recall my dentist's office overlooking the eddy below the falls and the spray from the falls on cold winter days as we hurried across the marble bridge. I can remember the smell of new books at the Vermont Bookstore, the huge piles of shoe boxes at the Lazarus Department Store, and the strangeness of the train going under the street.

My family left Middlebury many years ago, but we children have visited one by one, keeping track of the changes. In 1986, my wife, Danielle Jeanloz, and I bought a weekend home in Benson, and I renewed my connection to Middlebury as a nearby town, learning the new stores and restaurants and watching the changes in the campus landscape.

We initiated *Around Middlebury* after we had written a similar book on Chatham, Massachusetts, where my mother still lives. I have been collecting Middlebury postcards for only three years and have been amazed by their abundance and diversity. I had figured that there would be a need for such a book as we had written for Chatham, documenting local buildings and changes in the town scenes. It was not long before I discovered that Middlebury history is far better documented than our beautiful tourist town on the Cape. Middlebury and its neighboring towns have a wealth of histories, documenting buildings and town events. There are numerous theses and other personal projects focused on the full range of cultural and social issues that have made Middlebury and its neighboring towns what they are today. We have used these works extensively in this project and want to note our particular admiration for the Andres *Walking History of Middlebury*, the *Historic Architecture of Addison County* book, the Lake Dunmore, Salisbury, and Otter Creek books by James and Max Petersen, *At Home in Vermont: A Middlebury Album* by Nancy Graaf, and the remarkable recent work by Bain on the college. The county is truly lucky to have strong historical societies in apparently all towns and active research and archival facilities.

Special thanks go to Bob Cushman and Dick Hubbard, who were willing to discuss Middlebury history and to share their stories with me. And thanks to Bill Powers, whose interest and perseverance for accumulating the visual history of Lake Dunmore and Silver Lake inspire a fellow collector, and to Gena and Mahlon Teachout, for their shared enthusiasm for postcards and local history. Thanks also to Nancy Rucker, who was willing to provide resources at the Sheldon Museum, and to the staff of the Ilsley Library, whose Vermont Collection should provide all of us who love Vermont with endless and fascinating reading. We appreciate the assistance of Dick Hubbard, Bob Cushman, Beatrice Zaremba, and Dorothea Jeanloz, who read portions of the text and made helpful suggestions for its improvement. We also thank Jeanne and Peter Bartholomew for their interest and support for this project.

While this is not a scholarly work, it is not our intention to create or perpetuate inaccuracies in local history. We have attempted to limit our discussion to good, solid information. We are aware that there are likely to be errors in content and take full responsibility, seeking correction when appropriate.

I have a long and happy attachment to the Shoreham and Middlebury area. Much of what I am, as a conservation biologist, I owe to my upbringing by parents who saw history all around them and to the rich historical and natural Addison County landscape in which I spent my earliest years. It is our hope that those who have assisted in this project, in whatever way, are pleased with the result. Looking at Middlebury and Addison County (and, oh yes, Brandon) from a slight distance, it is remarkable that the long history, by U.S. standards, is so evident in the structure and details of all the communities today. Somehow, to me, this project has helped to connect Middlebury's earliest days—when there were only a few cleared openings along Otter Creek—to the vibrant towns we now know so well. The people of Addison County have found creative ways to blend past features and new needs into an optimistic way of living in this strikingly beautiful setting.

—Robert E. Zaremba, June 2000

One

OTTER CREEK AND THE MIDDLEBURY FALLS

When the first Europeans saw the Middlebury Falls and the lowlands stretching to Lake Champlain, a great forest covered the land. Travel was slow, and it was easy and dangerous to get lost. Otter Creek was the main highway into the new frontier. The longest river within Vermont, Otter Creek was used by Native Americans, explorers, early settlers, and military campaigns. Along Otter Creek and its tributaries, a series of waterfalls became the centers of settlements that have since grown into villages.

By 1905, when postcards first appeared, Otter Creek had long ceased to be the highway of western Vermont. The waterfalls were the focus of local industry and became the subject of numerous postcards. The creek itself was also a tranquil feature of many country cards.

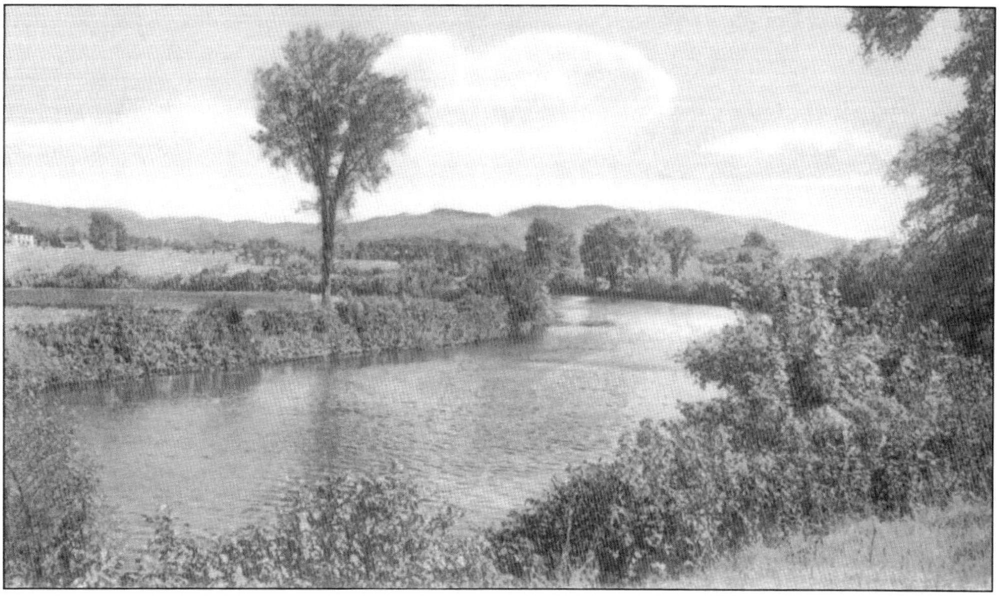

Otter Creek is a slow-moving, shallow stream that originates in southern Vermont and drains many of the western slopes of the mid-state and southern Green Mountains. Originating in the hills near Dorset, Otter Creek runs the length of both Rutland and Addison Counties. It is at the center of the Southern Lake Champlain Valley in Vermont.

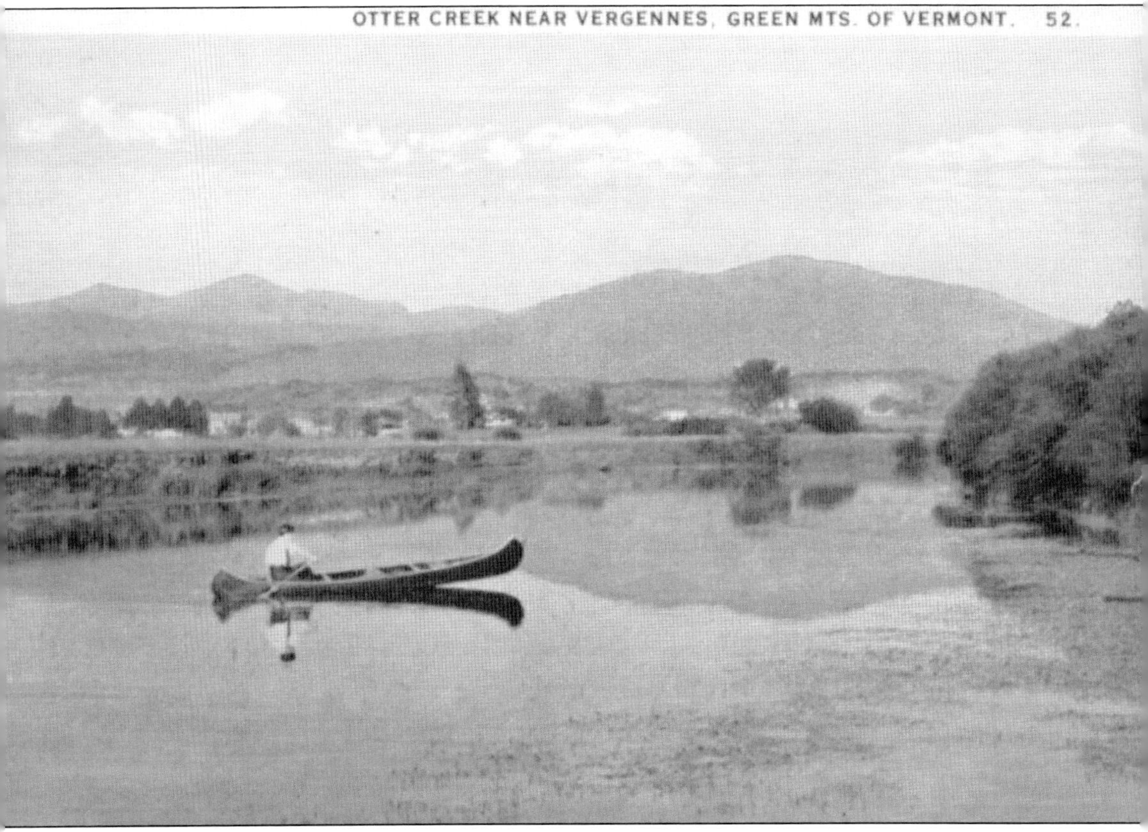

From Pittsford in Rutland County northward to its mouth in Lake Champlain at Ferrisburg, Otter Creek crosses the fertile Champlain Valley, with its low, undulating foothills of the Green Mountains. Along most of its course, the floodplain of Otter Creek is broad and flat. The creek crosses many large clay deposits and runs grayish-brown during spring floods. This postcard, produced in the early 1930s by the C.W. Hughes Company, shows an Otter Creek scene near Vergennes. The same scene was also produced by Hughes with a caption that it is located near Rutland. Those who made postcards demonstrated broad flexibility in meeting their clients' needs.

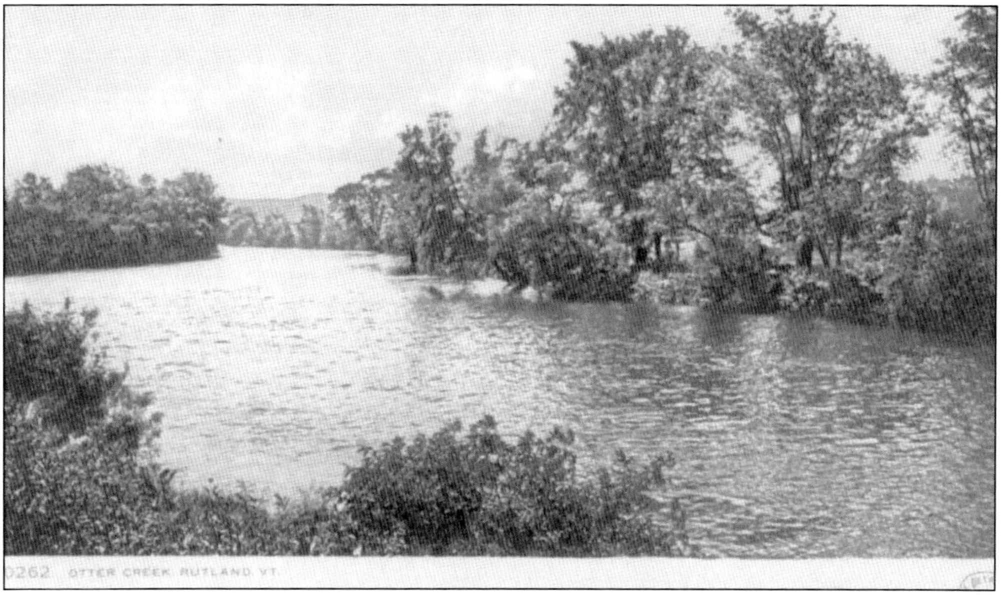

During early European exploration of western Vermont, Otter Creek was the main highway through the dense forest connecting the southern Vermont valleys to Lake Champlain and points north. The earliest roads were constructed along the creek borders but were abandoned when extensive upland sites were cleared and became easier to use for travel during spring floods.

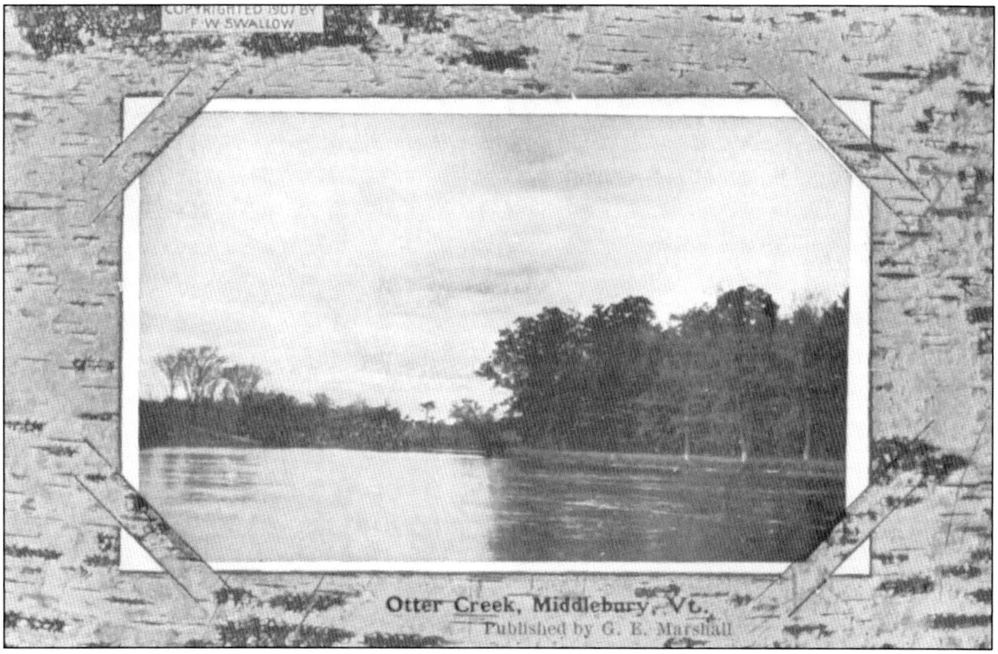

This 1907 scene, produced by the Swallow Company, shows the creek and adjacent woods set in a birch-bark frame. It was part of a series of Vermont postcards made to appear to be a part of a scrapbook.

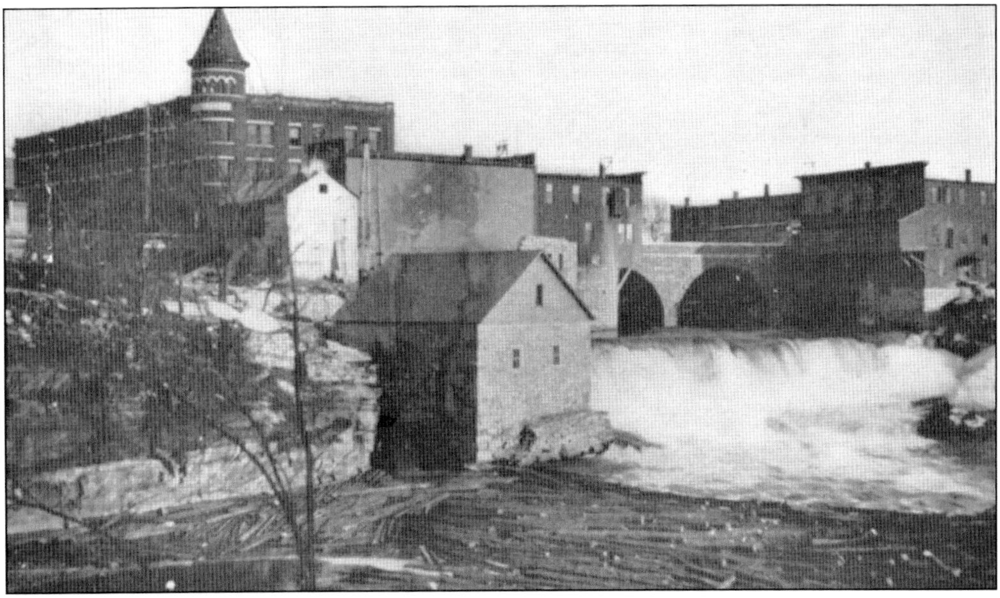

The section of Otter Creek with the Middlebury Falls was the first site of major development in the Middlebury area. During the period from 1760 to 1800, many mills were built that used waterpower from the falls. Several of these early mills were destroyed during major floods, and others burned. Mill owners were often prominent citizens who appear to have recovered quickly from seeming disaster, often with new and inventive solutions to their problems.

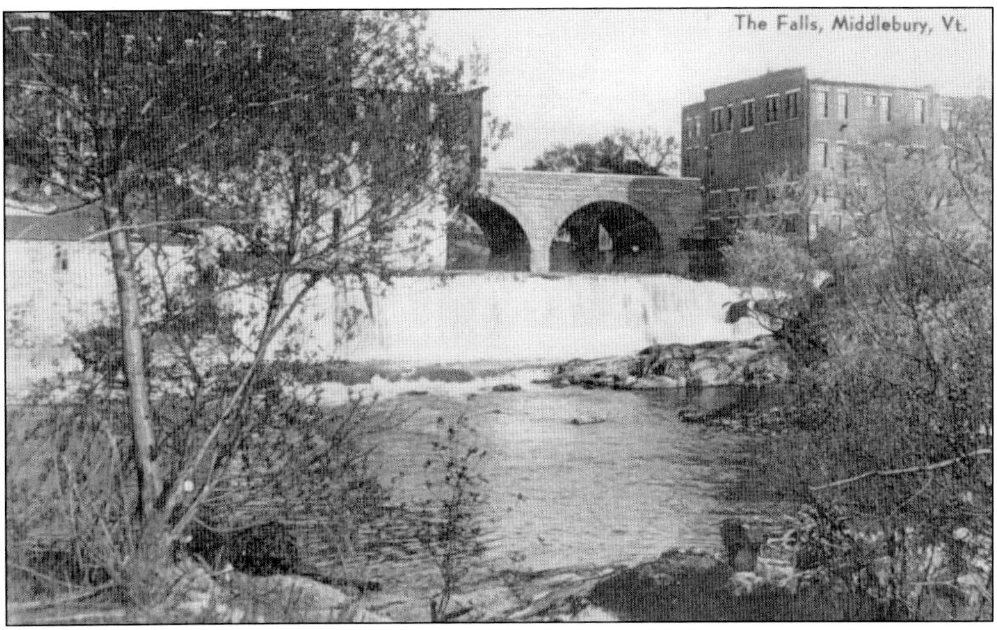

Middlebury began to develop other industries that used waterpower from the falls *c.* 1800. After the Champlain Canal opened in 1823, products from Middlebury could be transported around the affluent county towns and even to major population centers, including Troy, New York, and distant New York City. At the time of this postcard, *c.* 1925, most of the early uses of power generated from the waterfall were already in the past.

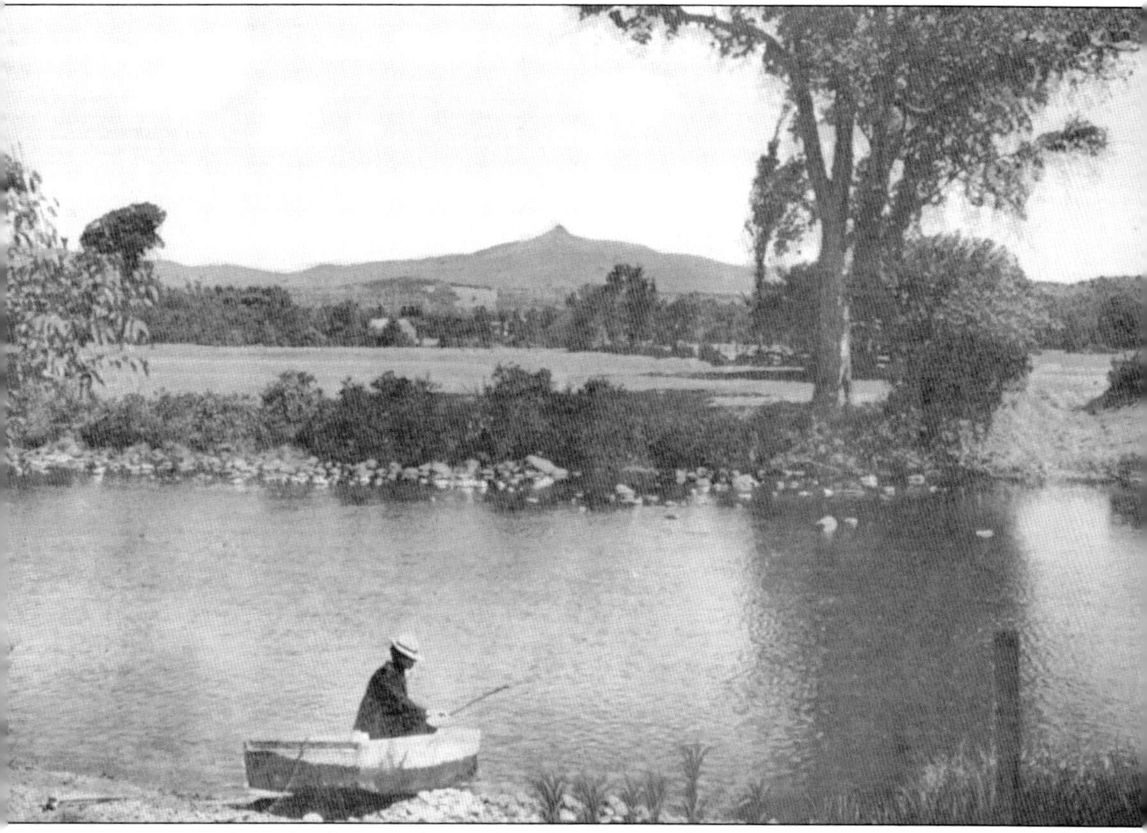

For many years, Otter Creek was a dirty and neglected part of the Middlebury landscape. Recent efforts to buffer the stream border and to decrease pollution have improved water quality and encouraged a broader range of uses of the creek. Some of the most extensive and interesting natural areas in Addison County are found associated with Otter Creek. These wetlands were difficult for farmers to drain, but trees were frequently cut during the coldest months of the winter, when ice made travel through the wet soils possible. Several parts of the forest are now protected for conservation and support numerous populations of rare plants.

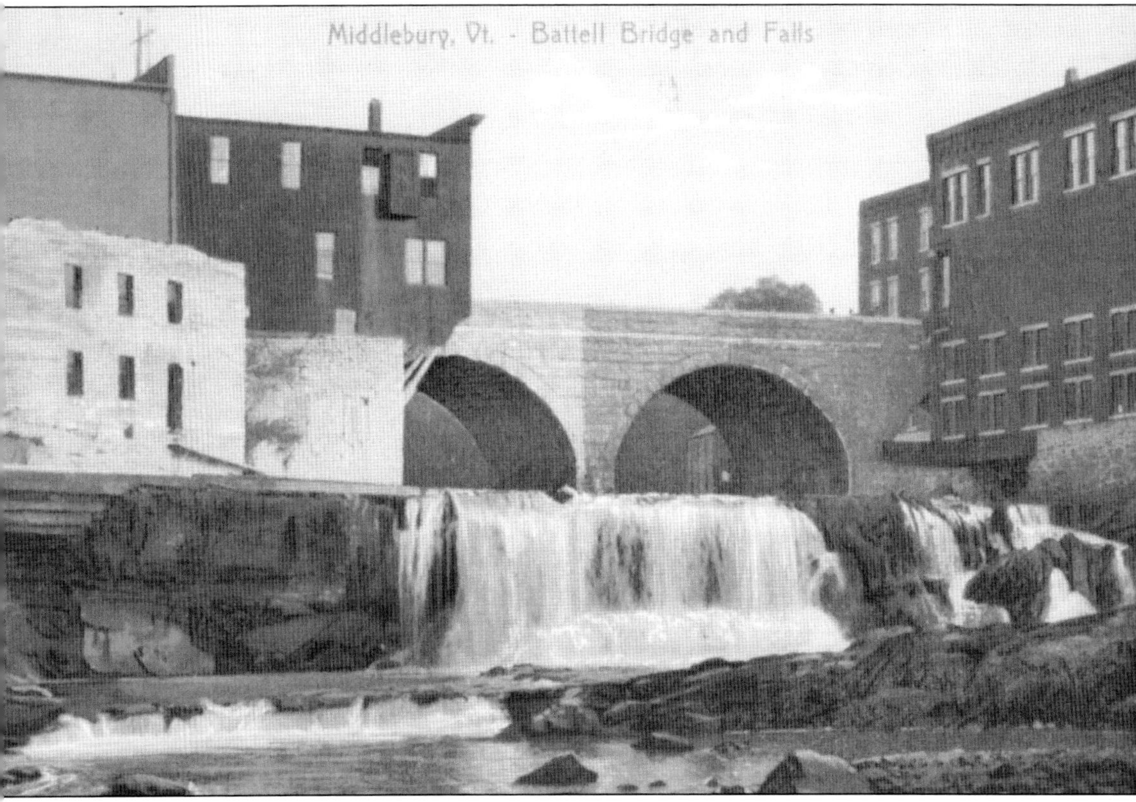

Many of the brick buildings along the west side of Main Street were constructed following the series of devastating fires that culminated in 1891, when most of the buildings immediately north of the bridge burned. Even the bridge, which was made of wood, was badly damaged and needed to be replaced. The stone building remnant on the left is a fragment of the cotton mill that once used the falls to generate power for a factory, which employed 500 people.

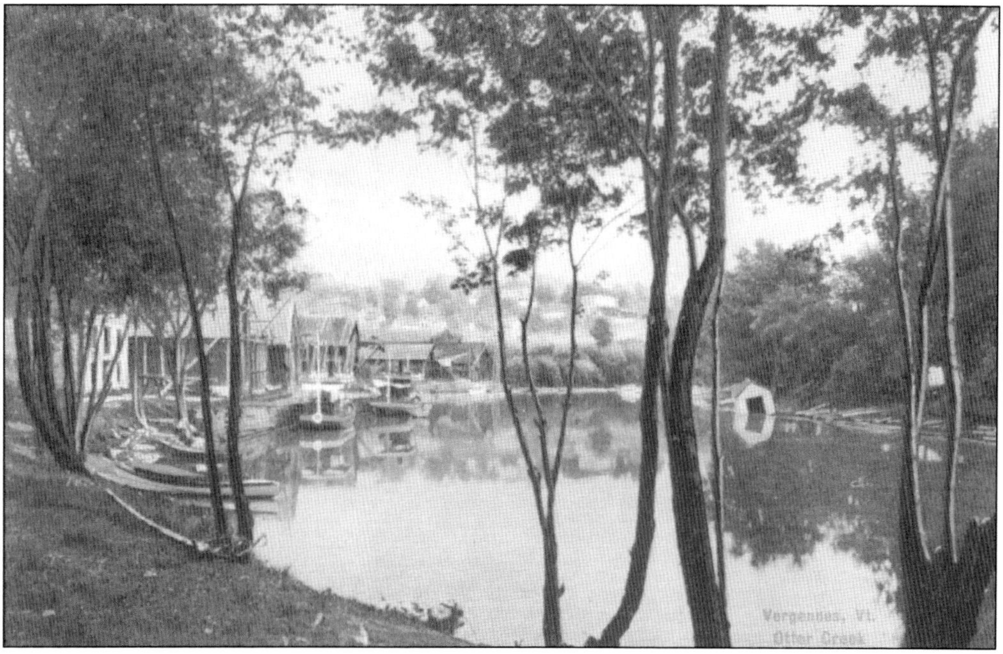

The American Champlain fleet was built along this section of Otter Creek in 1814 by Commo. Thomas MacDonough, who sailed from Otter Creek to defeat the British navy at Plattsburgh. The Vergennes shipyard later produced many of the steamboats that served Lake Champlain for nearly 100 years.

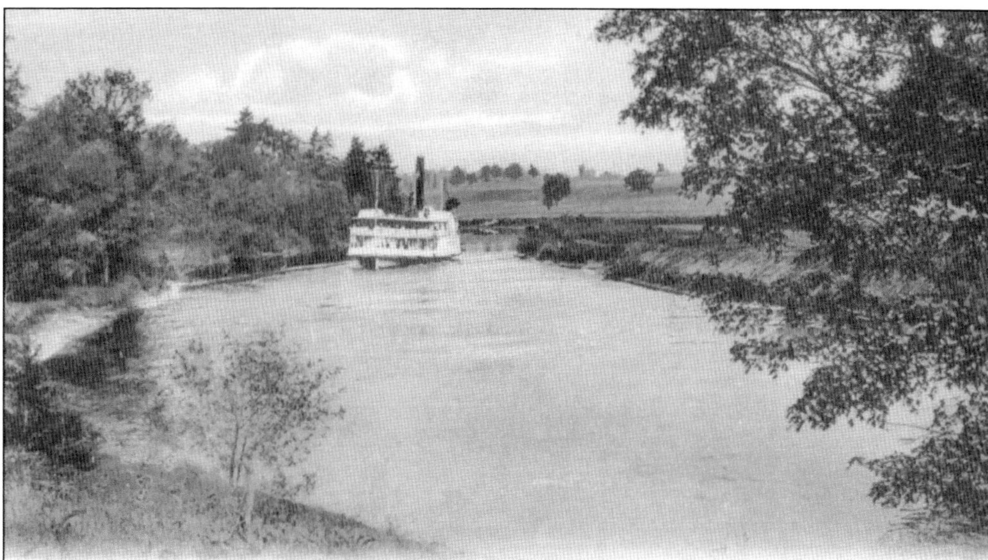

Steamboats were able to navigate the 7 miles between the mouth of Otter Creek at Lake Champlain and the Vergennes Falls, crossing the rich farmland of Ferrisburg. This *c.* 1910 view of Otter Creek shows a steamboat that made regular excursions from Lake Champlain to Vergennes, below the falls.

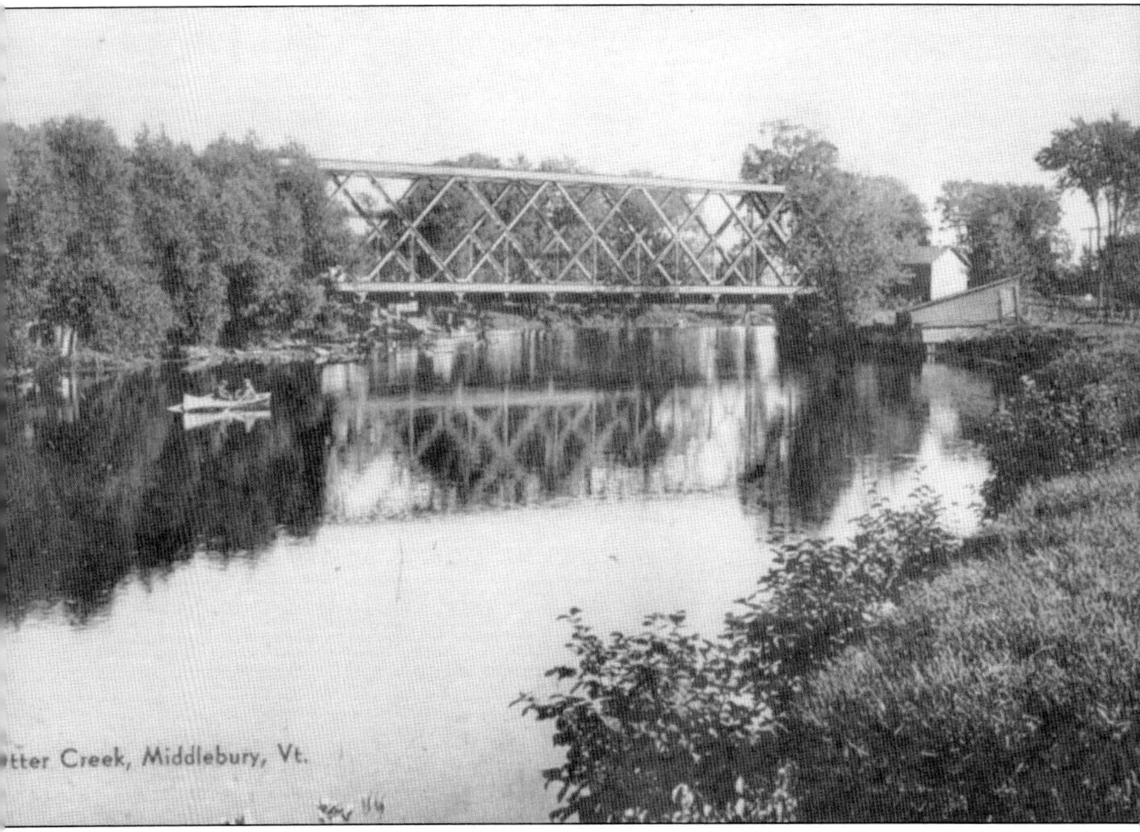

The iron railroad bridge over Otter Creek is located just upstream from the Middlebury Falls and carries trains across a quiet section of the creek. This bridge replaced an earlier covered bridge that collapsed in 1893 during the spring flood. A passenger train had successfully crossed the swollen creek and was soon followed by a train heavily laden with coal. The bridge fell during the second crossing, but surprisingly no one was seriously hurt. One of the early ferryboats run by Hop Johnson between 1783 and 1789 crossed the creek at this location. The first Middlebury train station was located on the east side of the creek just north of this bridge.

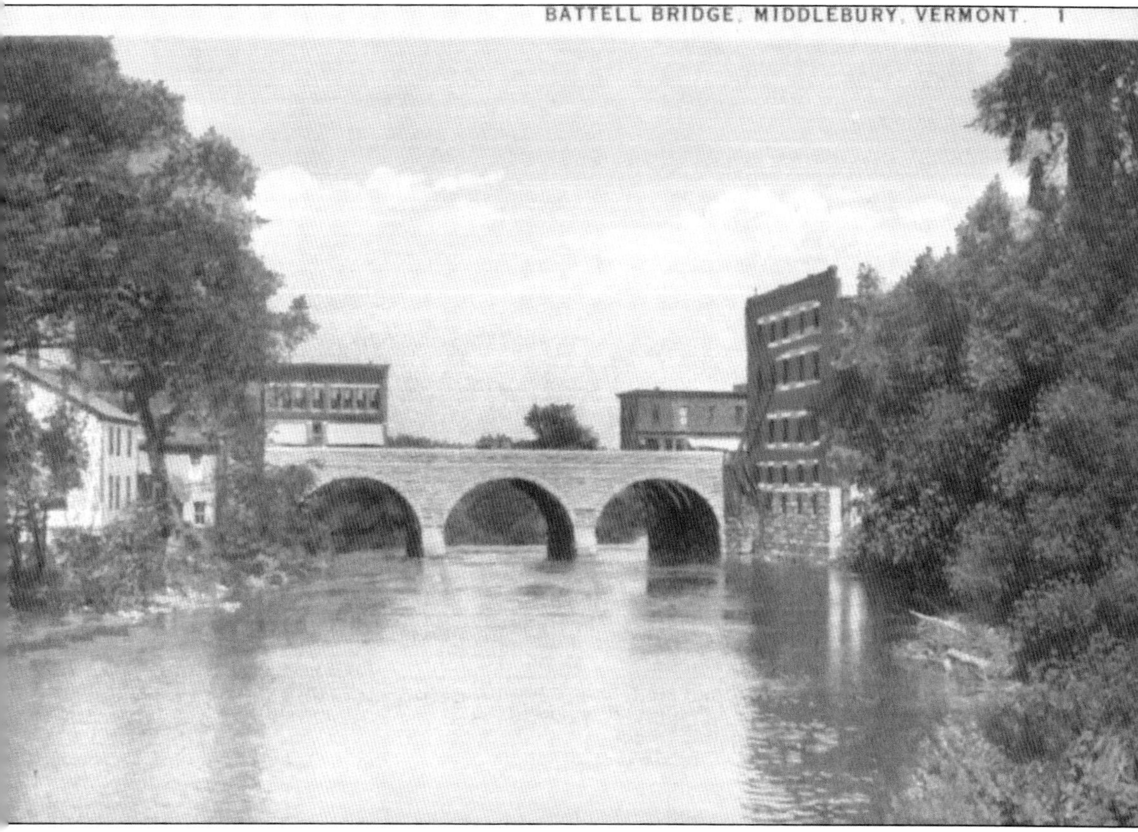

The Battell Bridge was constructed in 1892–1893 and replaced a series of precarious bridges that crossed Otter Creek above the falls. Joseph Battell, Middlebury businessman, promoted the construction of a stately stone bridge to unite the two sides of Otter Creek. Town discussion alternated between building a costly and elaborate bridge and a simple, but satisfactory, wooden bridge. Battell, a determined and affluent Middlebury citizen, finally persuaded the town by agreeing to pay personally for half of the construction cost. The completed design required that Main Street be elevated 10 feet, creating problems for existing buildings and sidewalks, which needed to be restructured.

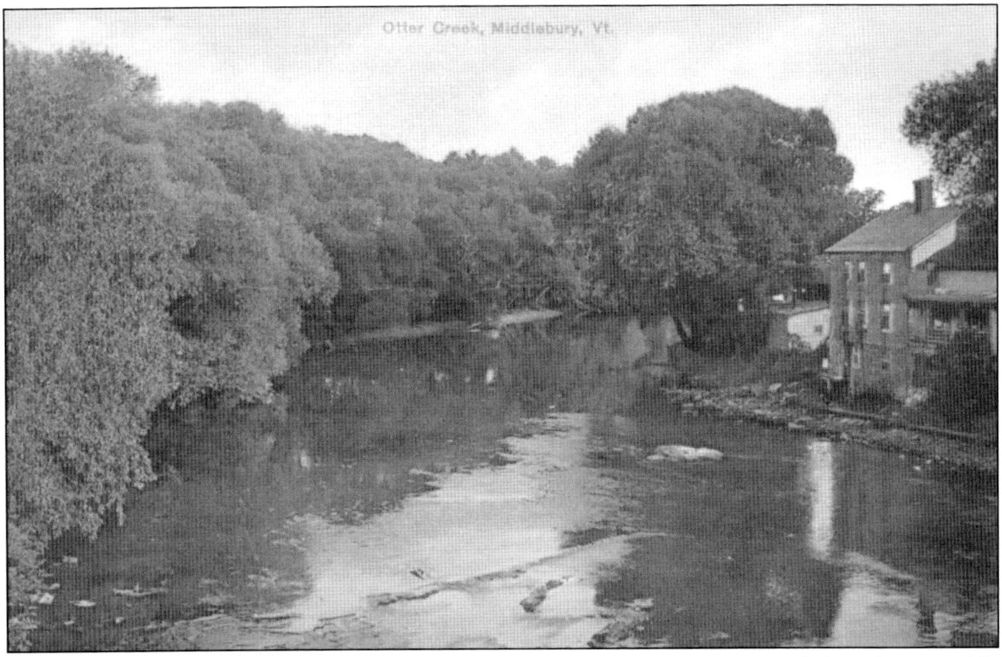

During quiet periods, when the creek runs clear, you can see portions of the white marble bottom of the creek bed above the falls. In 1802, Eban Judd began to quarry high-quality white marble from the stone ledge that defines the falls. He used power from the falls to cut the marble for a broad range of uses. The Vermont marble industry began at the falls. The building on the right, which was originally a mill, housed the town bakery for many years. Today, Woody's Restaurant is a stylish reuse of the old mill.

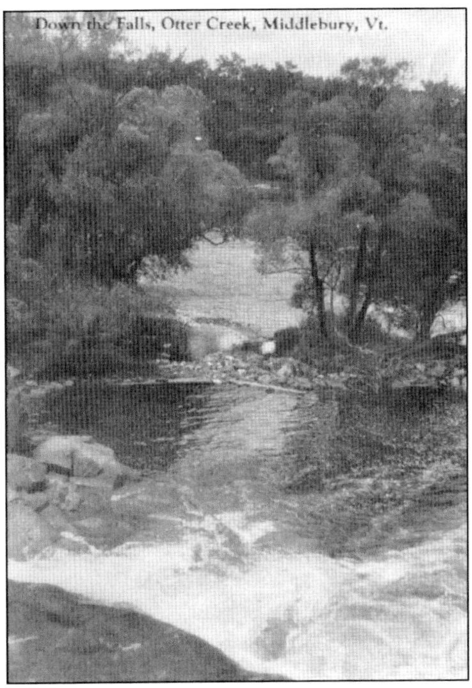

The view below the falls changes dramatically throughout the year and includes, during periods of high flow, a dramatic whirlpool. In the spring, large piles of wood, boards, and trees accumulate. For many years, these swirling masses of debris included colorful trash, papers, boxes, and the discarded goods of country life.

Two

MIDDLEBURY MAIN STREET AND MERCHANT'S ROW

All traffic moving through Middlebury from the south and west must cross Otter Creek and travel the short section of Main Street from South Main and College Streets to Merchant's Row. One of the signature views of Middlebury includes the Congregational church, the Battell Block, and the commercial and civic buildings along Main Street. Until 1950, when the Battell Tower was damaged during a late season hurricane and never replaced, the tower gave a rural French look to the center of town. There are dozens of postcards of this street scene, easily recognizable as Middlebury to anyone who has even made a casual visit. Surprisingly, little has changed in this portion of town in the past 75 years. Businesses come and go, the fountain and street features have changed, but the profile and character of Main Street have remained a comfortable constant for Middlebury, with the modern commercial and social changes focused along Route 7 to the south.

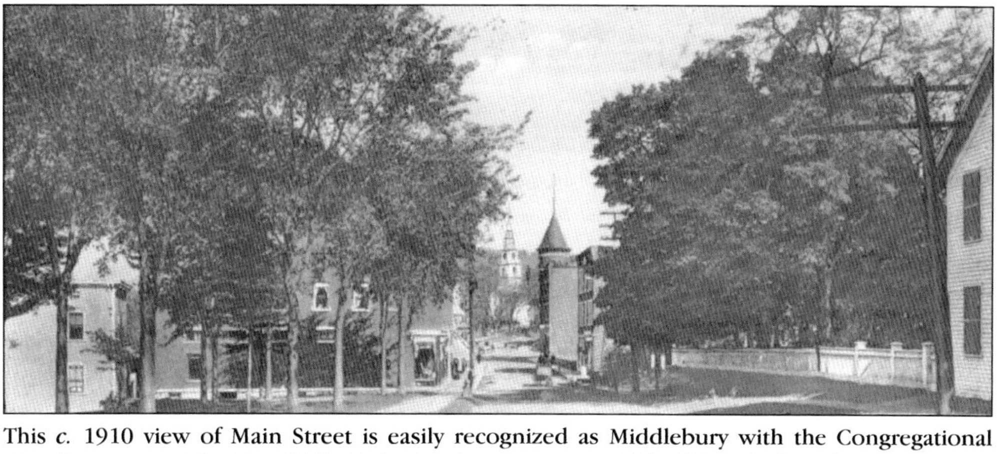

This *c.* 1910 view of Main Street is easily recognized as Middlebury with the Congregational church tower and the Battell Block. It also shows commercial buildings before the construction of the Ilsley Library. The house on the right was built in 1816 by Daniel Henshaw, who owned a nearby mill. Now known as the Osborne House, it was the first meeting place of the Episcopal Society, before the Episcopal church was built in 1827.

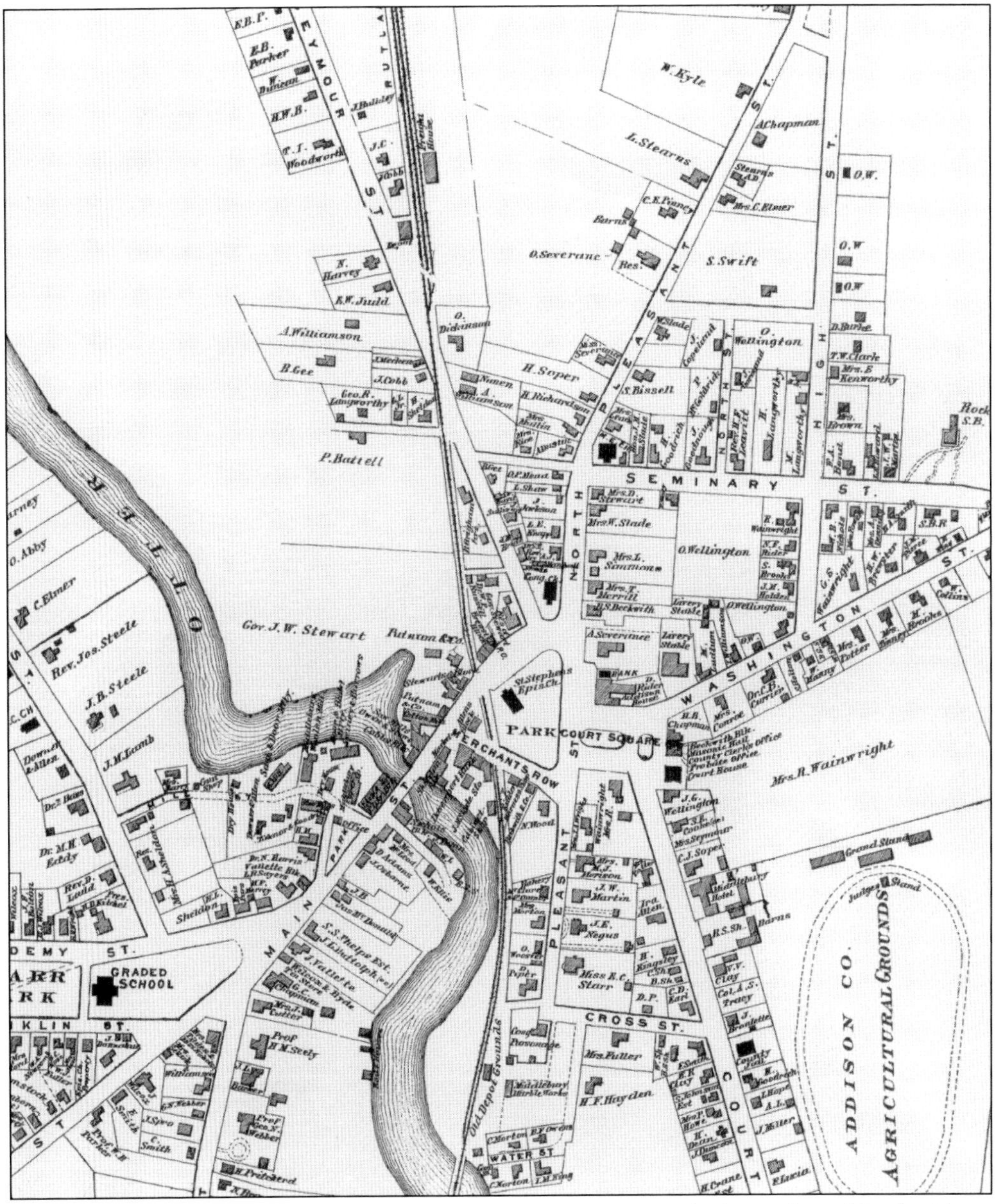

The village center developed around the Middlebury Falls and the early public buildings constructed around the park, which was donated to the town by Gamaliel Painter. It was Painter's fervor to support his businesses and civic interests that focused attention on the vicinity of the falls. This 1871 Beers map prominently shows the Addison County Agricultural Society Fairgrounds east of Court Street, the old railroad depot near Water Street, the active mills around the falls, and the houses lining the south side of Washington Street. While most of these features are now gone, this map is remarkably recognizable 130 years later, with most of the same buildings. The early village layout has remained successful, when many other town centers have become less functional.

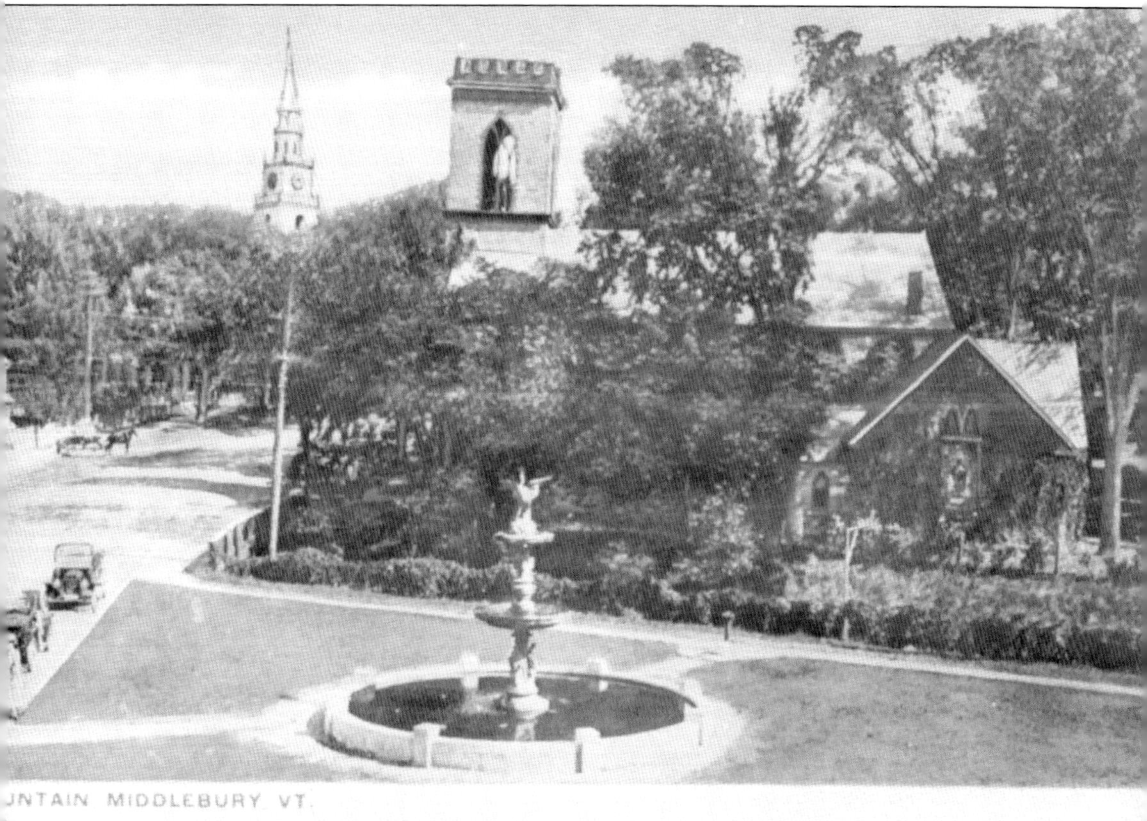

This view looking north from the Battell Block tower shows the Battell Fountain, the Episcopal church, and the Congregational church *c.* 1915. The fountain was constructed in 1908, a donation by Joseph Battell to Middlebury. The fountain originally stood 15 feet high and was supported by women and topped by an eagle. During windy periods, shoppers and their cars were sprayed with water from the fountain along Main Street and Merchant's Row. In 1938, the iron in the fountain was scrapped to make armaments for the war effort. In 1976, a new and smaller fountain was constructed on the site, using an old garden urn modified into a fountain. Between the fountain and the Episcopal church, the railroad line through the village is visible in an opening going beneath Main Street and Merchant's Row.

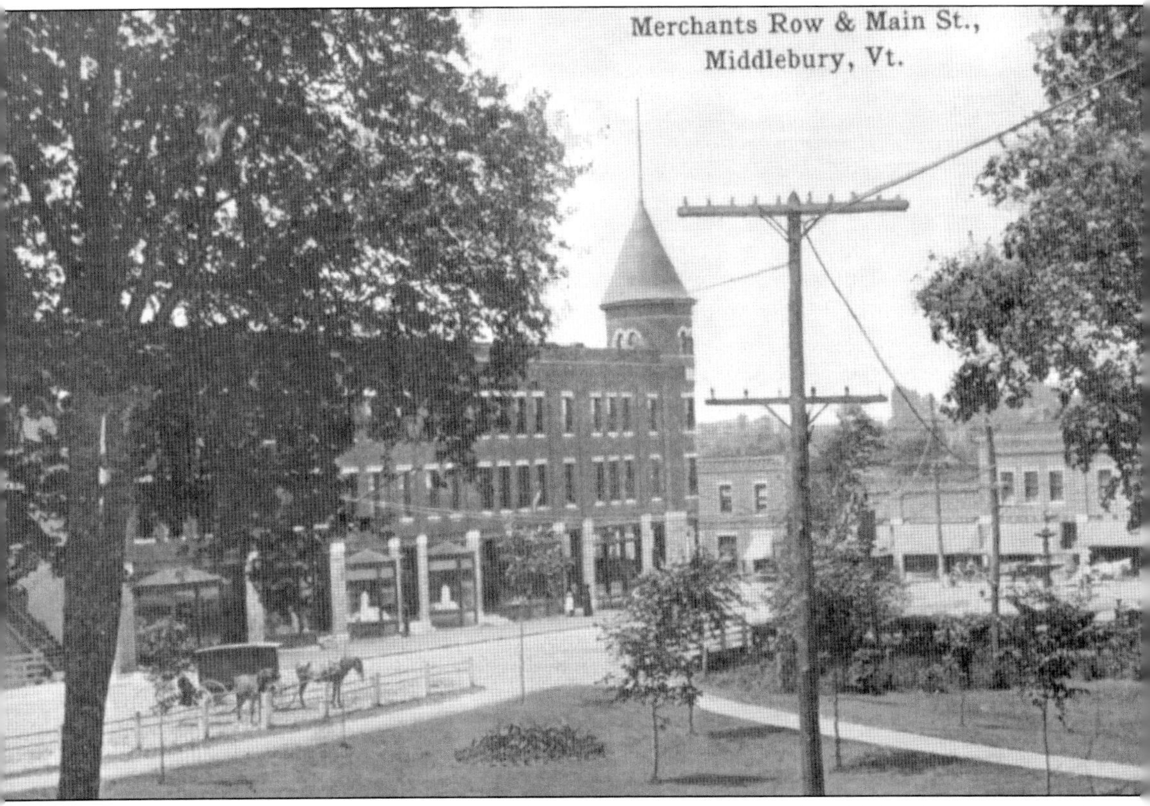

The view from the porch at the Middlebury Inn, sometime after 1910, shows the newly constructed Battell Block and commercial buildings on the west side of Main Street. This postcard was produced several times with and without telephone poles. The first-floor stores in the Battell Block included a dry goods store, a grocery, and a bank. During this period, many small trees were planted in the village green. The Battell Fountain is to the right. The new Calvi's store is one of the one-story buildings behind the fountain.

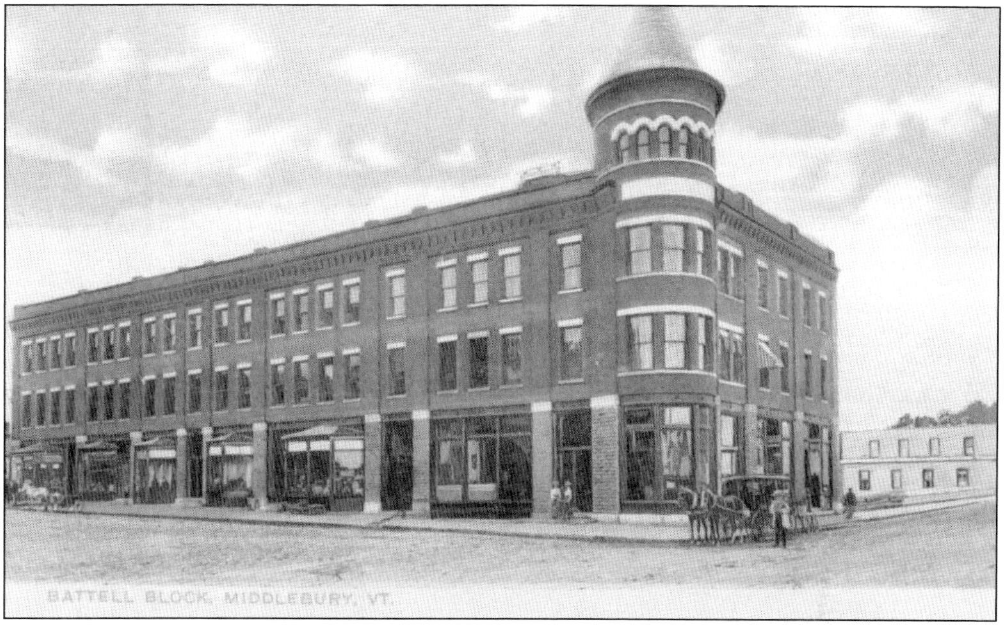

The Battell Block is located on a choice commercial site in Middlebury where all buildings had been destroyed in the 1891 fire. The massive structure was built by local businessman Joseph Battell in three stages, beginning in 1892. The section along Merchant's Row with the corner tower was completed in 1892, with the second section along Main Street attached to the tower added in 1895.

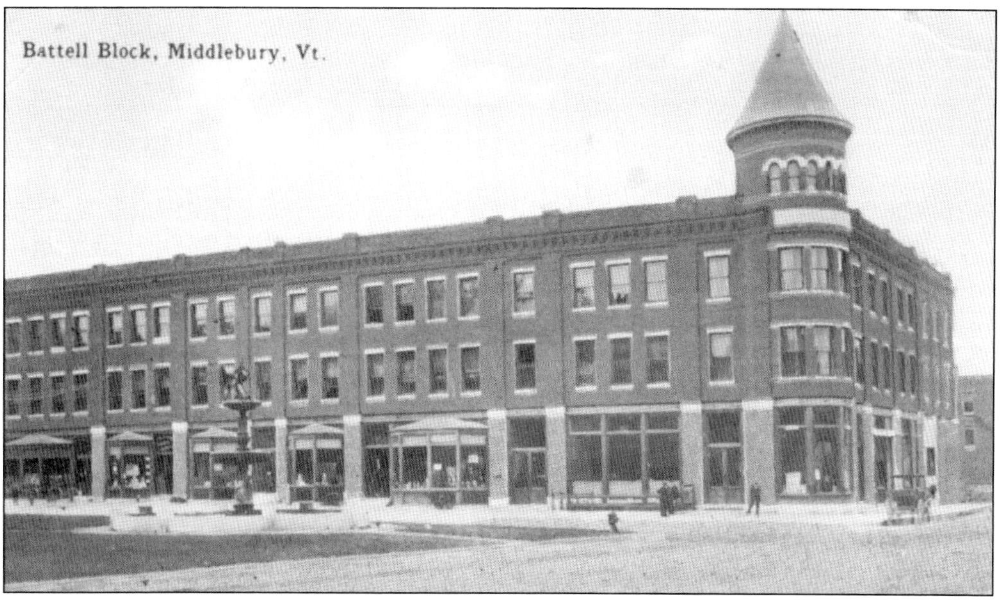

In 1915, a third section of the Battell Block was completed along Otter Creek and Main Street. The town post office moved into the ground floor of the new addition where the shop Dada is today. Joseph Battell's own home was on the second floor of this building and included the tower. He had a prominent view of commercial Middlebury and was for many years the most influential citizen in town.

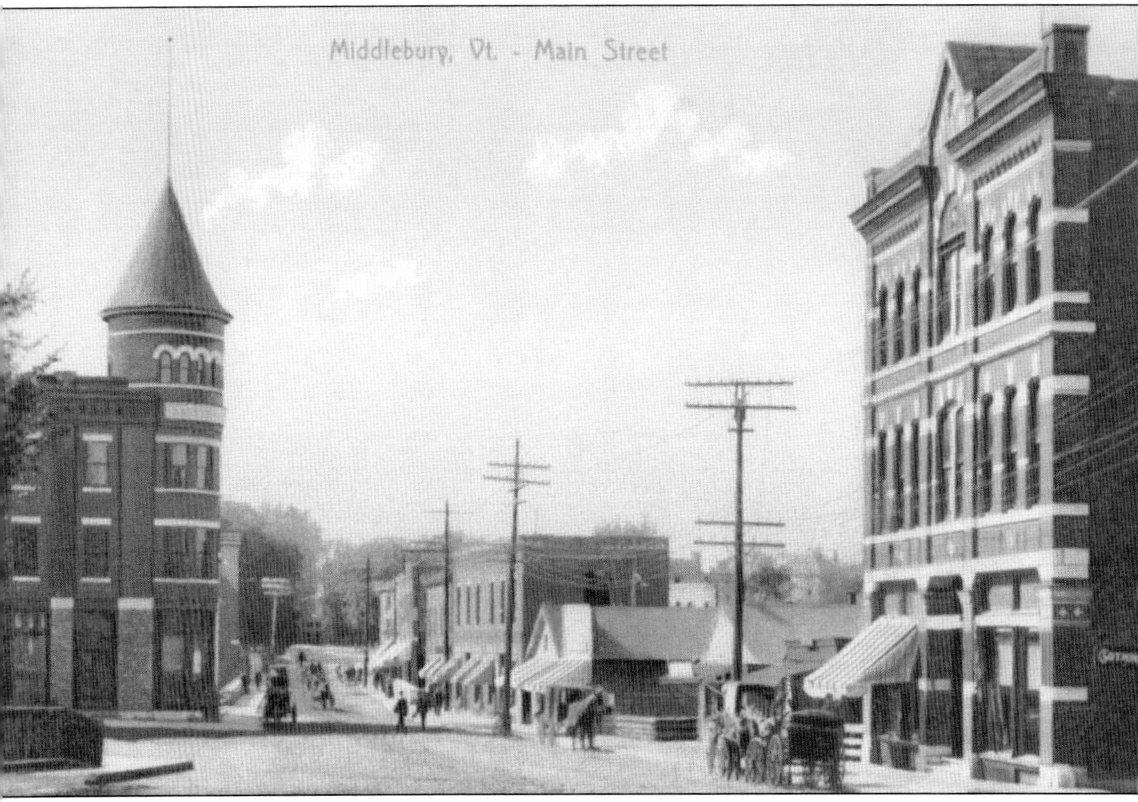

Across the street from the Battell Tower, a series of small wooden buildings, constructed soon after the 1891 fire, persisted for many years because Joseph Battell wanted to maintain the view of the Adirondacks to the west from his apartment. Calvi's store occupied one of these small buildings and was a popular meeting place for college students. Calvi's began as a shop selling fruit and ice cream in 1902 and moved to a new brick building in 1910. The Calvi family continued the business until 1998, when it was sold and remodeled. Sweet Cecily now occupies the old college hangout. On the right is the Beckwith Block, built in 1882–1883. This tall, imposing building of brick, marble, and granite was one of the premier buildings of Addison County for many years and survived the 1891 fire.

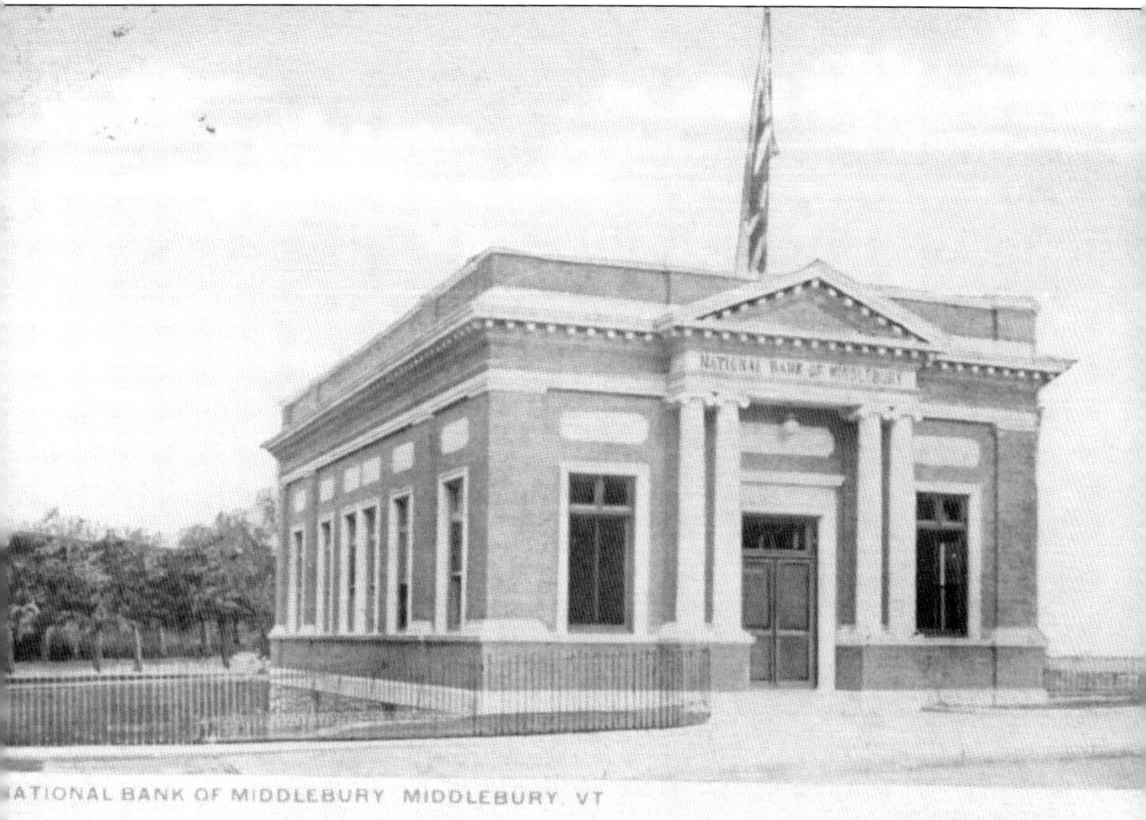

This view of the National Bank of Middlebury building shows the new bank shortly after it was built in 1910 as though it were located in an isolated part of Middlebury with no nearby buildings. The Beckwith Block to the north has been removed from the photograph, as has the brick building to the south. The bank is constructed in a Classical Revival style, a monumental form for a structure only one story tall. In a typical postcard enhancement, an oversized American flag was added to the image.

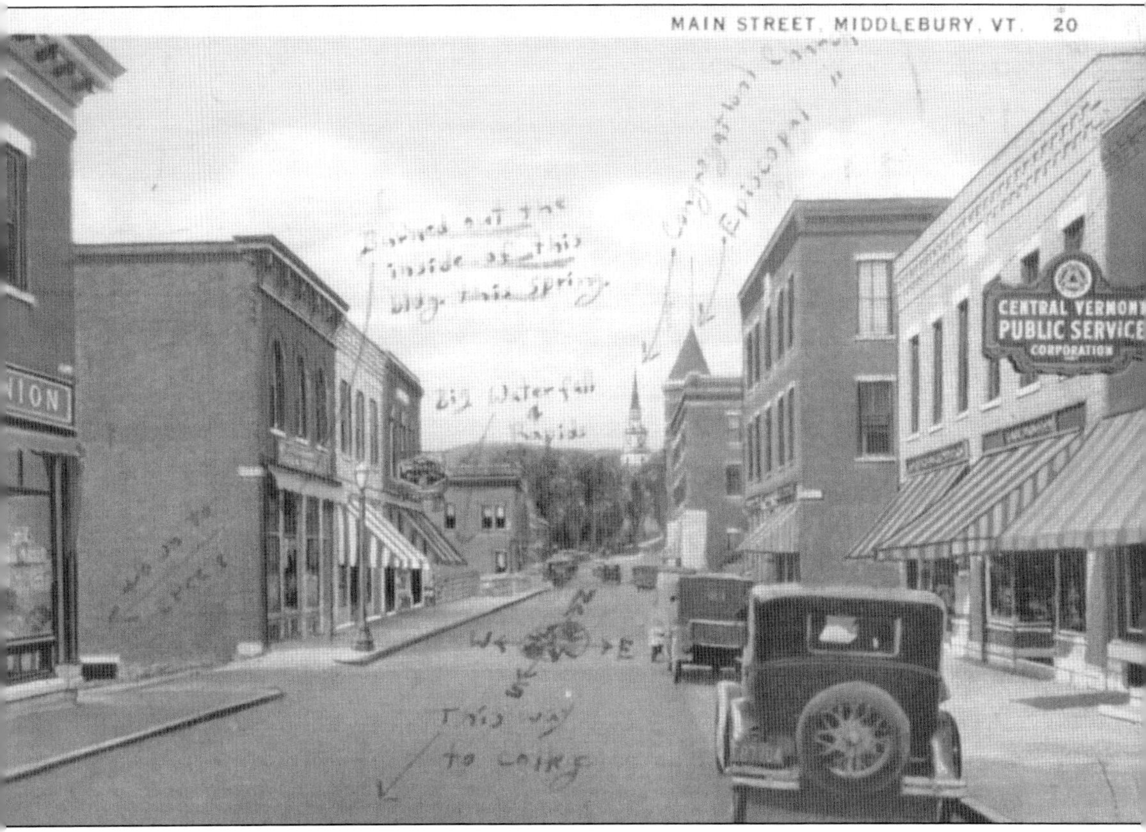

The view of Main Street of the 1940s had changed very little during the previous 30 years, with the Grand Union Grocery Store on the left and Central Vermont Public Service, the electric company, on the right. The power company generated electricity at the Middlebury Falls with its facilities in the old mill at the foot of Mill Street. Eventually, electricity generated at the falls was no longer economically justified, and the years of waterpower production at the Middlebury Falls came to an end. Central Vermont sold its generating building to the Town of Middlebury. This postcard, like many that were mailed, has some interesting annotations made by the sender.

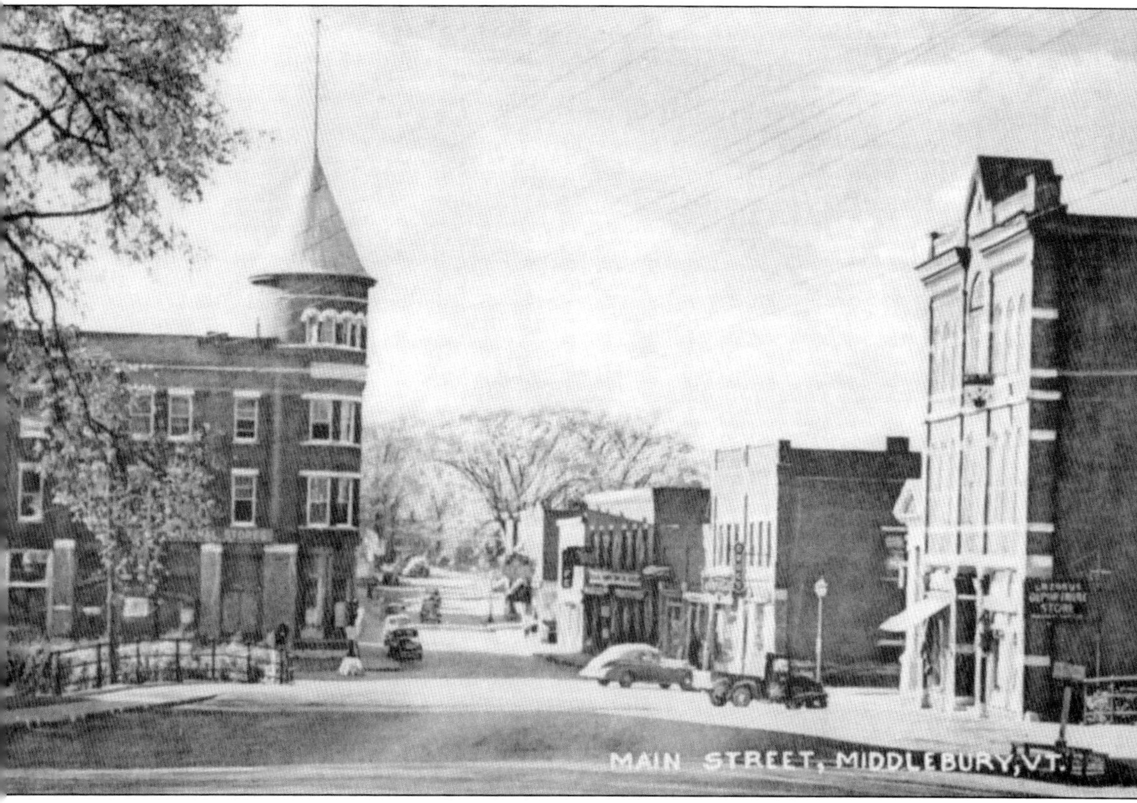

Main Street in the 1940s took on the prosperous look of 20th-century commercial development. The Rexall Drugstore now dominated the center of town, with the First National Grocery Store at the corner of the Battell Block. The iron railing to the left guards pedestrians from the railroad line that runs under Main Street. In 1950, during a severe hurricane that affected many of the villages in Addison County, the top of the Battell Tower was badly damaged; the tower was subsequently removed and never replaced.

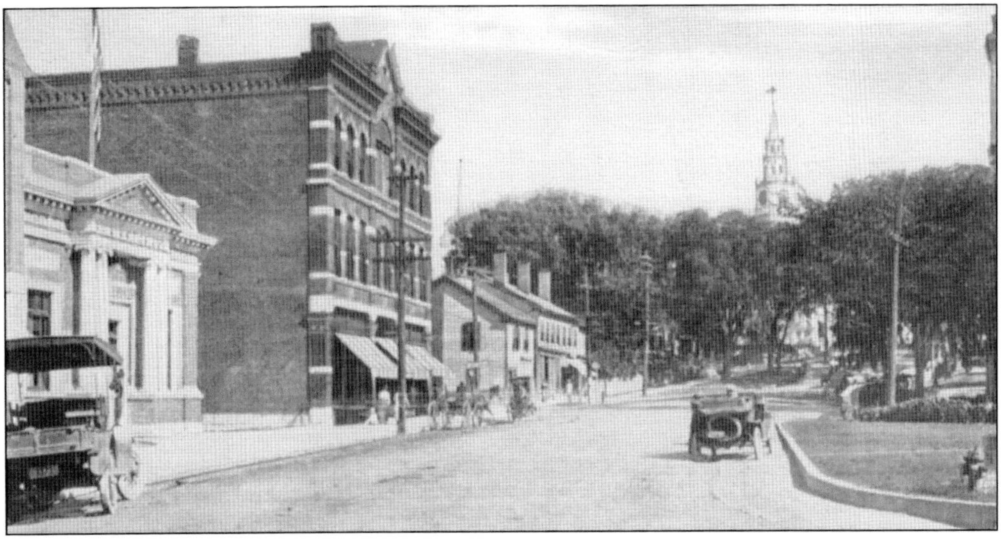

In this *c.* 1915 postcard, looking north from the Battell Block, the new bank and Beckwith Block dominate Main Street. The small wooden buildings in the center of the view are the fire station, built in 1856, and the Brewster Block, a pair of commercial buildings built in 1837. The Brewster Block housed the post office, the telegraph office, and several other businesses. These buildings were demolished and replaced by the new post office in 1932.

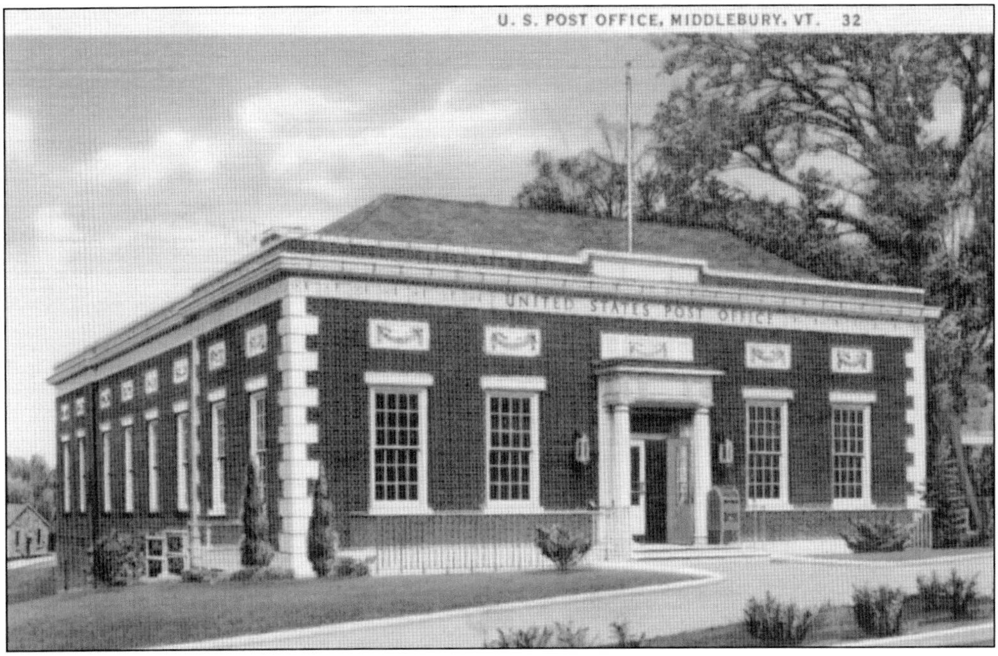

The Middlebury post office was built in 1932–1933. As another monumental building on Main Street, it was constructed of brick and marble with decorative swags above each window. Begun under the Hoover administration, the structure was nearly complete when Franklin Delano Roosevelt became president. The Republican postmaster inscription, already in the cornerstone, was quickly replaced by the name of the new Democratic postmaster, reflecting the changes in Washington.

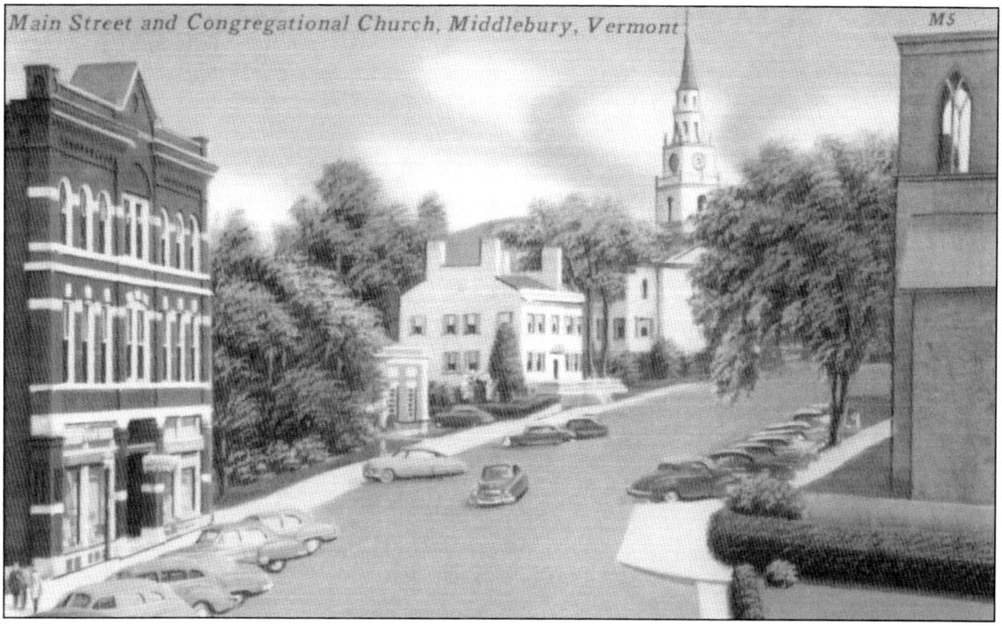

This view looking north from the Battell Tower in the 1940s shows the Beckwith Block, the post office, the Community House, and the Congregational church, with the Episcopal church to the right. The card is severely altered, removing detail from the street and buildings and adding features such as the mass of trees between the Beckwith Block and the post office. This linen postcard is typical of a series of almost cartoonlike cards produced between the late 1930s and the early 1950s.

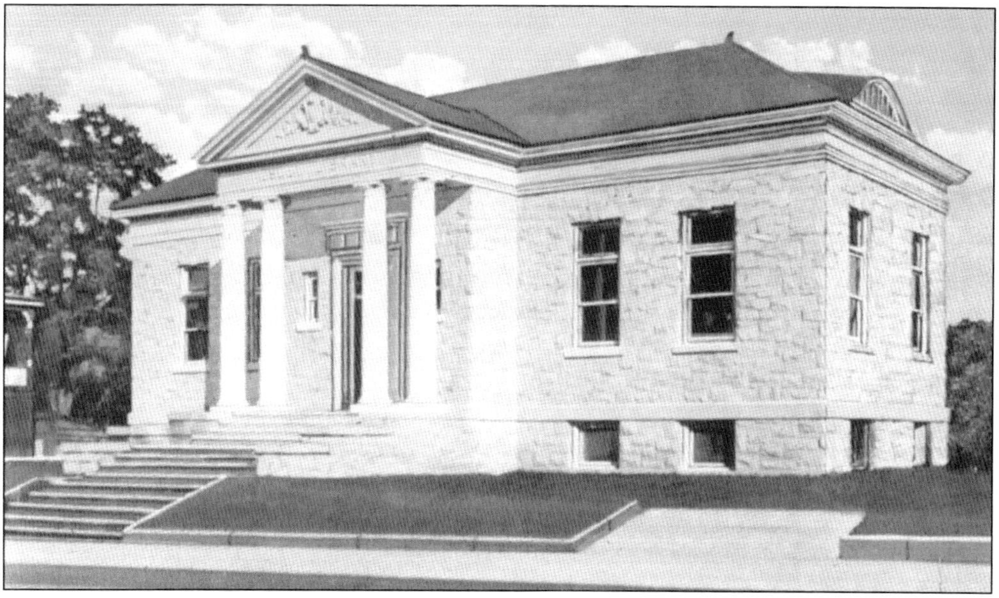

The Ilsley Library was built in 1924 with money donated by Col. Silas Ilsley, who also donated funds for the Civil War Monument at the head of Merchant's Row and for the Baptist church. The Ilsley was the first public library building in town, replacing several small libraries at scattered locations around the village. The library has been expanded twice—in 1972 and in 1998.

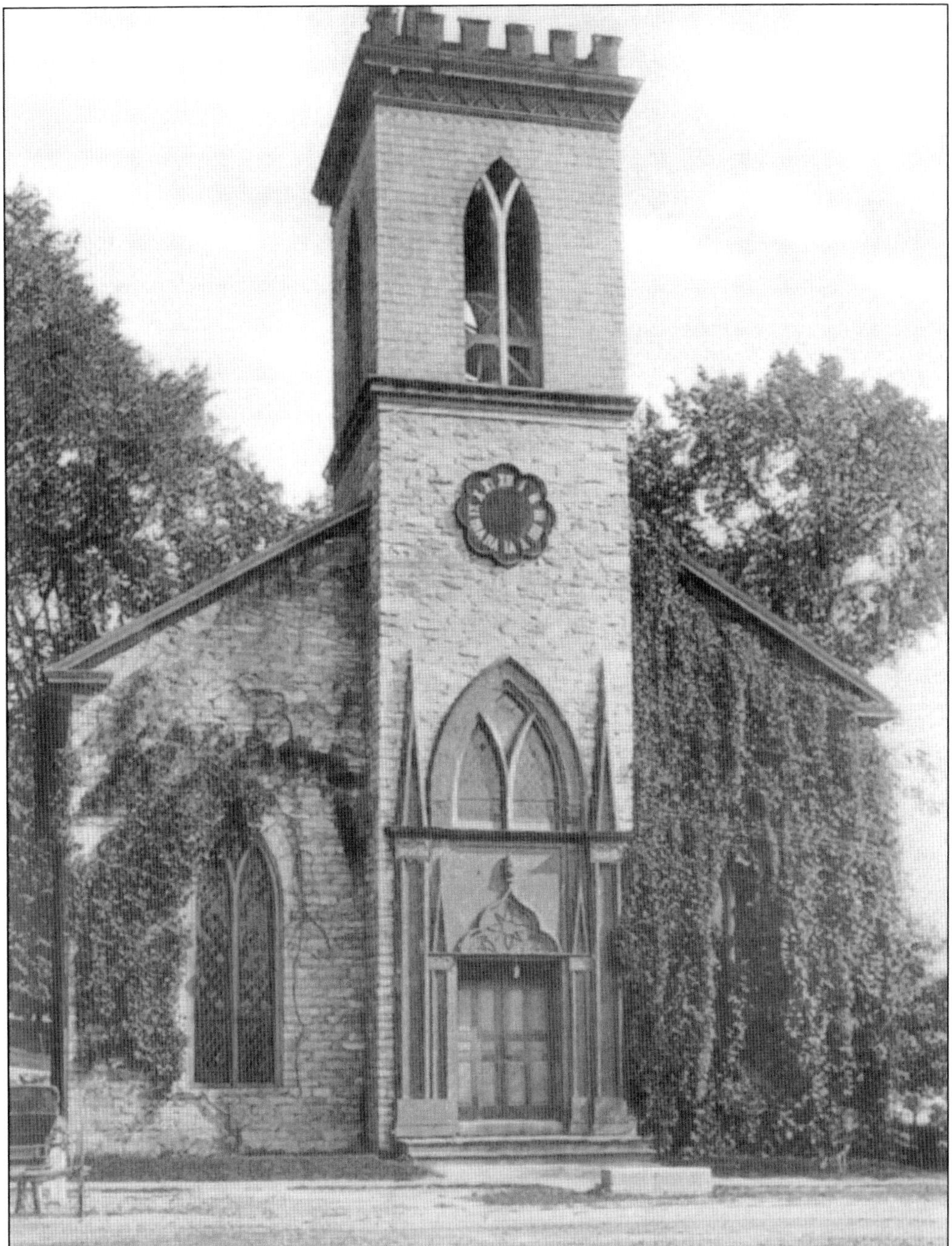

The Episcopal church was constructed in 1826–1827 in a Gothic style that had recently been introduced to New England. Permission was granted to build the church on the village green, but only if it were made of stone and brick, part of the conditions of the original Gamaliel Painter deed. The elaborate door surround was an ornate feature of the distinctive church. A small chapel was added to the south side of the building in 1879 and appears to have been removed from this postcard. Card manufacturers often blurred out portions of the photograph that they considered unbalanced or unattractive. Note the fuzzy appearance on the right side of the card.

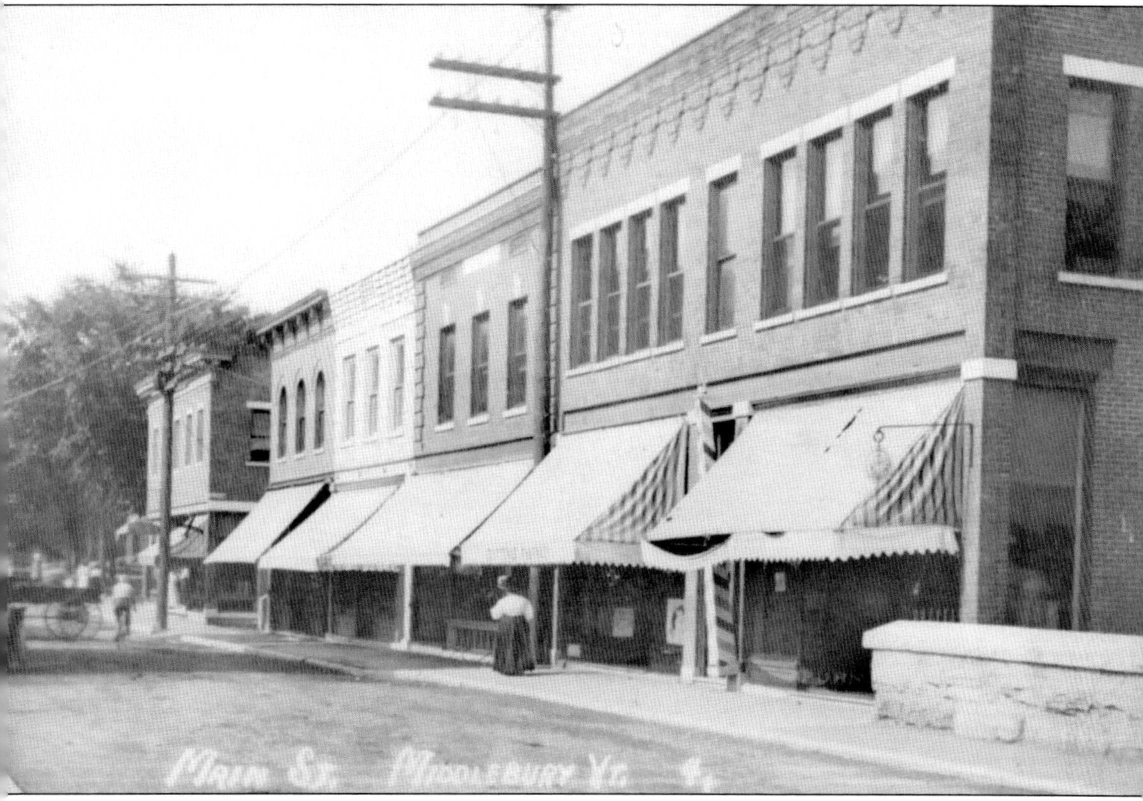

A series of commercial buildings was constructed between 1900 and 1910 along the west side of Main Street south of the Battell Bridge. Each of these buildings had commercial space on the first floor, with storage in the basements and apartments and offices on the second floors. For many years, Farrell's Clothing Store and the Grey Shop were located in these buildings. (Courtesy of Beatrice Zaremba.)

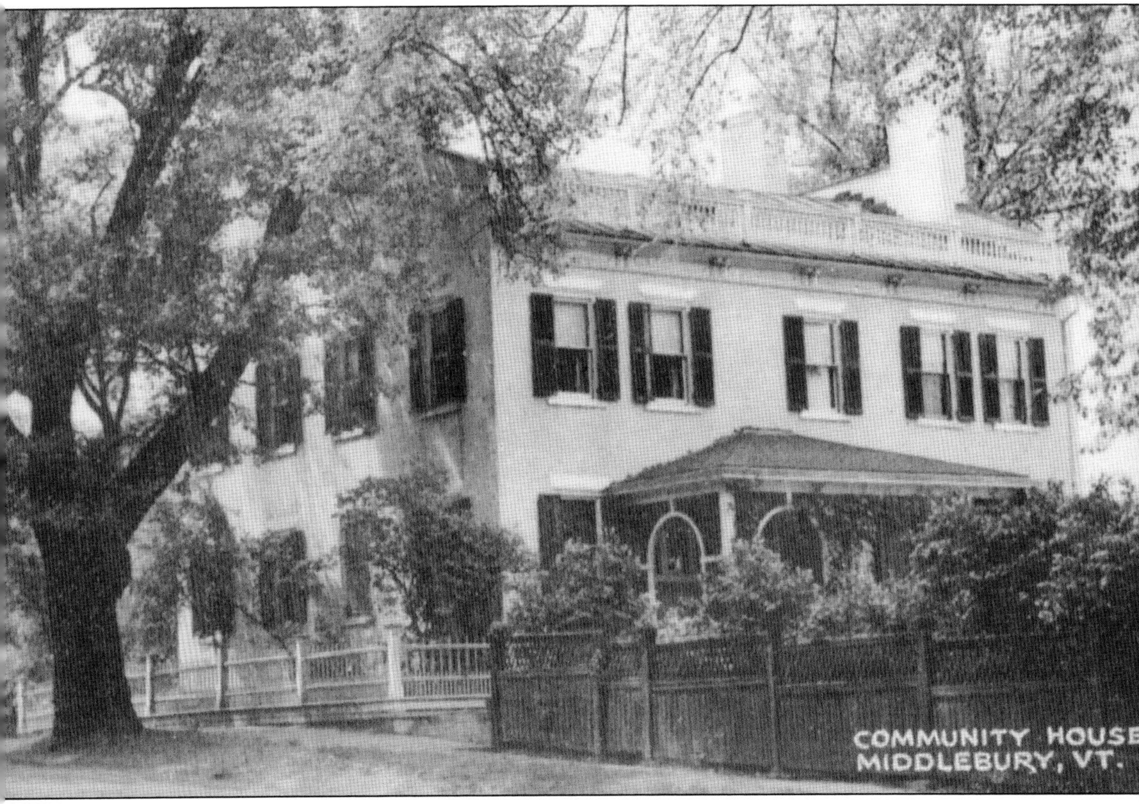

One of the most substantial houses in Middlebury was the Seymour House at the corner of Main and Seymour Streets. Horatio Seymour was postmaster, educator, businessman, and U.S. senator from Vermont. He built his brick Federal-style home in 1816–1817. Seymour's son-in-law Phillip Battell, the father of Joseph Battell, further modernized the house and passed it on to his son-in-law John Stewart, who became a Vermont governor and a U.S. senator. John Stewart's daughter Jessica Steward Swift donated the house and its contents to the town in 1932.

Three

THE TOWN OF MIDDLEBURY

Since its earliest days, the center of Middlebury has been focused around the Gamaliel Painter landholdings between the falls and the Congregational church. Painter's interests and ambitions defined many of the prominent locations in town. His home between Court and South Pleasant Streets on Court Square was at the center of commercial activity on the main road connecting Middlebury to Vergennes and Lake Champlain to the north and Rutland and points south. Across the street to the north from his home were the county courthouse and the principal tavern in town. The Congregational church was on the north side of the village green, which he deeded to the town in the late 1700s with the provision that it remain open and that only stone and brick structures be built within its boundaries.

The early tavern was replaced in 1826 by the Vermont House, which became the Addison House and finally the Middlebury Inn. The second courthouse and Masonic Hall were nearby on Court Street. The Addison County Agricultural Fairgrounds was developed in the 1840s east of Court Street with its entrance only a few hundred yards to the south of the courthouse. Nearly all parts of the large and important fairgrounds complex are now gone. Most other prominent town features, except those at Middlebury College and Porter Hospital, are within only a short walk of what Gamaliel Painter envisioned as the proper village configuration more than 200 years ago.

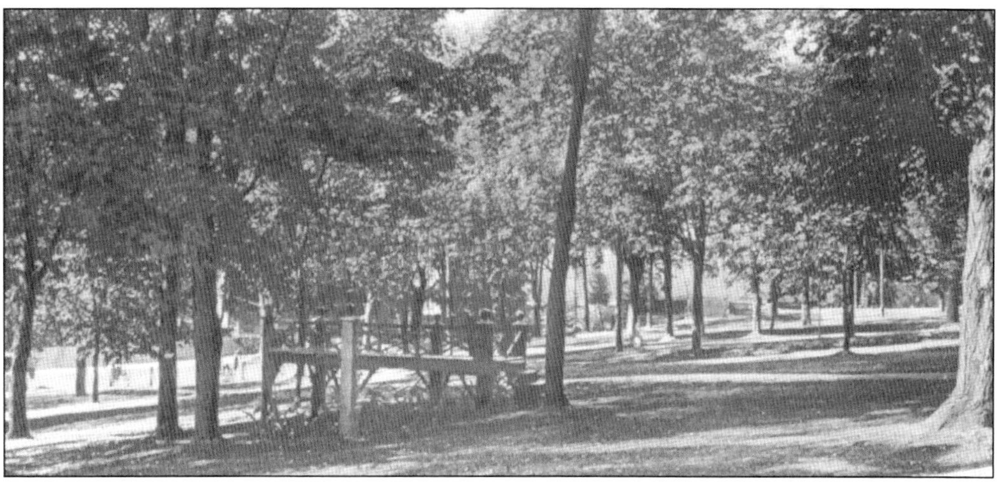

The village green is the central feature of the town. Everyone passes by the small park when visiting the commercial part of Middlebury. Although there are hundreds of postcards including a small section of the park, few focus on the park itself. In its earliest days, the village green was the site of public punishment, such as floggings, as well as of celebrations. Throughout the past 100 years, town bands have also played at a series of bandstands, such as this one shown *c.* 1915.

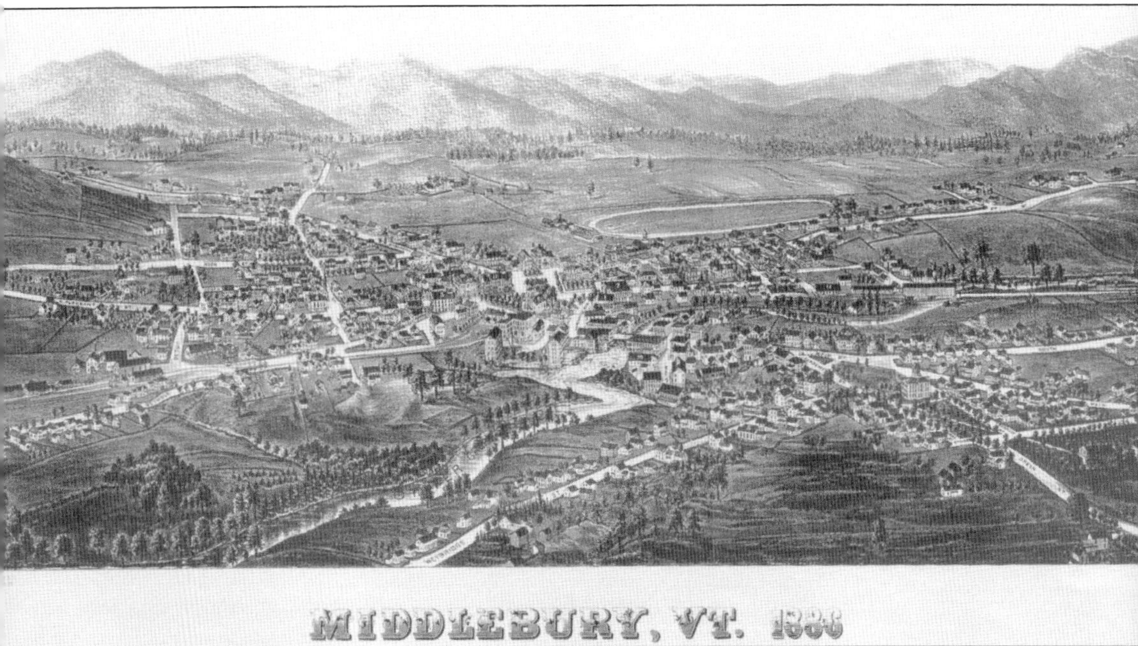

Civic pride ran high in the late 19th century and was evident in a series of panoramic views of many of the villages of the Northeast. This aerial scene of Middlebury was assembled in 1886 by Lucien Burleigh of Troy, New York. It includes remarkable details of buildings and the general landscape of Middlebury. Notable in this view are the Addison County Agricultural Fairgrounds, the covered railroad bridge over Otter Creek, the concentration of mills around the falls, and the open farmland on what later became the North Campus at Middlebury College. At this time, the Beckwith Block had only recently been completed. It was another five years before a major fire swept through much of the commercial center of town, leading to a new appearance for Main Street and Merchant's Row.

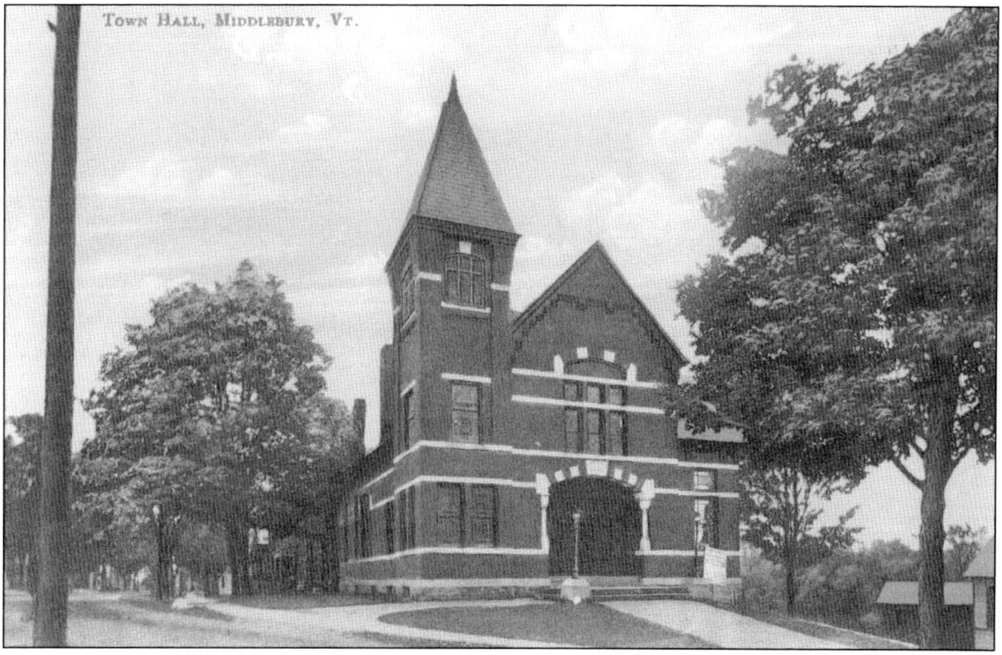

In 1883, Middlebury constructed a new town hall at the corner of Merchant's Row and South Pleasant Street. Built in a Romanesque style, the town hall had a large auditorium for town meetings, a vital part of life in all New England towns. The town hall was used for plays, musicals, and early movies, and in later years it was even used as a furniture store.

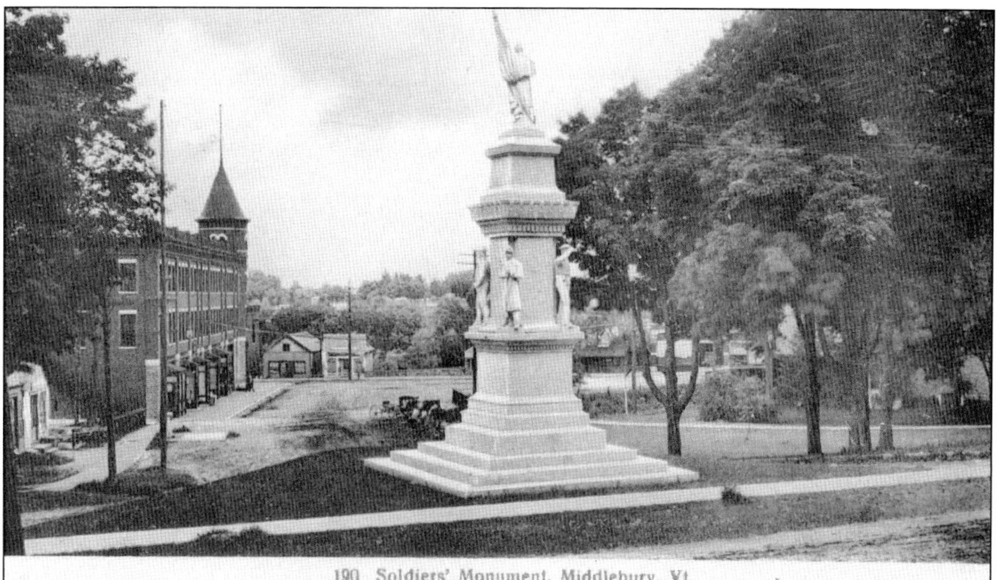

In 1905, Middlebury commemorated its Civil War soldiers with an impressive memorial at the east end of Merchant's Row. Built with funds from Col. Silas Ilsley, the monument depicts the four branches of the military. The only name that appears on the entire monument is that of Ilsley.

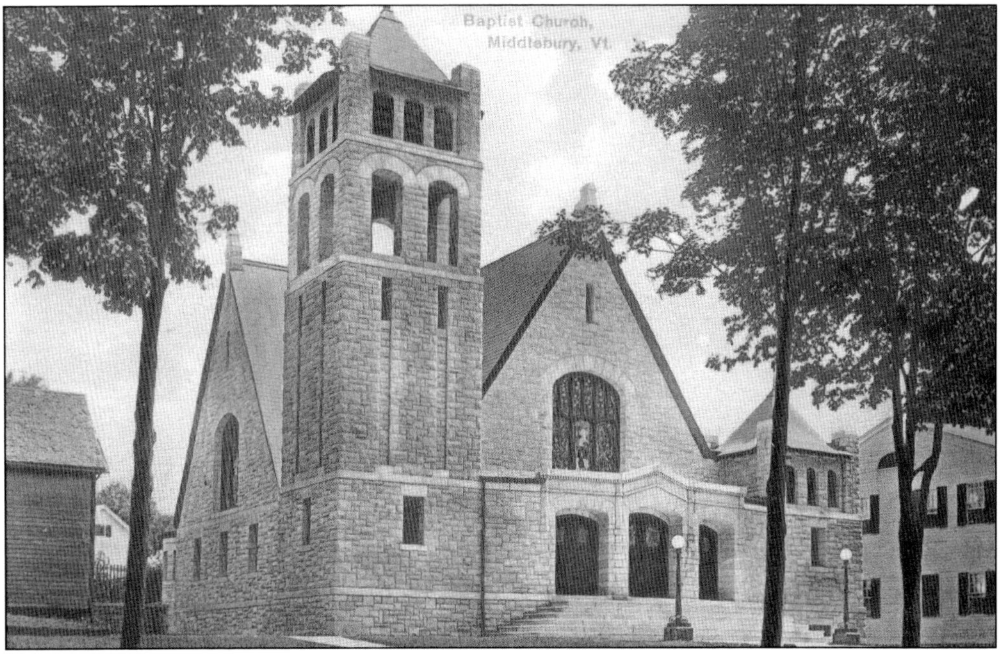

Col. Silas Ilsley also turned his attention to his church, the Baptist church, building a new structure in 1905–1906 on South Pleasant Street that rivaled the other grand churches in town. The church is constructed of Brandon marble with Gothic influence throughout. The house to the right was built in 1801 and has served as the home of two Middlebury College presidents.

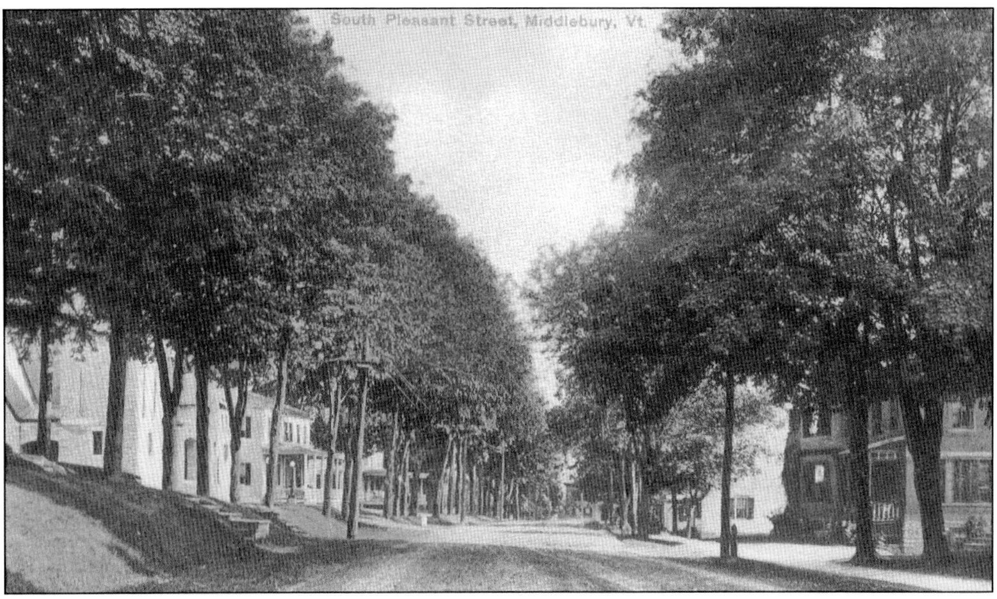

South Pleasant Street is a quiet, tree-lined road near the very center of Middlebury. Many of the leading families of the village had homes along South Pleasant Street. The building on the left is the Baptist church. The second building on the right burned in 1999 and was cleared in the winter of 2000. The first Middlebury home of educator Emma Hart Willard was on South Pleasant Street.

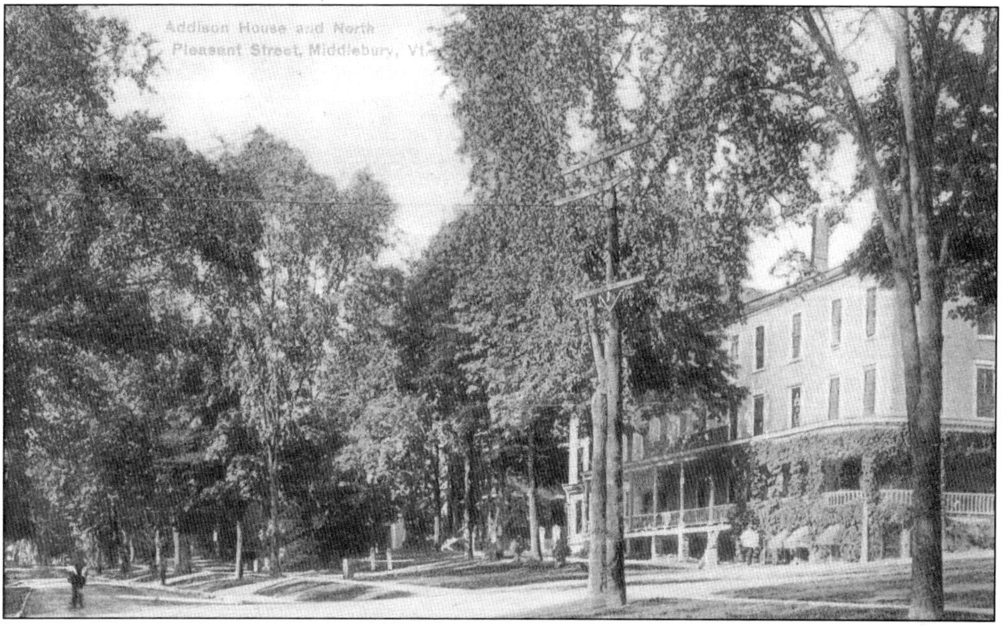

The Addison House was constructed in 1826, with the name the Vermont House, at the height of land above the village green along the main turnpike. A replacement for an earlier tavern, first built in 1794 and destroyed by fire in 1816, the Vermont House was one of the leading businesses in town. It was renamed the Addison House in 1852. The Addison House was painted a distinctive yellow with broad porches and a tall cupola. Over time, the inn suffered from disrepair and a critical need to be modernized.

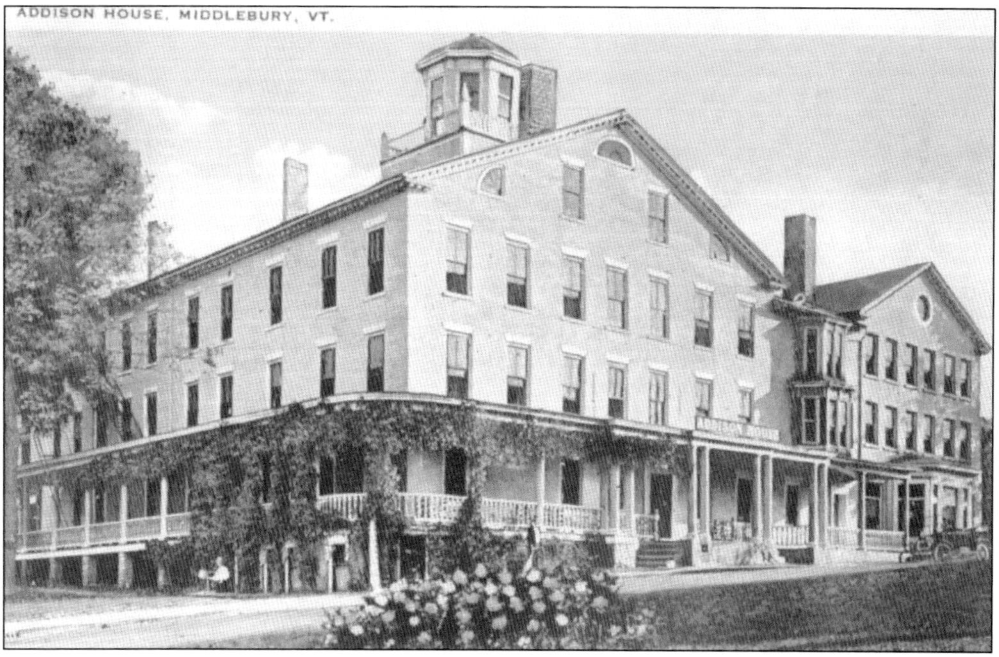

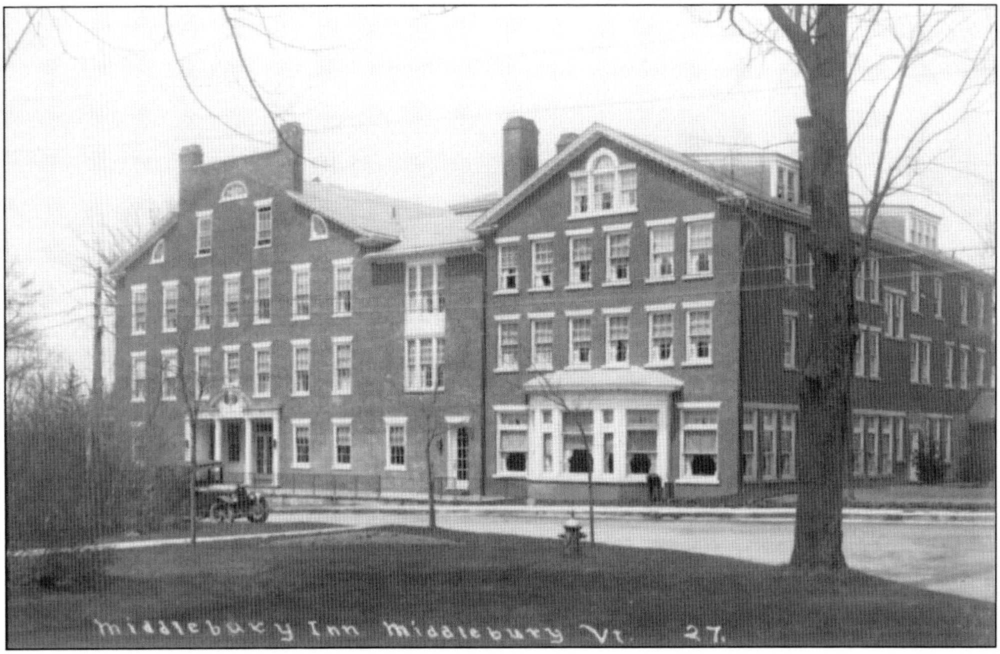

The Addison House was purchased by the Treadway Hotel chain in 1926 and transformed into the Middlebury Inn. The porches and cupola were removed, and the yellow paint was sandblasted away to expose the original brick. The roofline was also altered slightly. Victorian details were changed and the prominence of the inn among Middlebury boardinghouses was restored. Over time, porches were added and distinctive striped awnings were hung during summers. Since 1927, more than 100 postcards have documented the changes of the appearance of the inn and even some of the interior features.

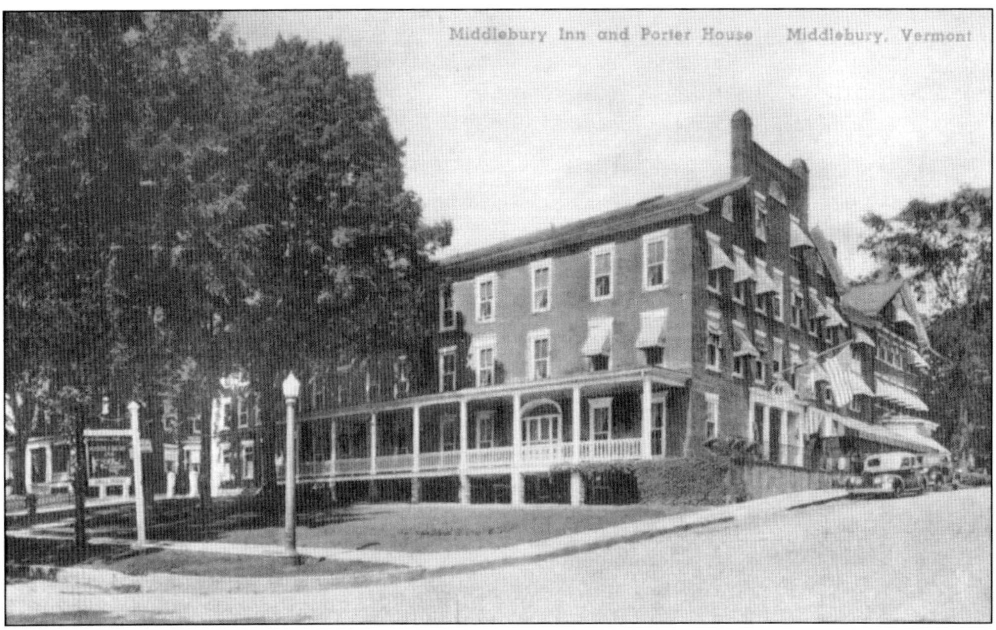

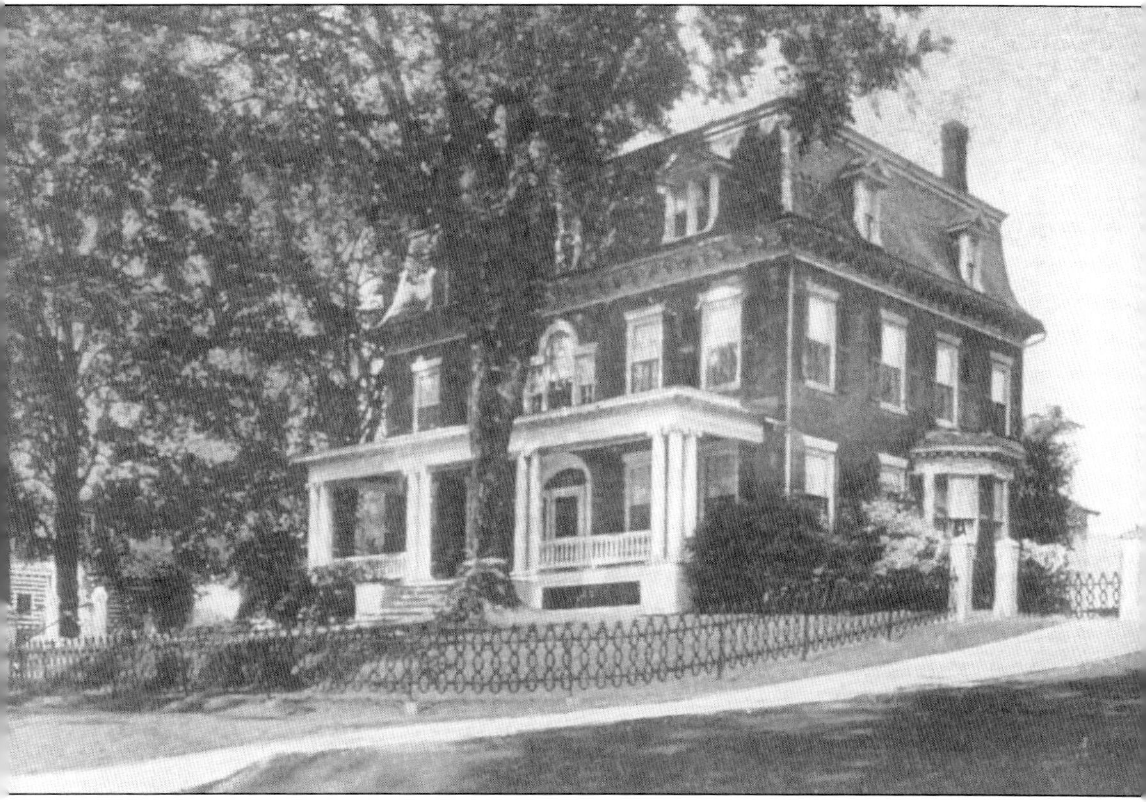

North of the Middlebury Inn along North Pleasant Street is the Wainwright home built in 1825 by Jonathan Wainwright, who with his brother Rufus Wainwright began a foundry at the base of the Middlebury Falls to manufacture iron goods. Rufus Wainwright purchased the Painter home after Gamaliel Painter died in 1819. The brothers' business expanded quickly. In 1826, after a fire destroyed their mill, they relocated to the vicinity of the Pulp Mill Bridge and continued their successful business, primarily producing stoves. The elegant Wainwright home was modernized in 1881 with numerous changes to the exterior, including the addition of a mansard roof. In 1941, the home was purchased by the Middlebury Inn and has since been used as an annex.

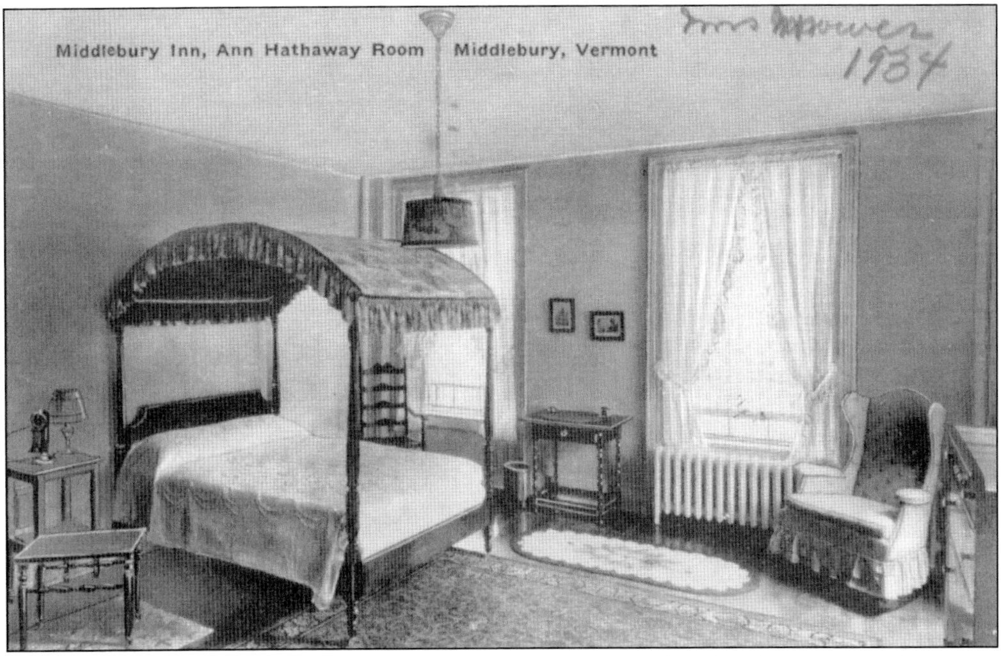

A series of postcards of the Middlebury Inn from the 1930s and 1940s documented changes in the inn, which featured antiques, a homelike atmosphere, and modern conveniences such as the telephone. The Middlebury Inn successfully competed with the Sargeant Hotel and, eventually, with the developing motels along Route 7 by investing in modern features and developing strong ties to Middlebury College.

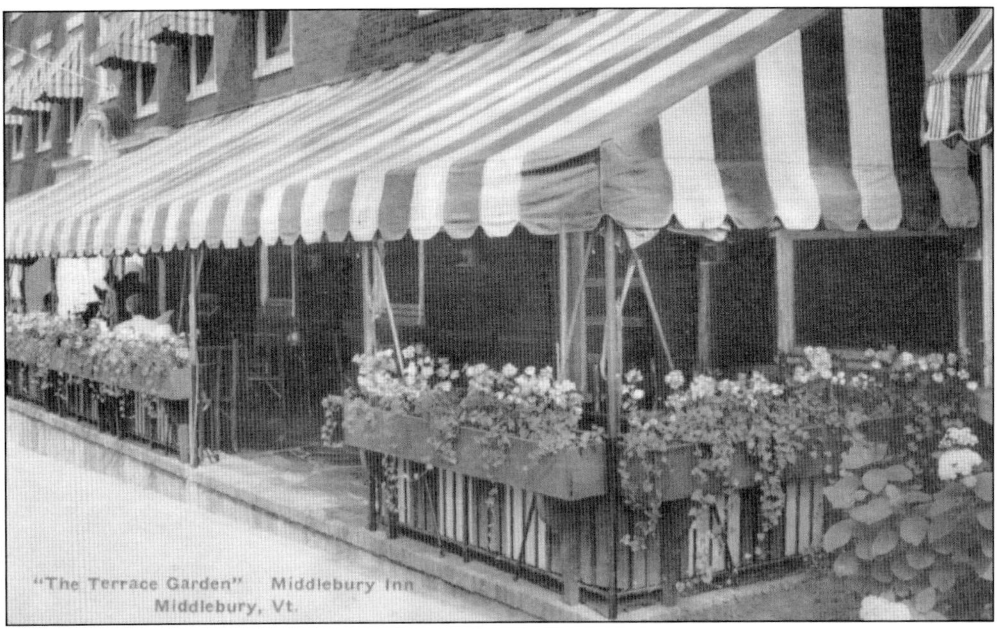

Over time, the Middlebury Inn restored the porches removed from the old Addison House, creating a setting for visitors to watch life along the busy main highway. Today, the traffic is slow but continuous, as nearly all vehicles moving through Middlebury must pass near the inn.

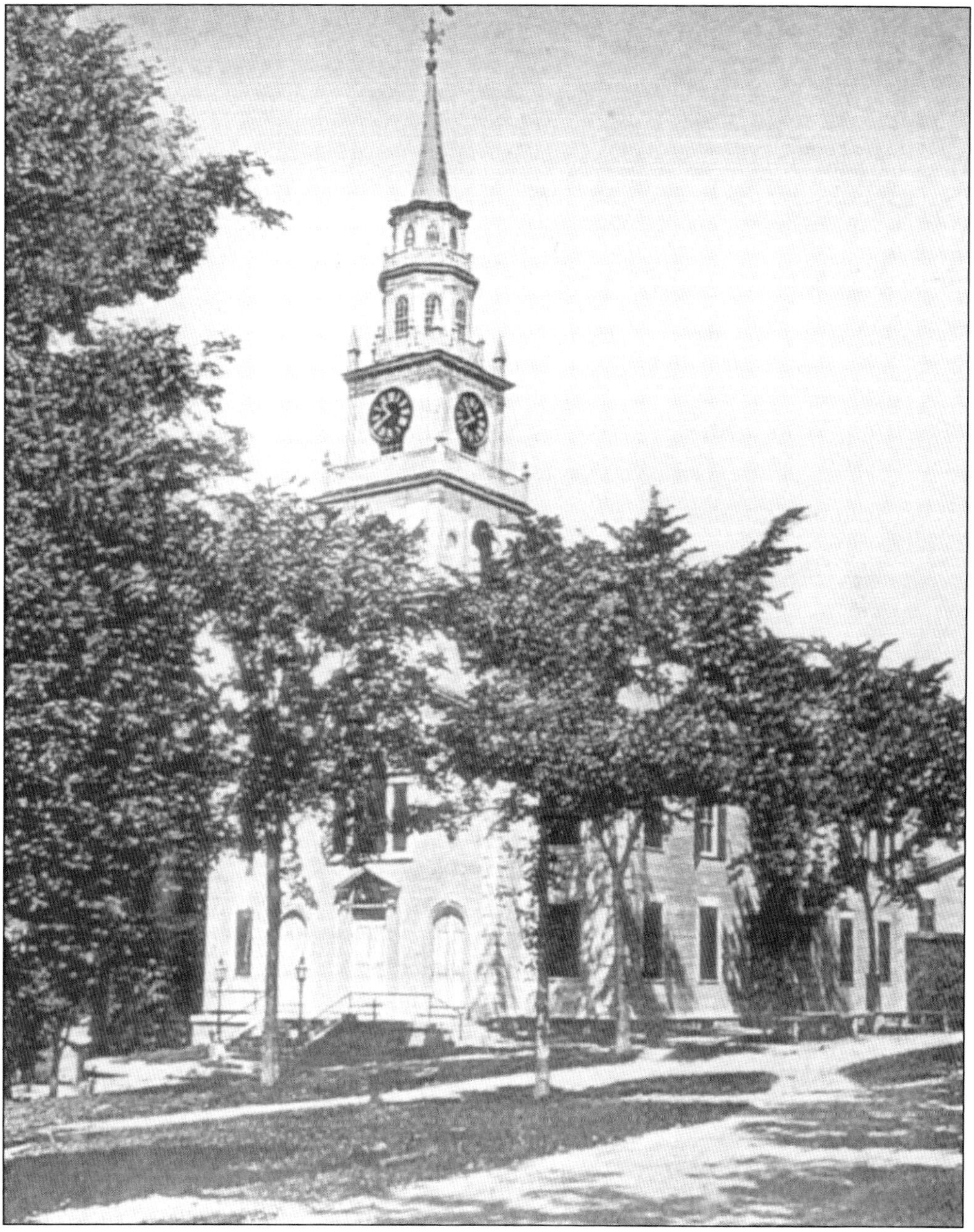

The oldest church in town is the Middlebury Congregational Church, prominently located at the north end of the village green. The congregation was first organized during early settlement of the town, with the construction of the church beginning only in 1806. The prominent location on the village green, overlooking the business district, was chosen along the main turnpike and further solidified the village green as the center of town. The church has been a prominent feature in many Middlebury postcards, varying over time only in relation to the size of the surrounding trees. The spire of the church is constructed as a series of interlocking, tapering structures, which give added strength to the tall tower. The tower has withstood numerous storms, when many other major towers in town and throughout the region were damaged.

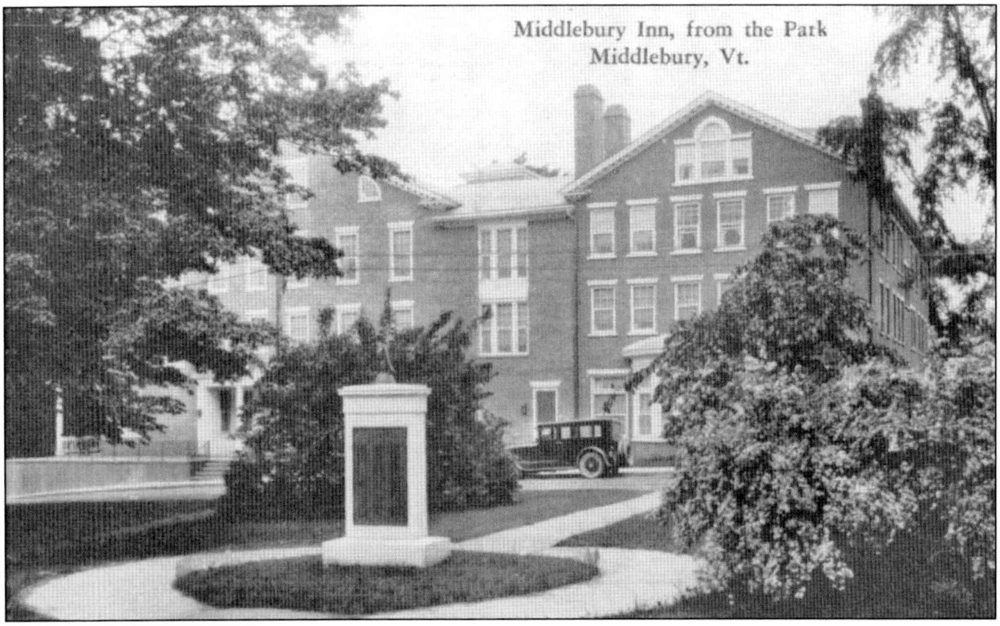

Following World War I, Middlebury sought once again to honor those who served in battle. Noting that the Civil War Monument did not name specific individuals lost in the war effort, a new monument that honored soldiers in all earlier wars was constructed in Court Square at the location of the first county courthouse.

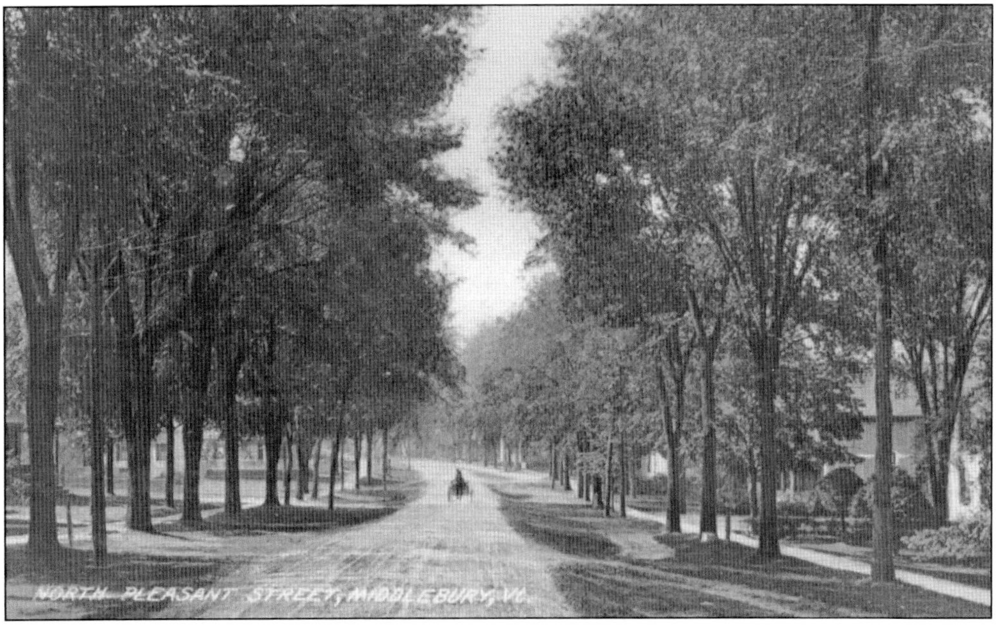

This street view shows the entrance to town from the north along Pleasant Street. A wide avenue lined with trees and sidewalks, Pleasant Street offers a green and pleasant setting for the village situated in an otherwise agricultural landscape. This view from Elm Street looking south shows the houses just north of the Methodist church.

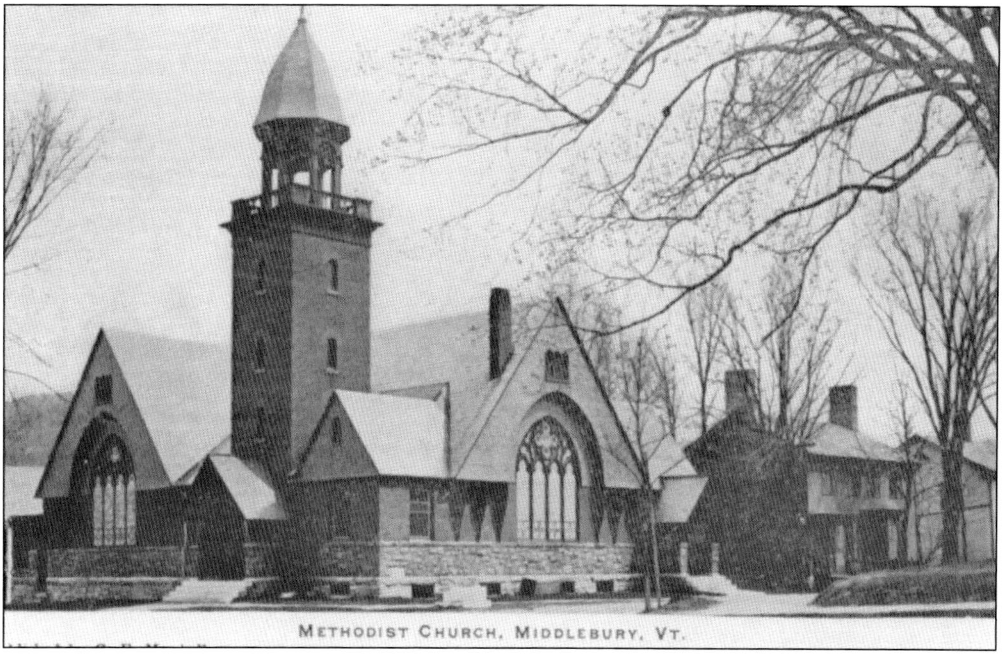

The Methodist church was constructed in 1892–1893 on the corner of North Pleasant and Seminary Streets. With its dramatic geometric features and forceful use of stone and brick, the church is considered one of the best examples of late-Victorian architecture in Vermont. The building to the right was constructed in 1815 by cabinetmaker Hastings Warren, who led local troops in the Battle of Plattsburgh in the War of 1812. Warren built his new home of brick, after losing two nearby wooden buildings to fire. His home was torn down in 1975 to make way for the church parking lot.

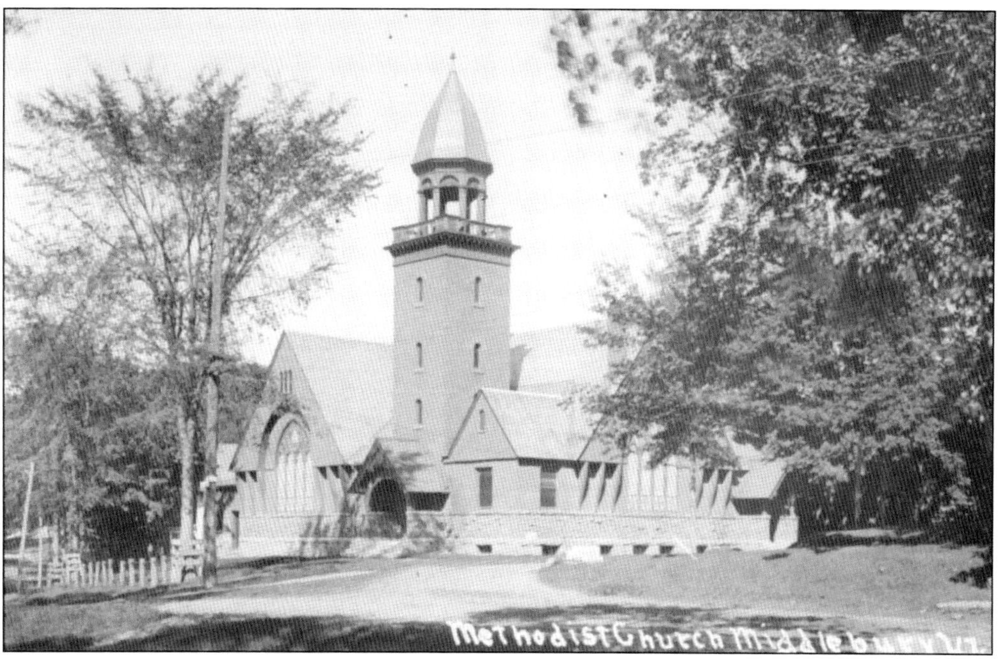

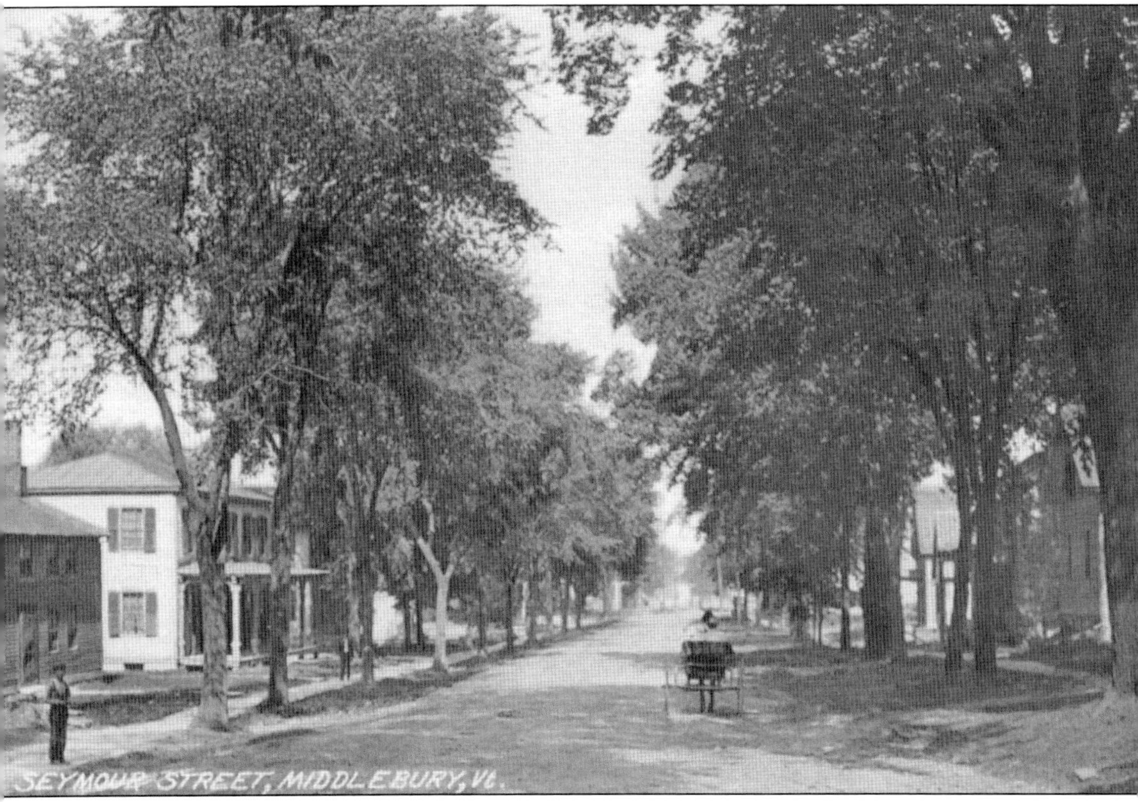

Seymour Street connects the village green with the railroad station, the Pulp Mill Bridge, and points north. It was a section of the Waltham Turnpike laid out in the early town plan, connecting Middlebury to Vergennes. The building on the left is the oldest house in Middlebury. It was constructed on Court Street facing Court Square by Simeon Dudley in 1787; it was expanded by Gamaliel Painter soon after he returned to Middlebury following the Revolutionary War. Painter built himself a new and grander home, moving this house to what is now 7 Seymour Street. The building to the right of what is called the Oldest House is one of a series of three early houses torn down in the 1967 to make way for a Middlebury National Bank building.

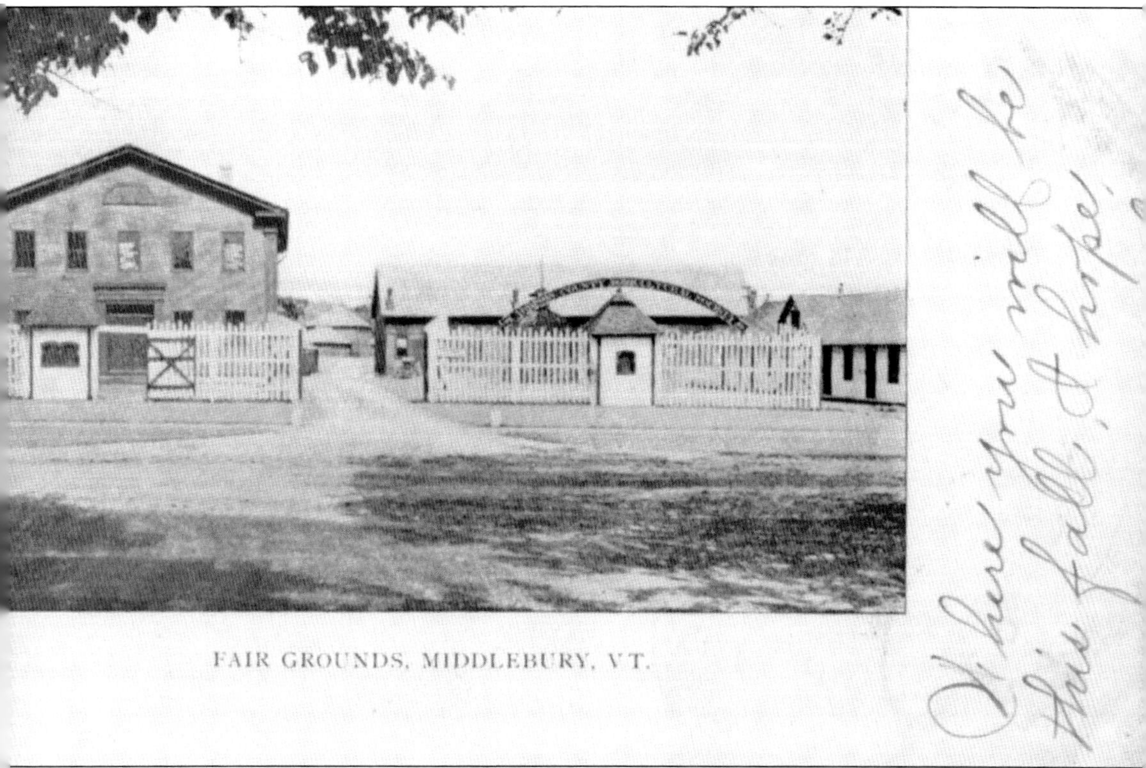

In 1796, Middlebury became the county seat of Addison County, displacing Vergennes. The first courthouse, a simple wooden Colonial-style building, was constructed on Court Street, on what is now called Court Square. It was moved in 1814 across Court Street to make way for the alignment of the new Centre Turnpike. Always considered an uncomfortable building, it was moved again down Court Street to the entrance of the Addison County Fairgrounds, where it was used as a display hall until the fairgrounds closed in 1938. It was torn down in 1939. At the time of this postcard, the old courthouse was called the Exhibition Hall.

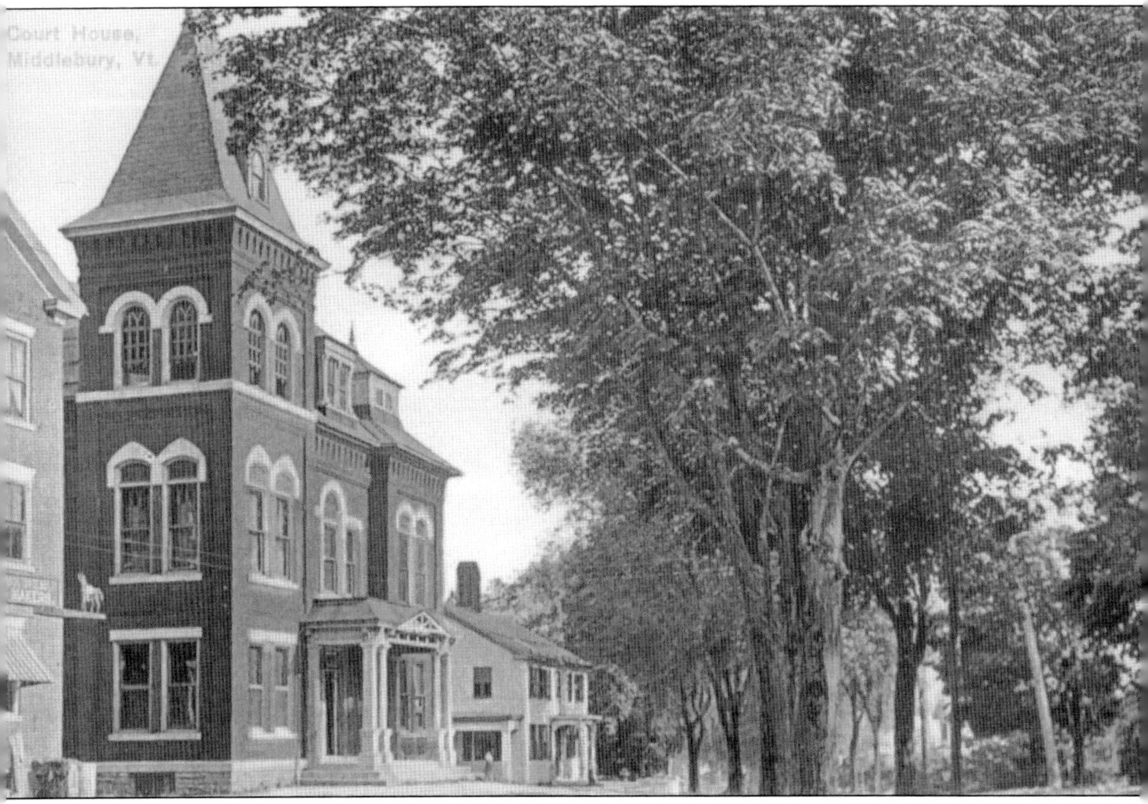

In 1882, a new courthouse was constructed of brick and marble, with Romanesque design and a late Victorian tower. It served the county for 110 years, until a new building was erected to the east. The building to the left is the Masonic Hall, built in 1823. The second courthouse is now owned by Middlebury College and is the home of the Center for Education Technology. The Masonic Hall has, over the years, had a series of uses. It is currently the home of the Vermont Community Foundation and the Vermont Folklife Center.

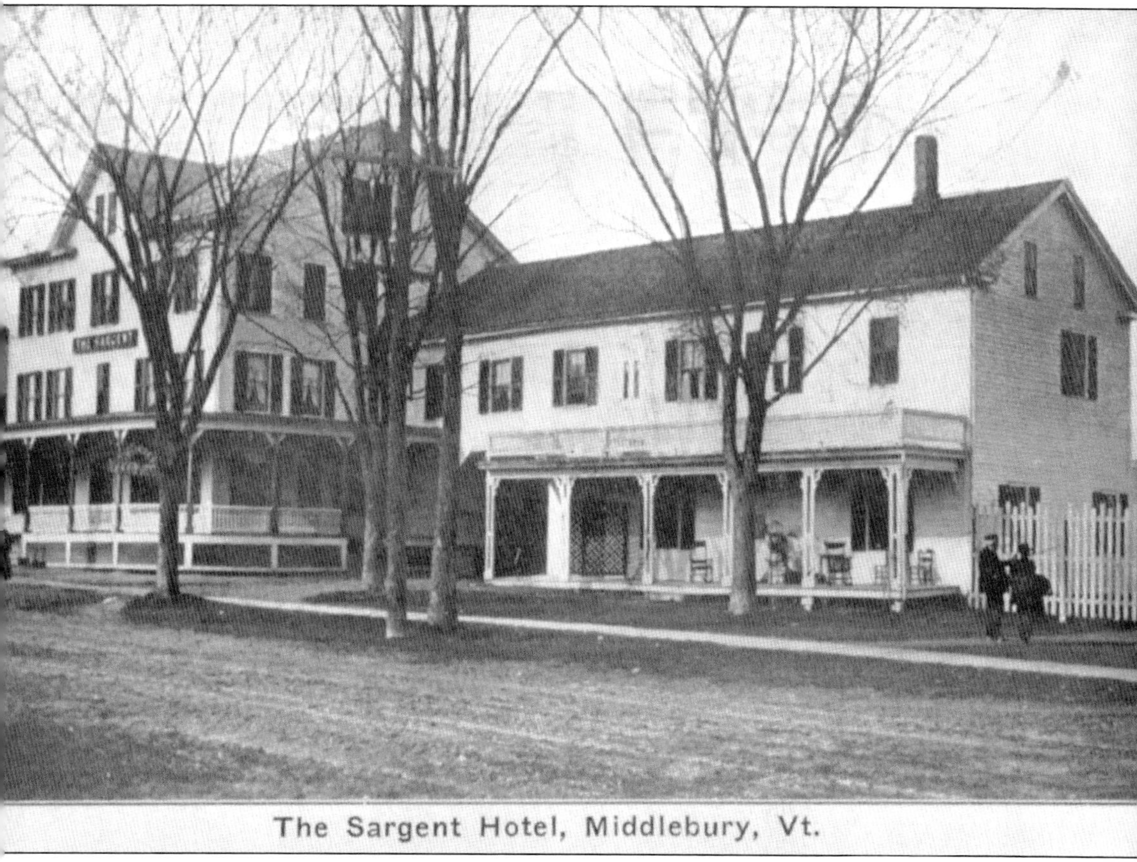

The Sargeant Hotel was first constructed in 1811 on Court Street along the stage route from Brandon to Vergennes and was an important stopover for businessmen and other visitors. Expanded several times, the hotel was in continuous use until the 1940s. It was the site of many events associated with the Addison County Fair. The building has been renovated several times in recent years and is now an assisted-living center. The wing along the right side of this image has been removed. This part of the Sargeant Hotel is currently the location of Milne Travel.

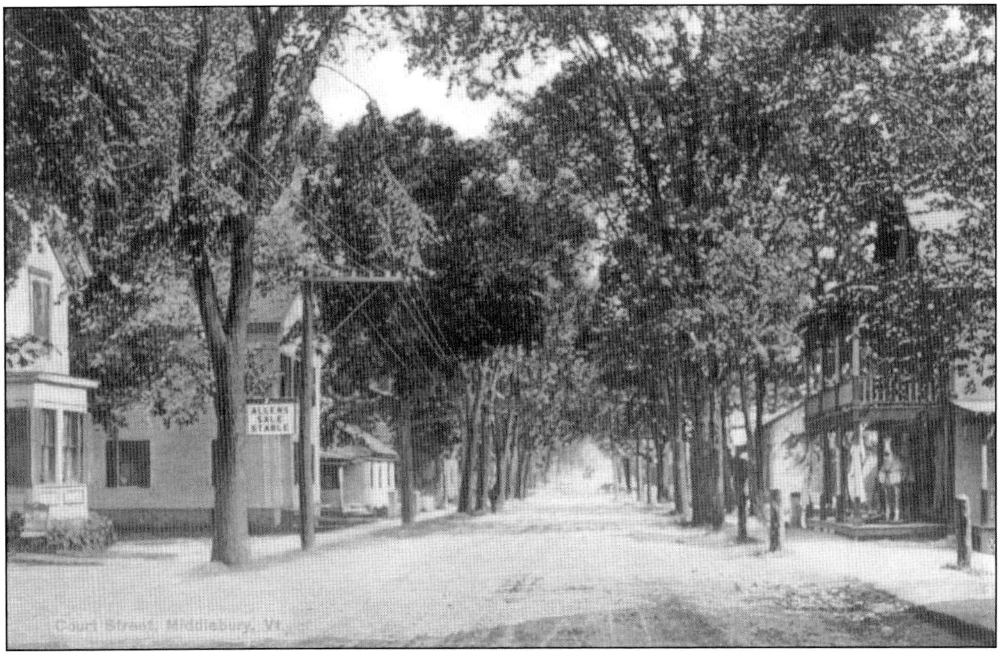

This postcard is labeled Court Street, but it is actually Washington Street. Postcard makers were often unfamiliar with their subjects. Allen's Stable was located in the building now occupied by the Middlebury Bagel and Deli. All of the buildings on the right side of the street have been torn down to make way for the Grand Union Grocery Store complex.

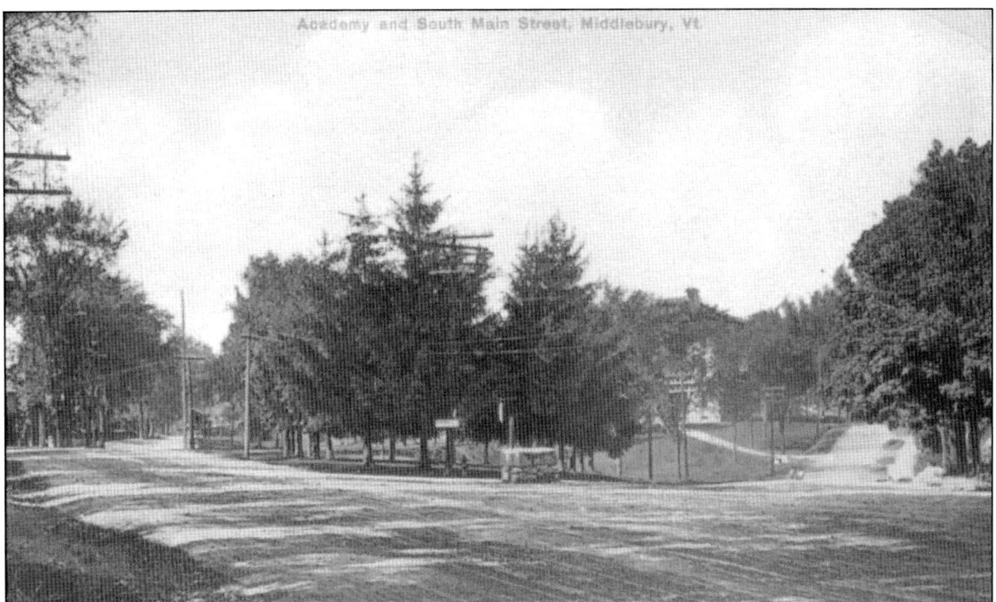

This postcard was mailed in 1909 and shows Storrs Park, defined by South Main Street on the left and College Street on the right. This park was the southern end of the commercial district and the edge of the Middlebury College campus. It was an ideal location to build a new high school for the town.

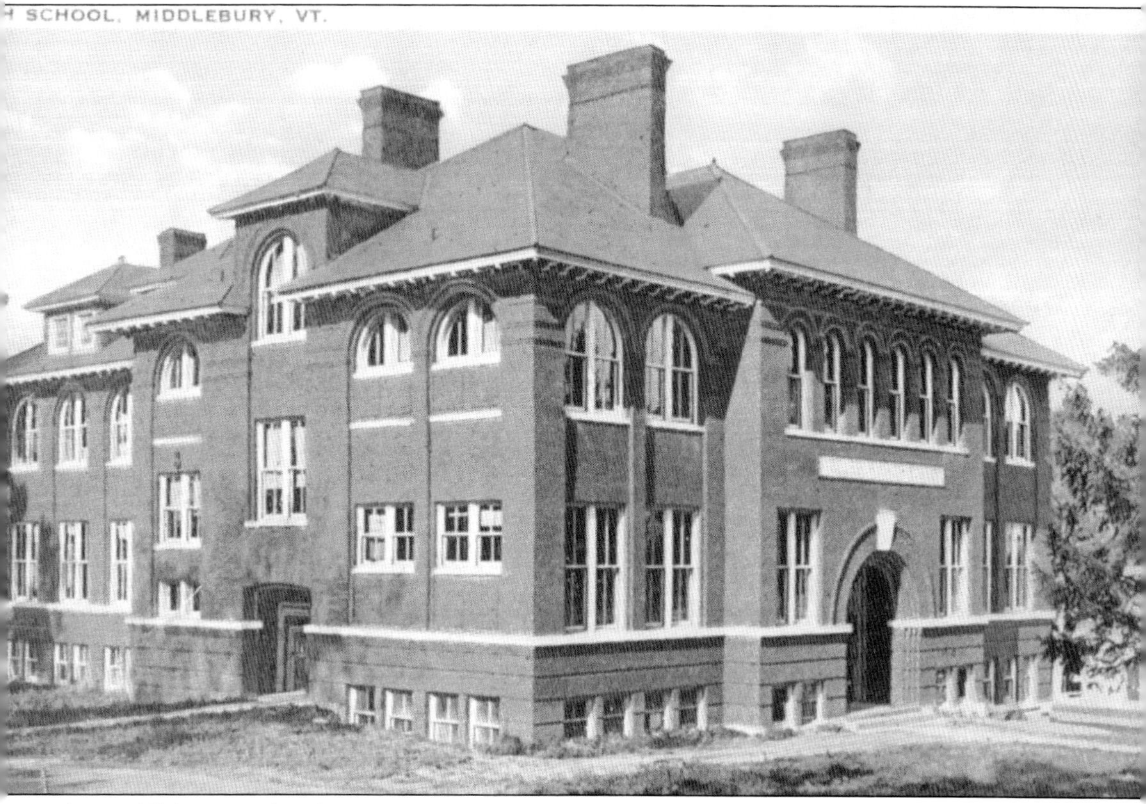

The Middlebury High School was constructed in 1911. An imposing building of brick, the school was near the elementary school, only a short walk for most Middlebury residents. In the late 1930s, a gymnasium was added to the south side of the structure. A fire in 1954 severely damaged the upper part of the structure. Rather than rebuild, a new high school was built off Court Street and the old school was reconstructed as a one-story building for use as town offices, which moved out of the old town hall at the top of Merchant's Row. Middlebury may be one of the only towns in New England with a gymnasium in its town office complex.

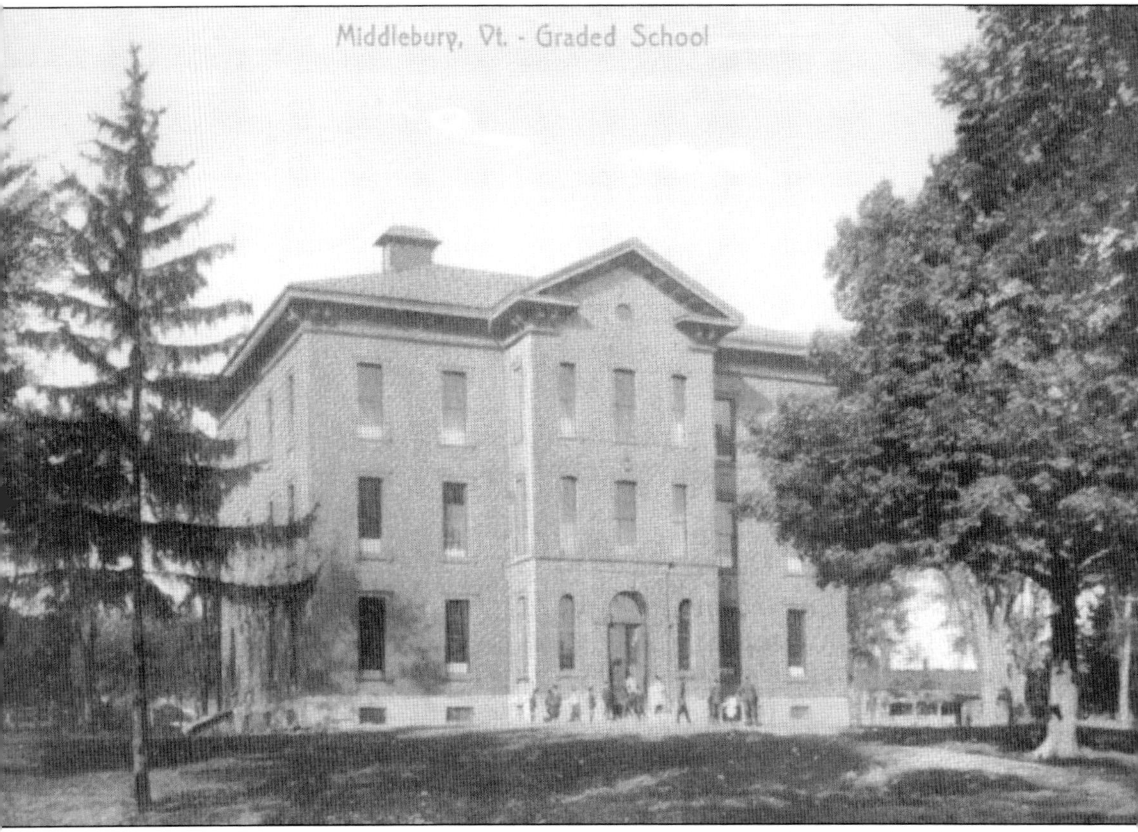

The Graded School or Old Academy Building is located on Academy Road and is now called the Twilight Hall. The current building is shown here *c.* 1915. The first Academy Building was constructed in 1798. For many years, all levels of education took place in the building, including the early years of Middlebury College, which moved in 1820 to Painter Hall. The 1798 building was torn down and a new Academy Building was constructed in 1867. It burned in 1904. A significant debate arose as to how to replace the important structure. Many advocated a new building in the monumental style of the period; others missed their school. Finally, it was finally decided to rebuild the school exactly like the earlier structure, with the exception of the original tall cupola.

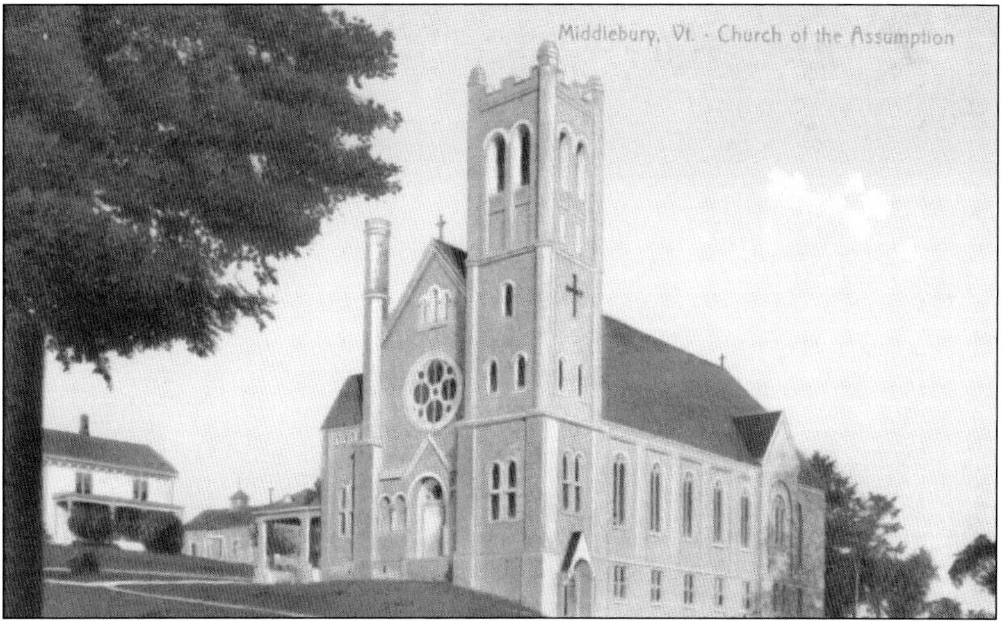

The Roman Catholic church, St. Mary's, constructed between 1895 and 1907 at the corner of College and Shannon Streets, is a monumental marble structure with elaborate stained-glass windows. Because much of the labor to build the church and interior features was donated by local craftsman, it took 12 years to complete the stately church.

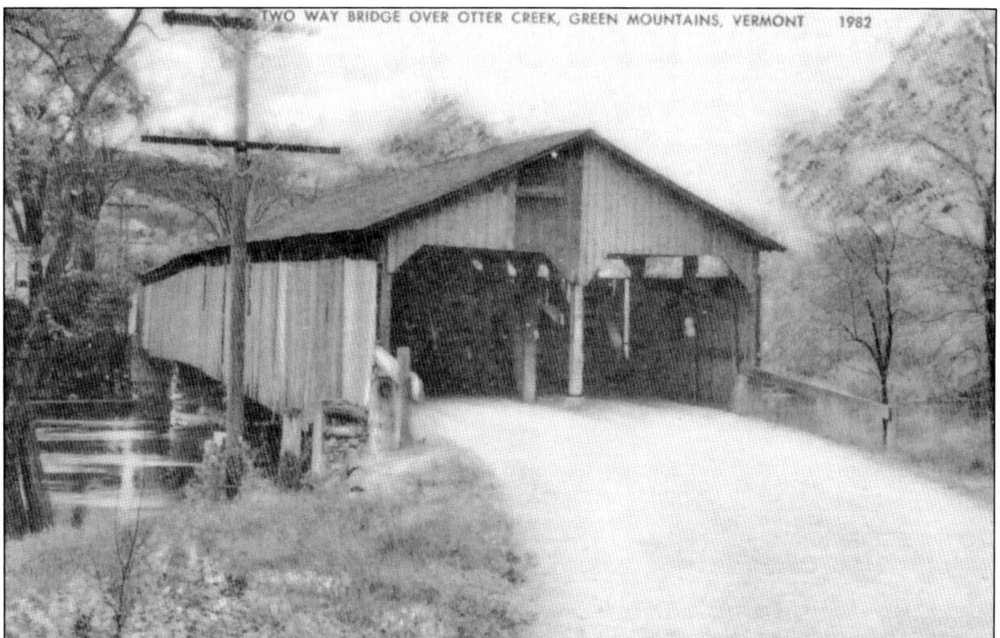

The Pulp Mill Bridge crosses a quiet section of Otter Creek downstream from the waterfalls. First built in 1808 and redesigned and rebuilt in 1820, the Pulp Mill Bridge is 199 feet long and one of only two double-covered bridges remaining in Vermont.

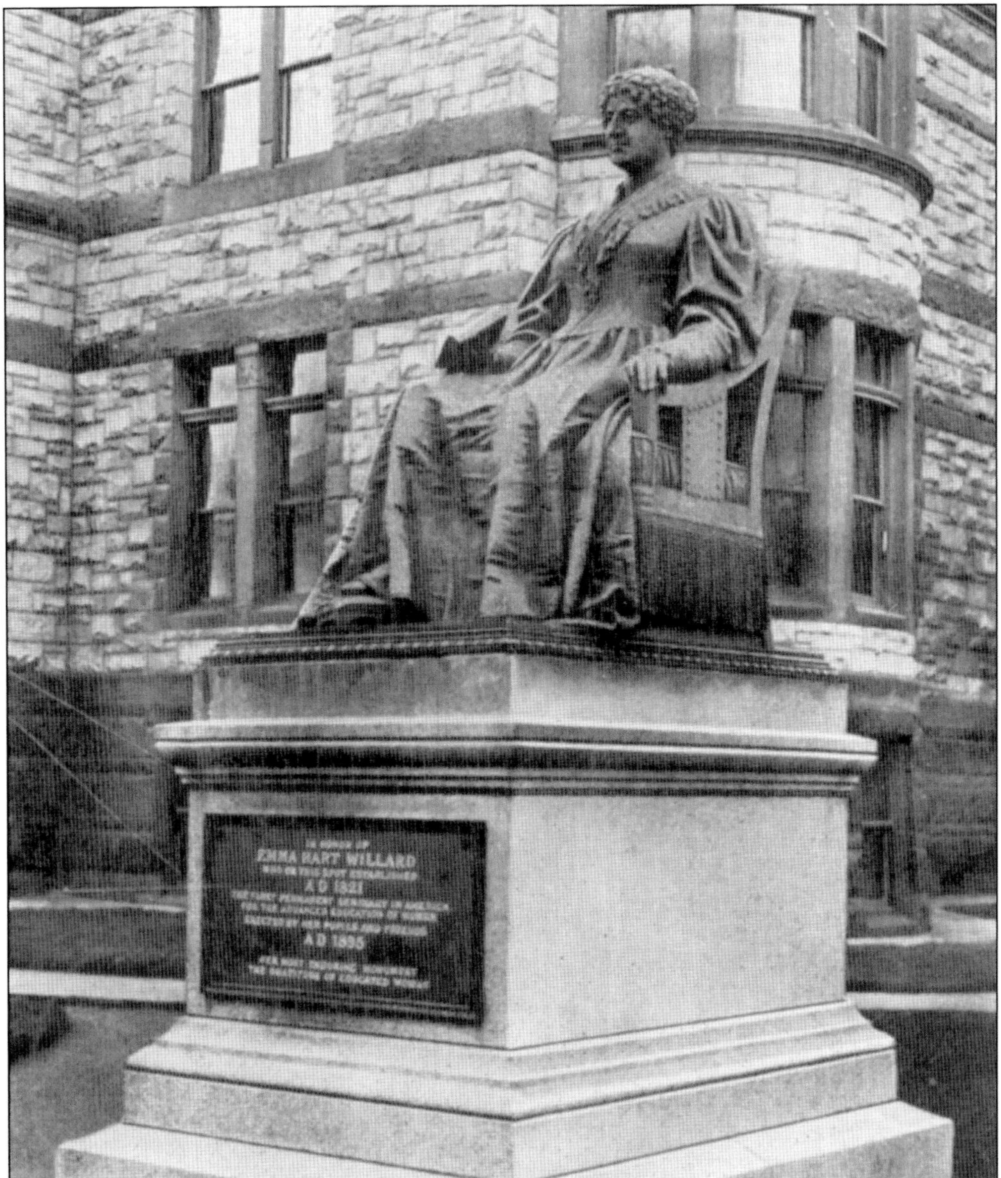

Emma Hart moved to Middlebury in 1808 to teach at the Middlebury Academy. Her early writings describe the vibrant intellectual and social community of the time. In 1810, Emma Hart married John Willard, a prominent doctor. John Willard was also a director in the Middlebury Bank. When the bank was robbed in 1814, the Willards were partly responsible for making up bank losses. To cover part of their costs, Emma Hart Willard opened a school in her large home. Long dedicated to the advancement of women's education, Emma Willard was concerned for the education of young women and drew the attention of local educators. In 1819, the Willards moved to New York State, where Emma began a school for girls. This monument to Emma Willard stands in front of the main buildings that were the Emma Willard School in Troy, New York. Middlebury commemorates Emma Willard's early work with a small monument erected in 1941 in front of the Congregational church.

Four

Middlebury College and Bread Loaf

Middlebury College began in 1800 at the south end of the village in the first Academy Building, an ambitious undertaking of the earliest town founders. The school has a long and colorful tradition developed from a series of supporters, many of whom experimented with new forms of learning in the beautiful country setting. Early women's education was a priority. At Middlebury, a new way to learn languages was developed by immersing students into the culture in an intense living and educational experience. Postcards were an important feature of college life, as a quick note from the undisciplined student correspondent or as a means of renewing old connections among alumni. The cards documented the changing campus scene, showing old venerated buildings, new structures, and campus events. Bread Loaf, the country retreat of Joseph Battell, was developed between 1866 and 1915. When Battell died, he bequeathed his 31,000-acre forest and hotel complex to the college. Bread Loaf Inn subsequently became the Summer English School and, finally, the site of the Bread Loaf Writers' Conference.

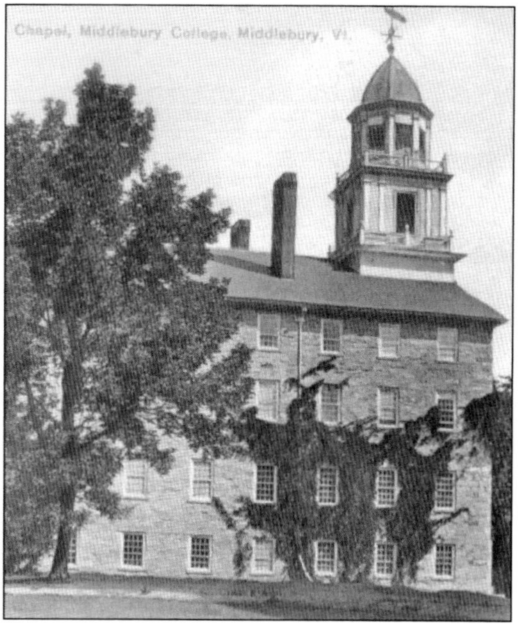

The Old Chapel was built in 1835–1836 as an all-purpose campus building, including classrooms, living quarters, a gym, a chapel on the upper floors, and faculty offices on the fourth floor. It was the subject of numerous postcards and has become the symbol of Middlebury College.

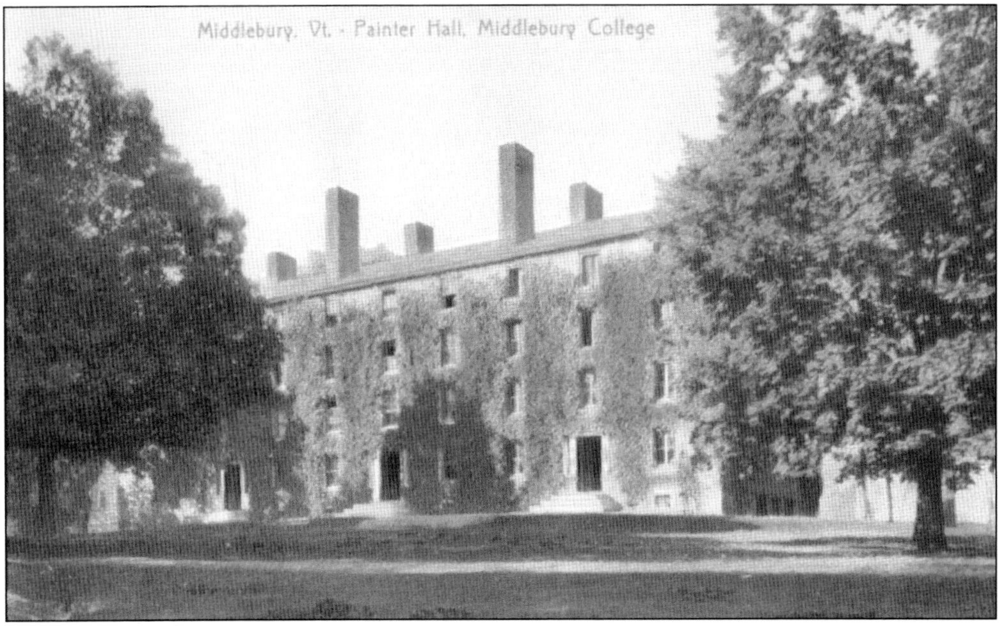

Painter Hall is the oldest college building in Vermont. Constructed between 1814 and 1816, using local limestone and marble, Painter Hall is designed like the mills owned by the college patrons who supported its construction. Built to serve many of the early needs of the growing school, Painter Hall has adapted to change well over the years. Today, it is used exclusively as a dormitory.

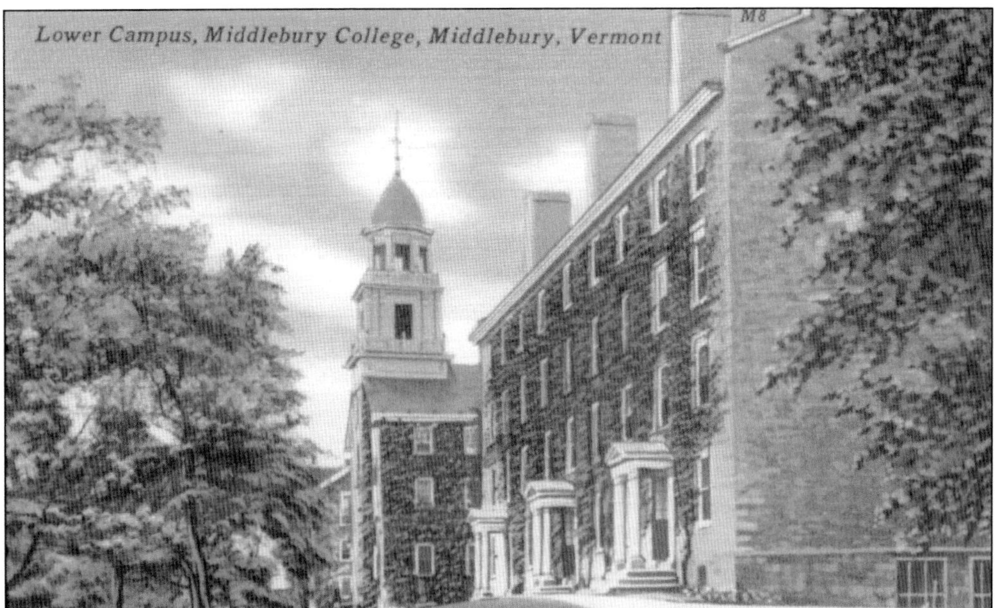

Part of the early Middlebury College plan included a series of three buildings, with stunning views of the Green Mountains, as the central focus of campus. In the early days of postcards, the Old Stone Row was a symbol of dignified collegiate life. The buildings were, however, constructed over a 50-year period, beginning in 1814, adhering to the original school plan.

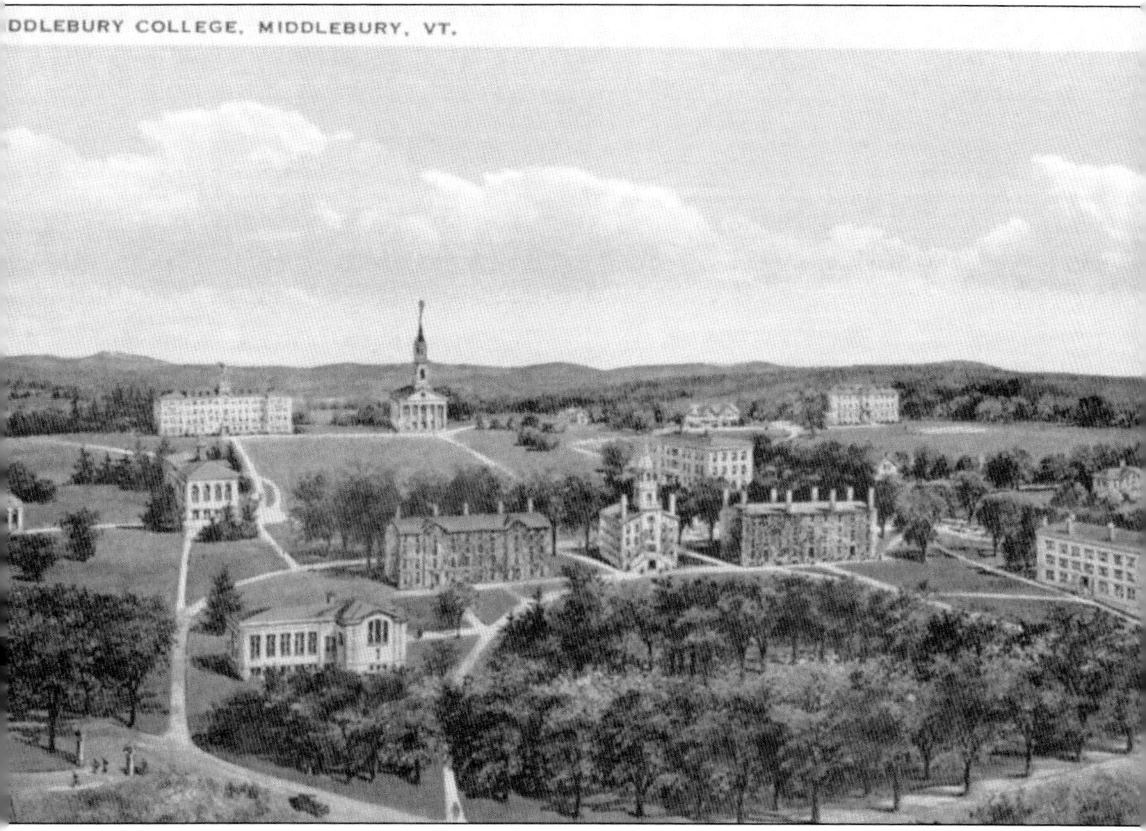

This aerial view painting of the Middlebury College campus, shown in a 1920 postcard, has become a standard image, representing the beautiful college in the Vermont countryside. The campus was set distinctly apart from the village of Middlebury, with dramatic views of the Adirondacks to the west and the Green Mountains to the east. Today, college-owned buildings are scattered through the village as well as on campus, and there are increased efforts to include local people in college events, decreasing the separation between town and school.

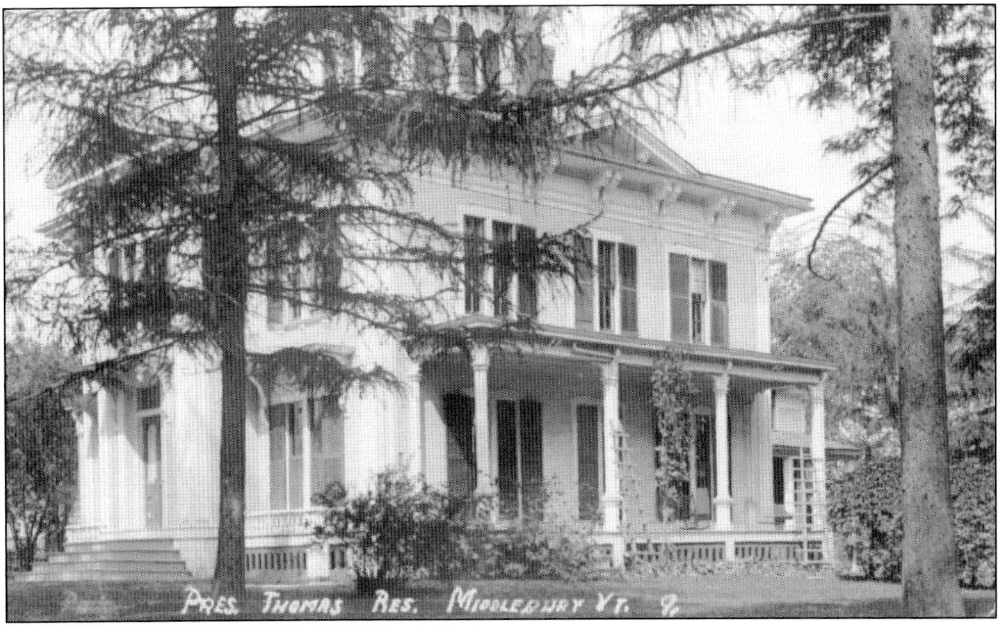

In 1867, Middlebury College president Harvey Kitchel built a Victorian mansion with Italianate details on the corner of Weybridge and College Streets near the edge of the college campus. In 1891, the Kitchel home became the first dormitory of the new women's college and was renamed Battell Hall. Today, the Kitchel house is a privately owned nursing home called the Addison House.

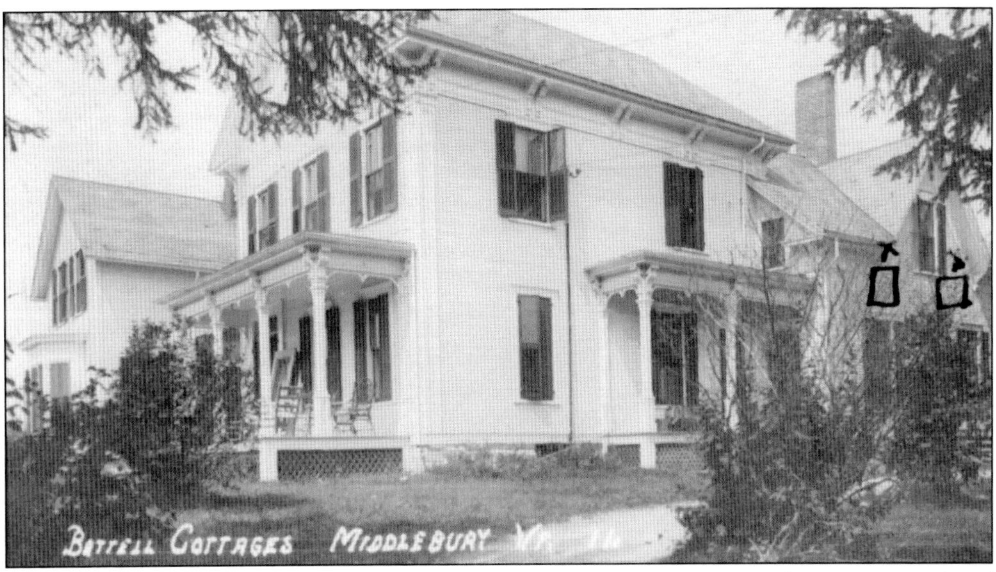

In 1909, Joseph Battell's charitable interests turned toward the women's college. He considered buying an 11-acre farm north of the school but was convinced by the college president that he should buy additional land along the ridge top that included a rundown farmhouse. The old house was remodeled into a dormitory, first called Battell Cottage and later named the Adirondack House for its spectacular view of the mountains. The 46-acre site that Battell purchased is now the North Campus.

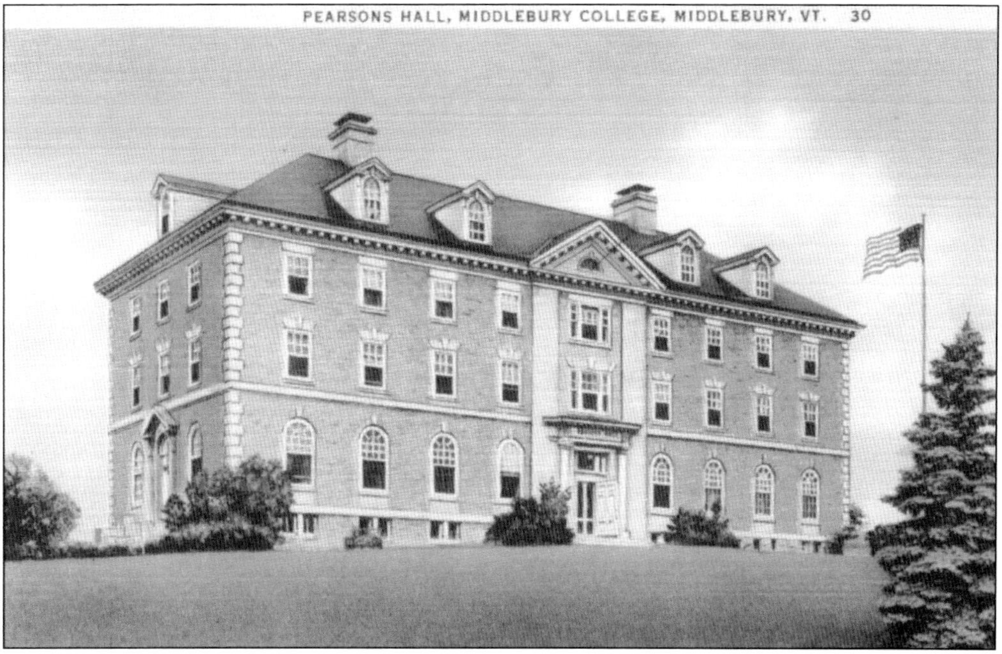

Just north of the Adirondack House is Pearsons Hall, built in 1911 as the first new building on the women's campus. With commanding views of both the Adirondacks and the Green Mountains, Pearsons Hall was the center of social life for the women's college. Today, the entire building is a dormitory.

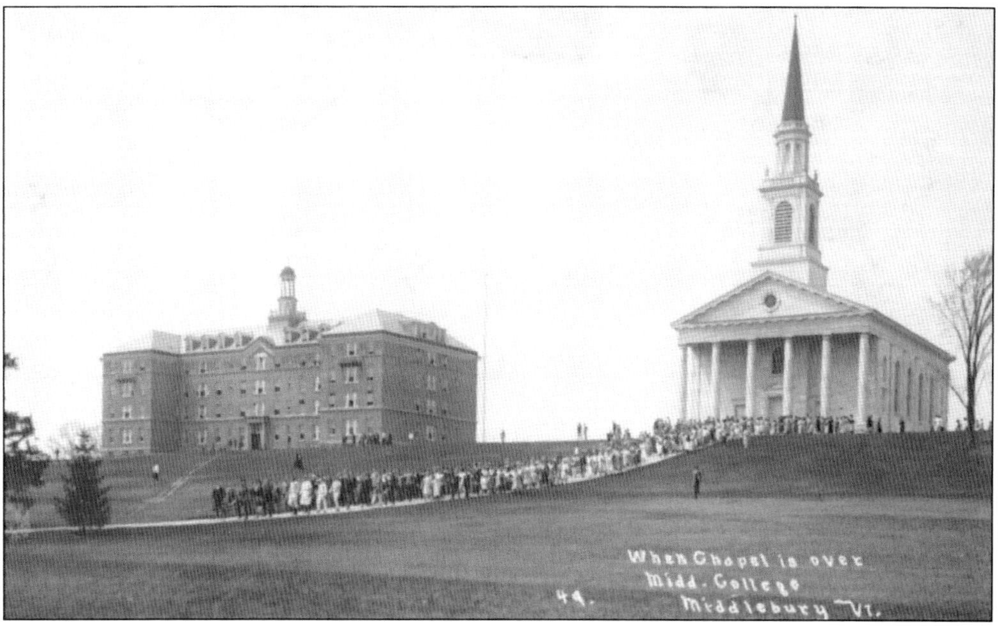

This real photo postcard of a stream of students leaving Mead Chapel, entitled "When Chapel is Over," has become a classic Middlebury College image from the 1930s. The chapel was built in 1916 with a major donation by former Vermont governor John Abner Mead, who grew up in nearby Fair Haven. The building to the left is Hepburn Hall, also built in 1916.

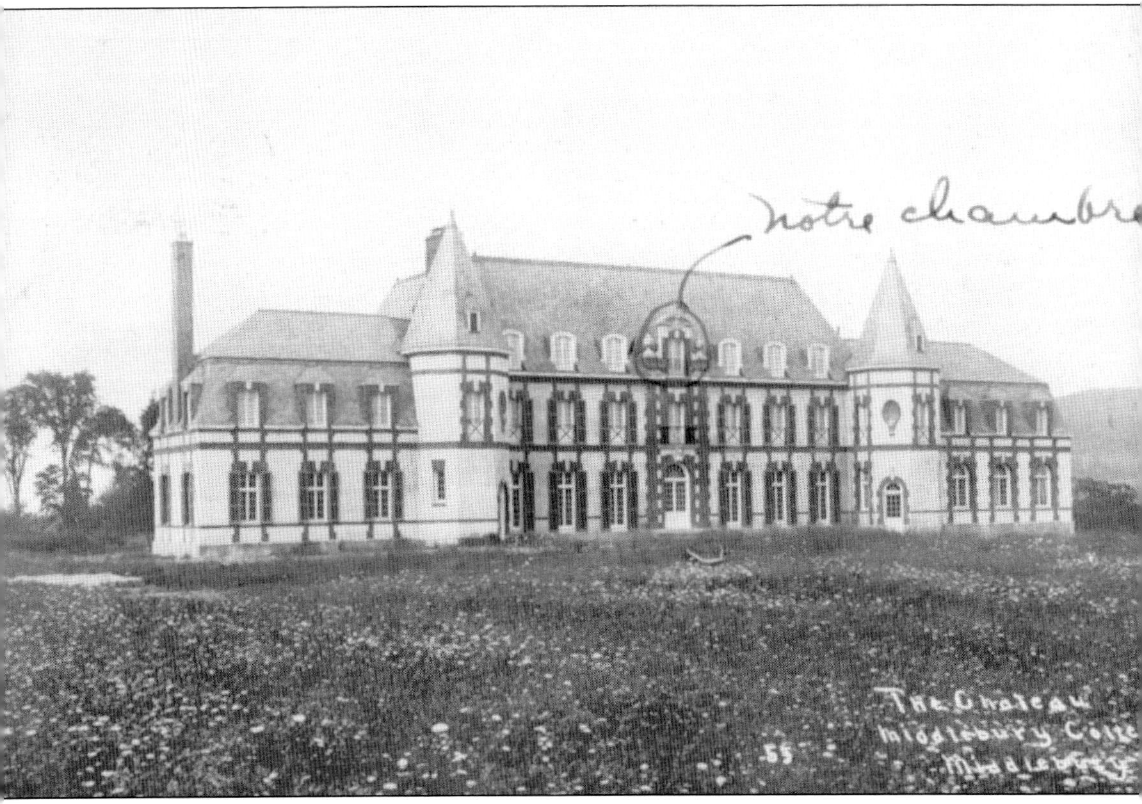

The Middlebury College Chateau was the first building specifically designed for the new college language programs. Built in 1925 with funds from the heir to the Proctor marble fortune, Mrs. John Proctor, Le Chateau was patterned after a mansion at the French Royal Palace at Fountainbleu. The Chateau was used for the intensive language program and was the site of all student activities, including a residence, classrooms, and dining hall space. The Middlebury Language School programs initiated a new form of learning a foreign language by immersing the students in a 24-hour exposure to the language and culture.

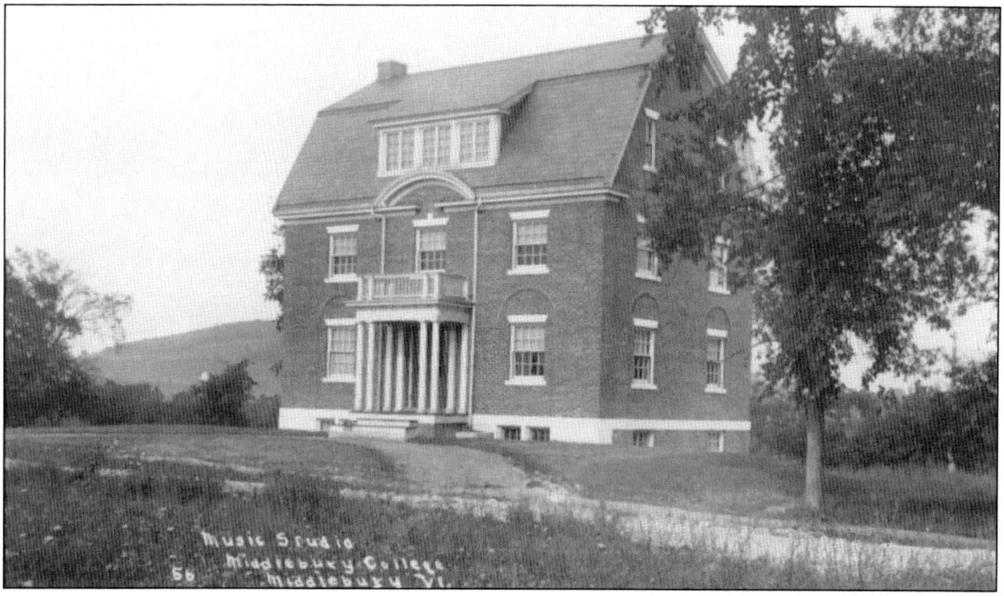

The Music Studio was, for many years, home to the Middlebury College music program, with classrooms, faculty offices, and practice rooms. Demolished in the 1970s to make way for the Wright Memorial Theatre, the Music Studio is one of the very few buildings lost to campus development. A remarkable number of early structures have found new uses on the well-planned campus.

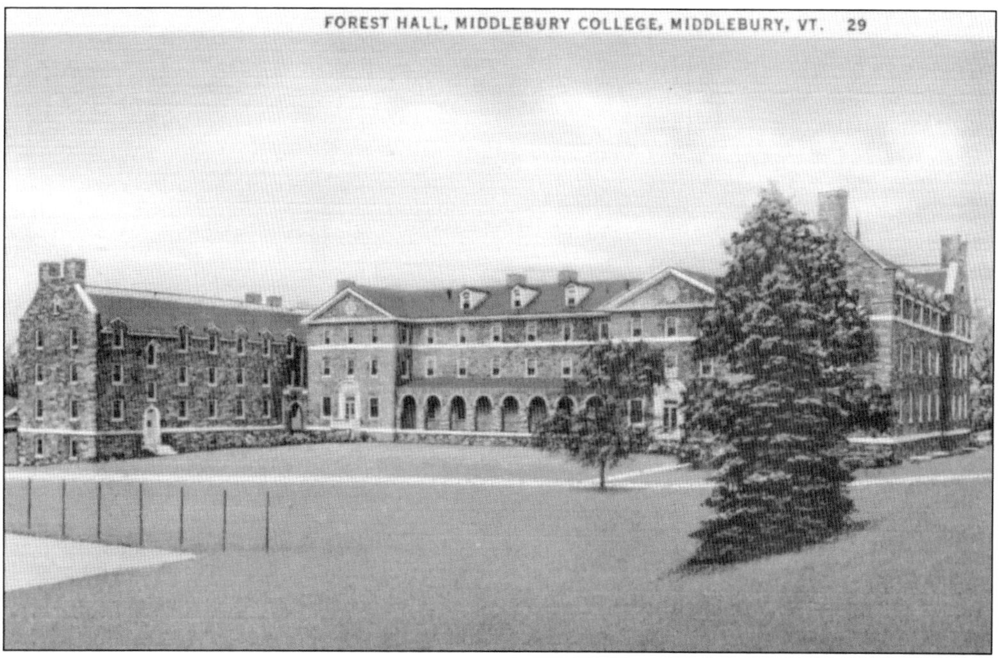

Businessman Joseph Battell continued to contribute to women's education at Middlebury beyond his death in 1915. In 1936, the college sold 21,000 acres of the forest left to the school in Battell's will to the U.S. government for inclusion in the Green Mountain National Forest. The $450,000 received by the college was used to build Forest Hall as the major women's residence.

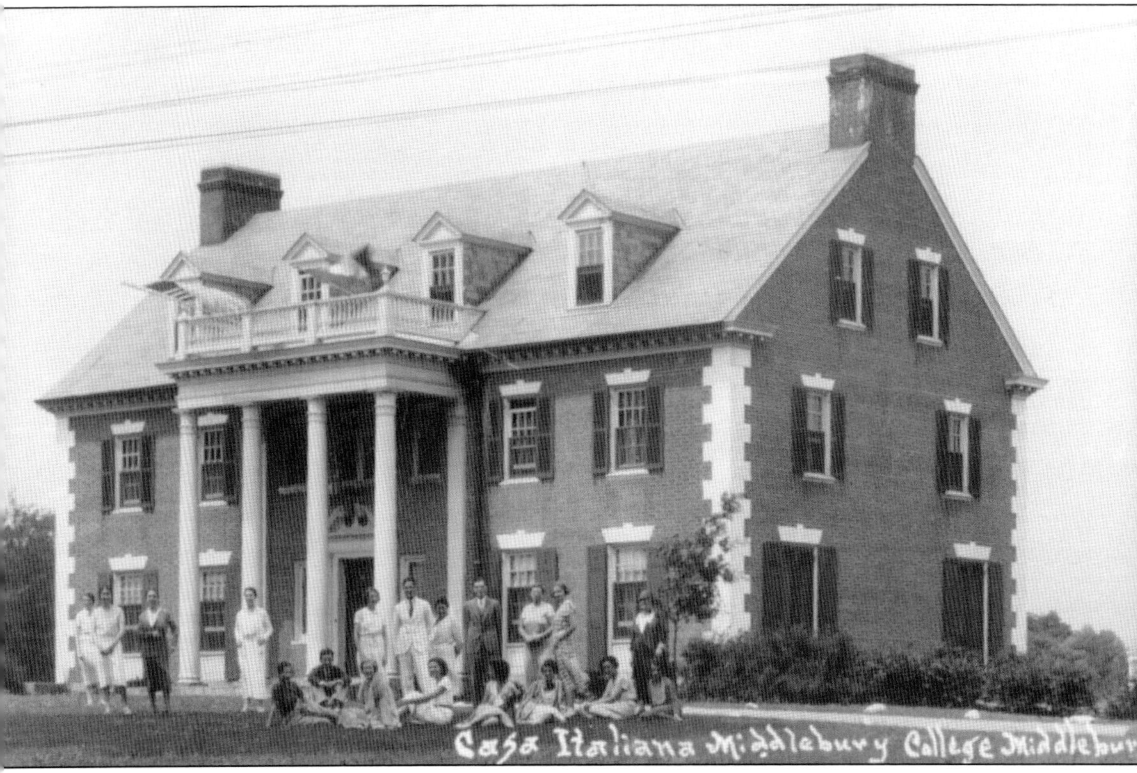

The DU House has long been a distinctive feature of the college along South Main Street, with Federal and Neoclassical features and its setting on a small rise above the road with minimal landscaping. The DU House was a popular and important college fraternity and, on occasion, was the summer home of one of the language programs. The Summer Italian Program is shown in this postcard. In the 1980s, the fraternities on campus were taken over by the college. Today, the old DU House is a student residence with several administration offices.

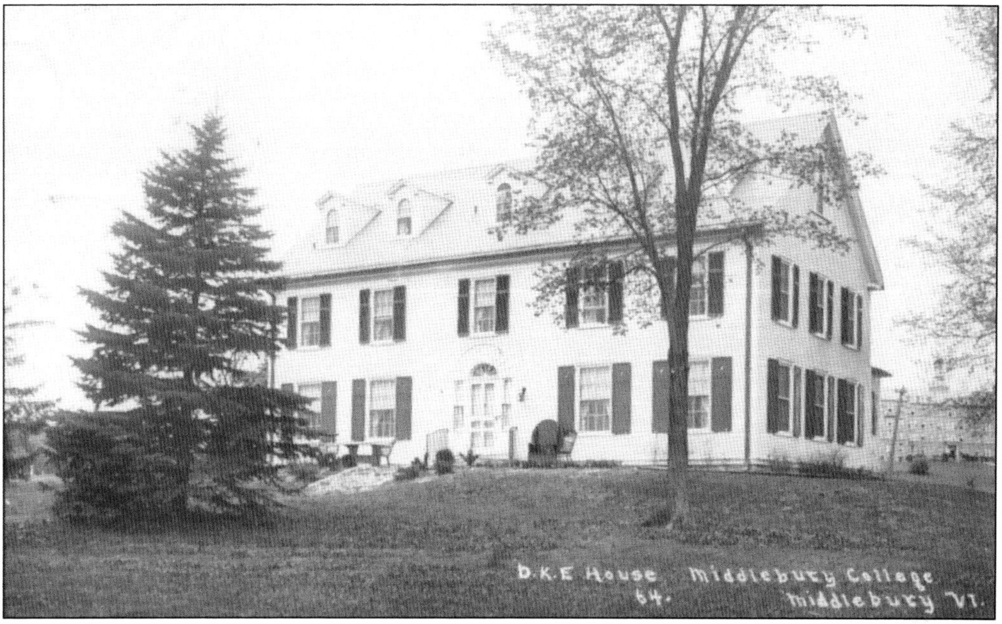

The DKE House, located immediately north of the DU House, was also an important social institution. In 1970, the DKE House, shown here in an early real photo postcard, burned in a dramatic fire. The fraternity was reconstructed with remarkably similar but much smaller features. The building houses offices and still has a room where the fraternity alumni meet.

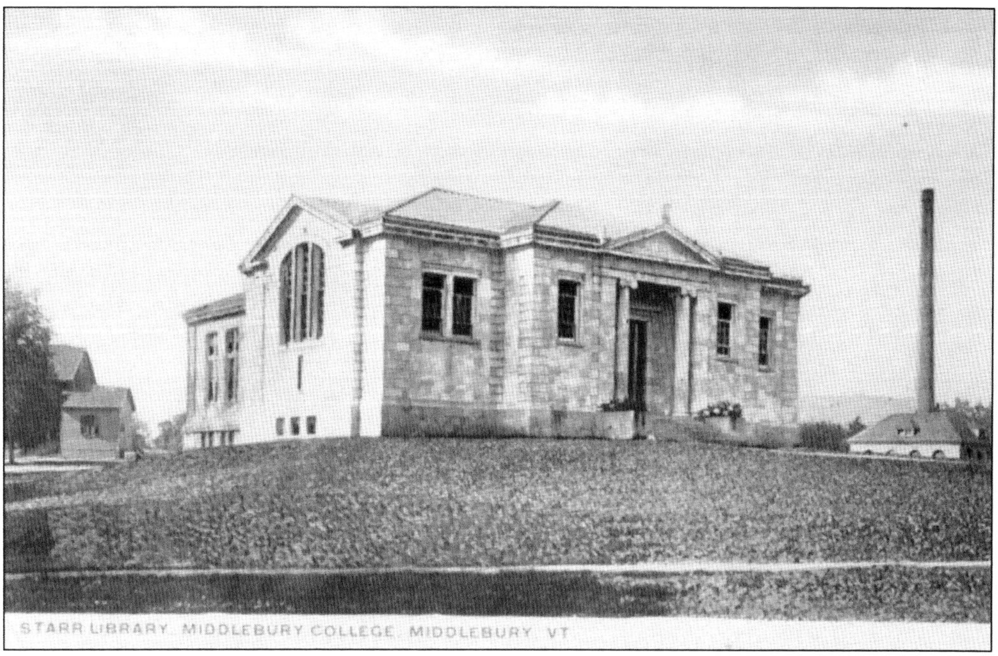

Starr Library was built in 1900, a dignified, classic marble structure, shown in this early-1920s postcard. It has been expanded three times to meet the needs of the growing college programs.

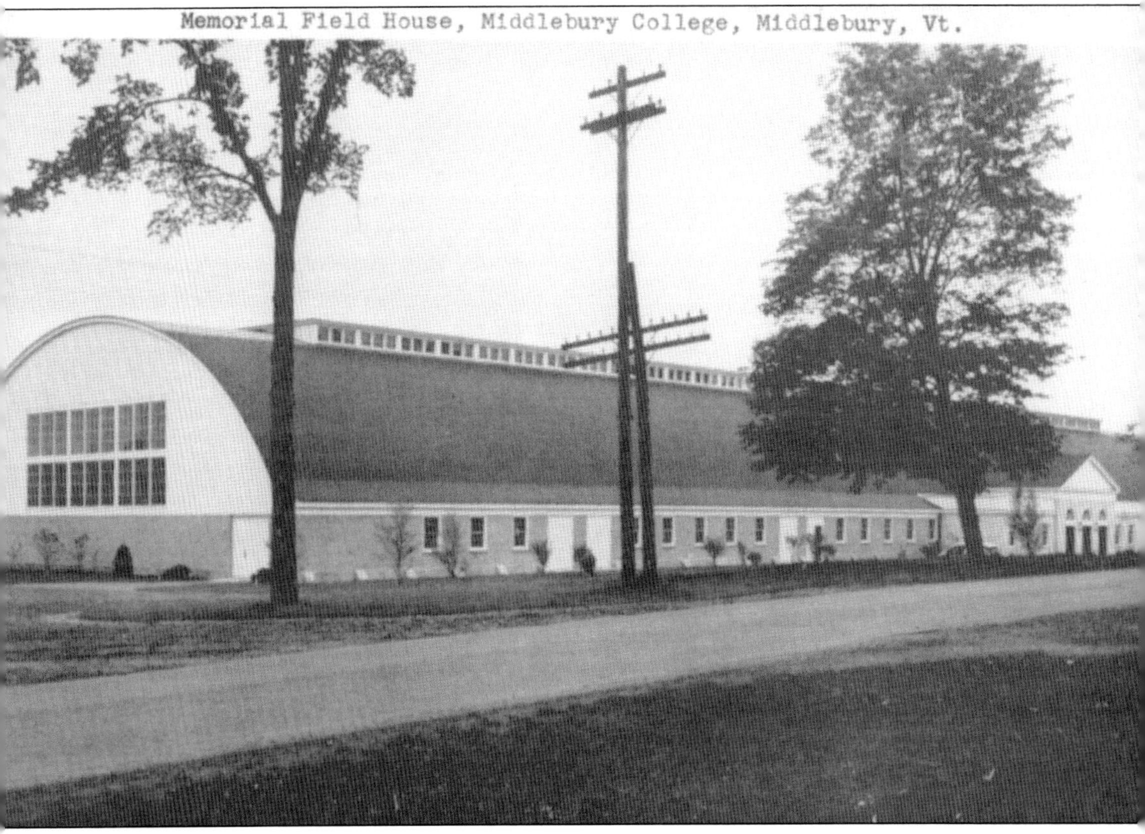

The Middlebury Memorial Field House was constructed with donations from 5,000 alumni in memory of Middlebury students who died in the war. The building was moved in 1949 from Griffiss Air Base in Rome, New York. For many years, the Middlebury Memorial Field House was the major feature along South Main Street, in the approach from the west. Today, it has been joined by a series of new, imposing structures, each a repetition of geometric forms that blends the shapes of the nearby mountains with many of the traditional building materials of the Middlebury region.

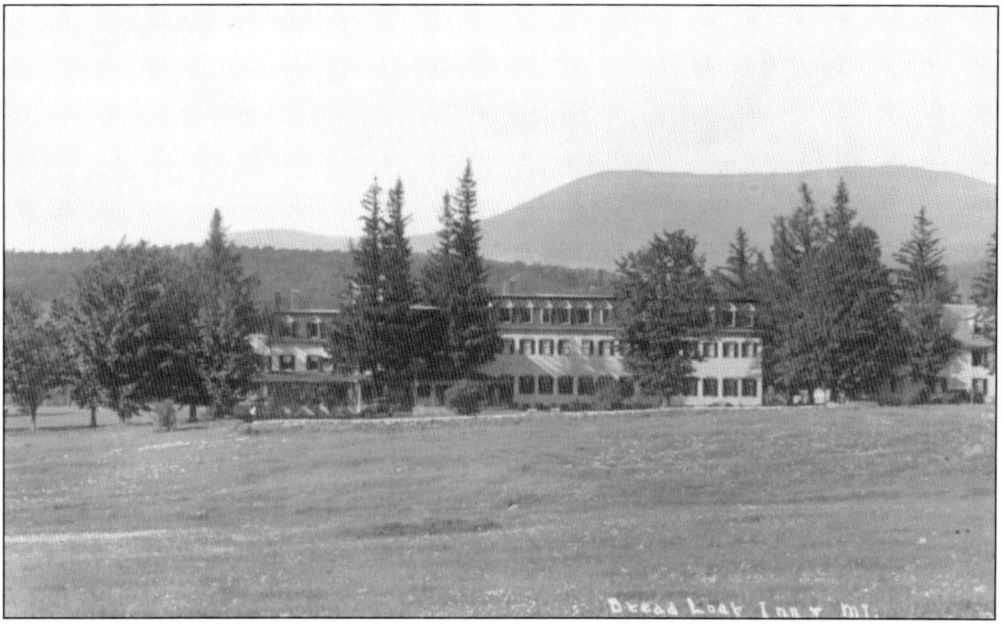

In 1866, businessman Joseph Battell began conversion of an old farmhouse into the Bread Loaf Inn, 12 miles east of Middlebury in the Green Mountains. With a dramatic view of Bread Loaf Mountain, the inn offered a cool retreat for Battell's friends and relatives. Soon, Battell realized that his attractive inn setting might be threatened by development. He began buying land. Over the next 50 years, Battell assembled the largest single land ownership in Vermont, a total of 31,000 acres. A tireless builder, Battell added cottages, a modern farm, and buildings for entertainment to the inn complex. When he died in 1915, the Bread Loaf Inn and the surrounding landscape were bequeathed to Middlebury College.

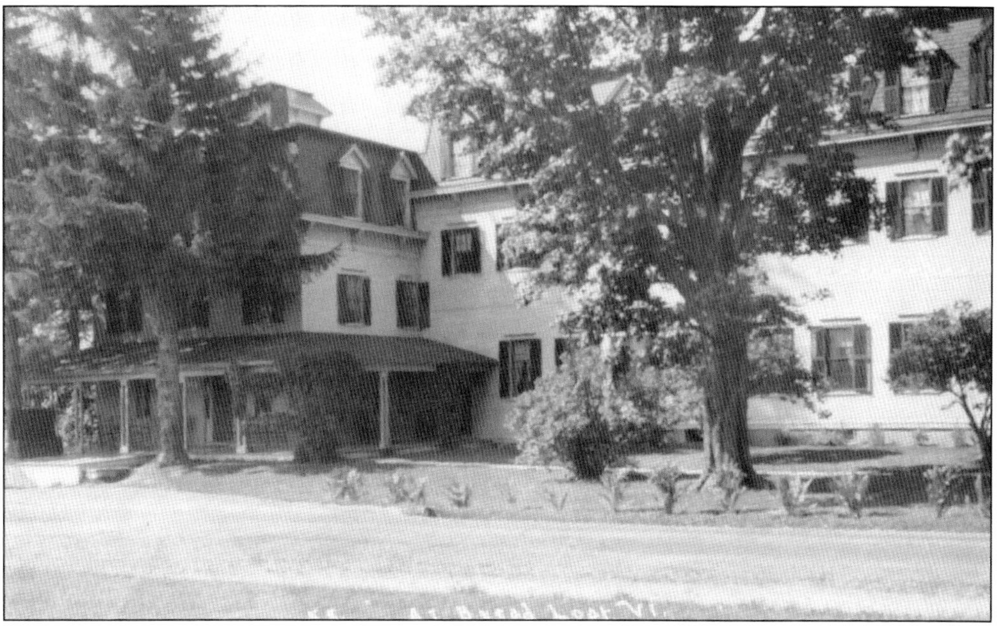

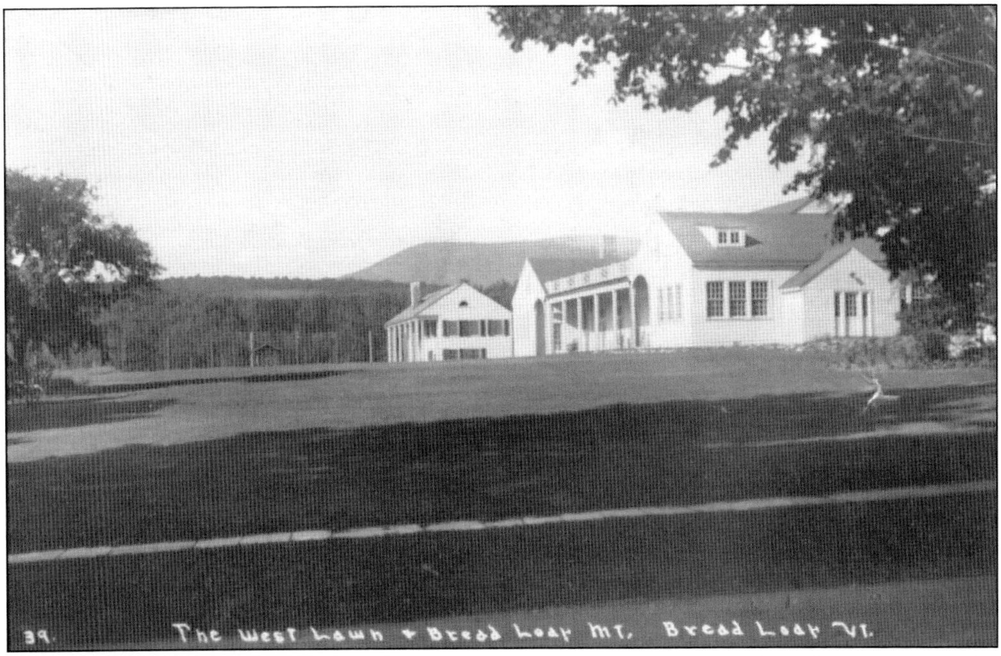

In 1919, Middlebury College moved its Summer English Program to Bread Loaf, restructuring the complex to include student housing, classrooms, a theater, and a library. In 1926, a new concept in education developed at Middlebury College: the Bread Loaf Writers' Conference. Throughout the summer, writers of all sorts—novelists, poets, essayists, and academics—gather at Bread Loaf to discuss writing techniques, publishing, and new ideas. Over the years, the Writers' Conference has been a stimulating and vibrant part of the Middlebury summer scene.

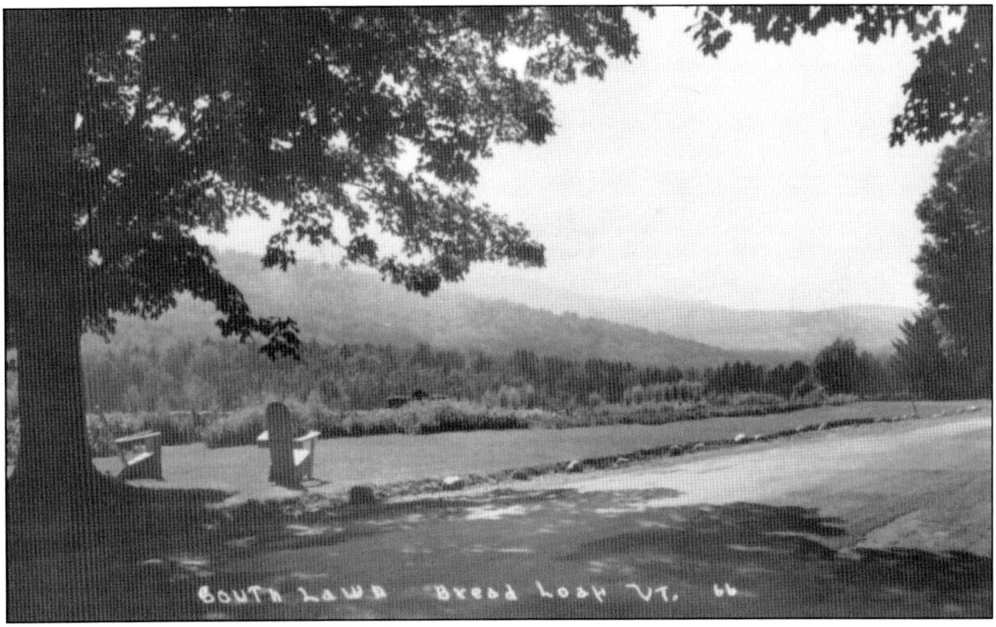

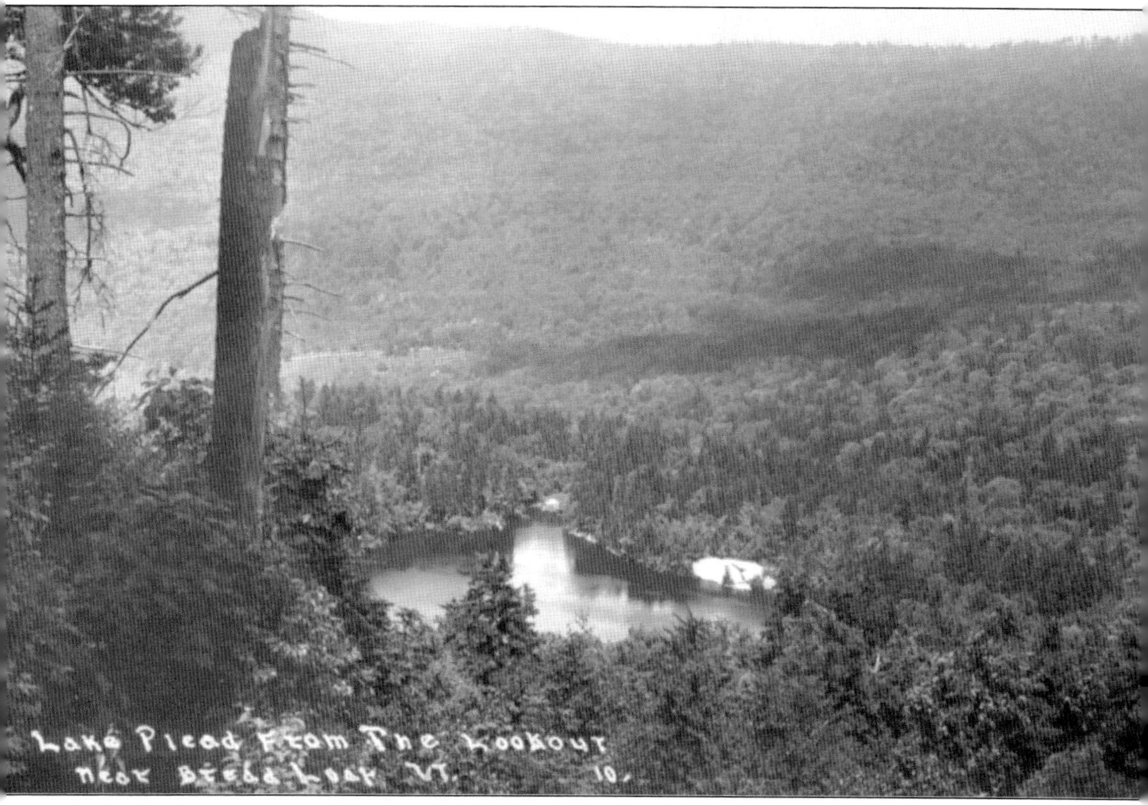

With its large forest holdings, Middlebury College also acquired major landowning responsibilities involving timber resources and a large complex of buildings. Initially, the college maintained the Bread Loaf Inn as a mountain resort. In 1936, the college sold 21,000 acres of the Battell Forest to the U.S. government for inclusion in the Green Mountain National Forest. Today, the national forest, with local headquarters 2 miles south of Middlebury on Route 7, offers miles of trails and recreational opportunities.

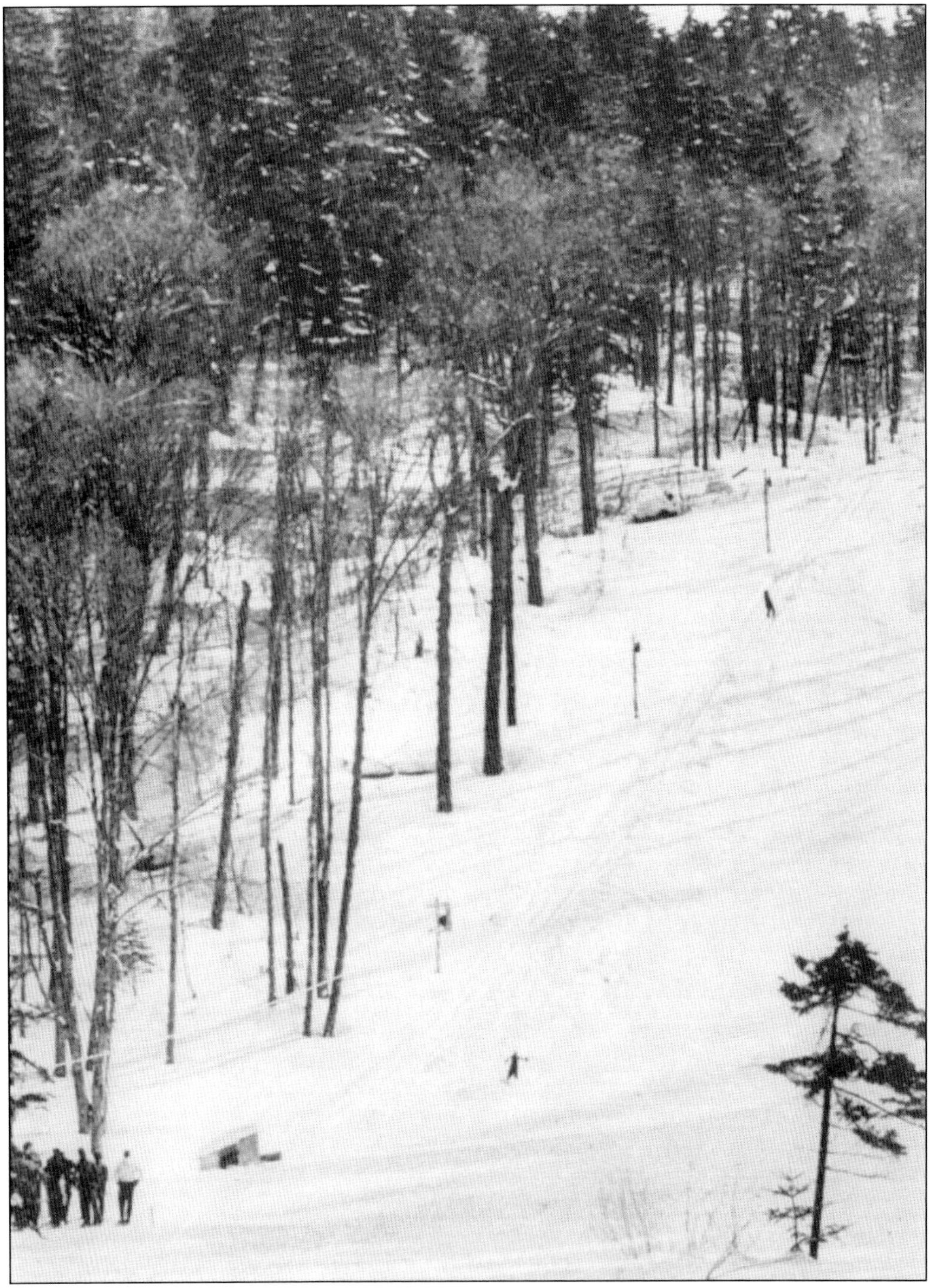

Until the 1930s, most skiing at Middlebury College took place on Chipman Hill near the village. In 1933, the Middlebury Ski Club began work on the development of a portion of the Battell Forest near Bread Loaf as an alpine ski area, patterned after trail systems at Tuckerman Ravine and Stowe. The Middlebury Snow Bowl trails were expanded in the 1940s with the construction of the Starr Lodge after the war.

Five

The Neighboring Towns

Middlebury lies in the foothills of the Green Mountains and is centrally located to serve the needs of the nearby hill towns to the east and the agricultural villages of the fertile Lake Champlain lowlands to the west. These towns were all connected commercially and socially to Middlebury, which was the seat of county government, as well as the center of commercial and intellectual life. For many years, Middlebury was also the site of the important and popular Addison County Agricultural Fair. Brandon, Shoreham, Bristol, and Vergennes, among others, were important villages in their own right but were dependent on Middlebury. Many of these towns were larger in the period from 1840 to 1860 than they are today. They were wealthy, with prominent citizens who participated in both state and national politics, and were leaders in agriculture and industry. Lake Champlain transportation was also important to Middlebury. Throughout the area, early industry focused on timber, quarries, and manufacturing; later, agriculture dominated.

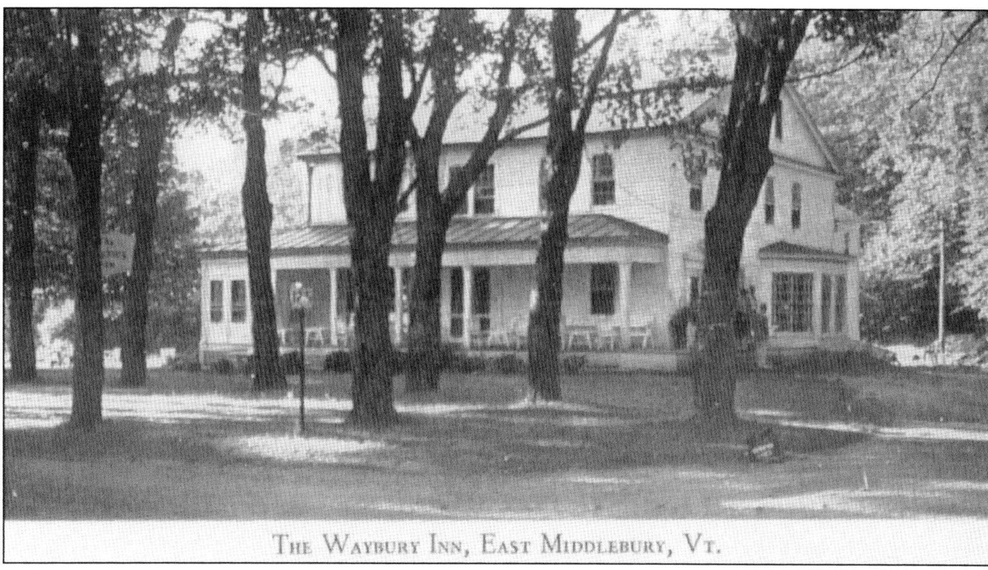

The Glen Tavern in East Middlebury was the first stop along the stage route for visitors after crossing the rugged Green Mountains. Built in 1810, the Glen Tavern, now called the Waybury Inn, has a long and successful history as a hotel and restaurant. The opening scenes of the Bob Newhart television comedy show of the 1980s used exterior shots of the Waybury Inn.

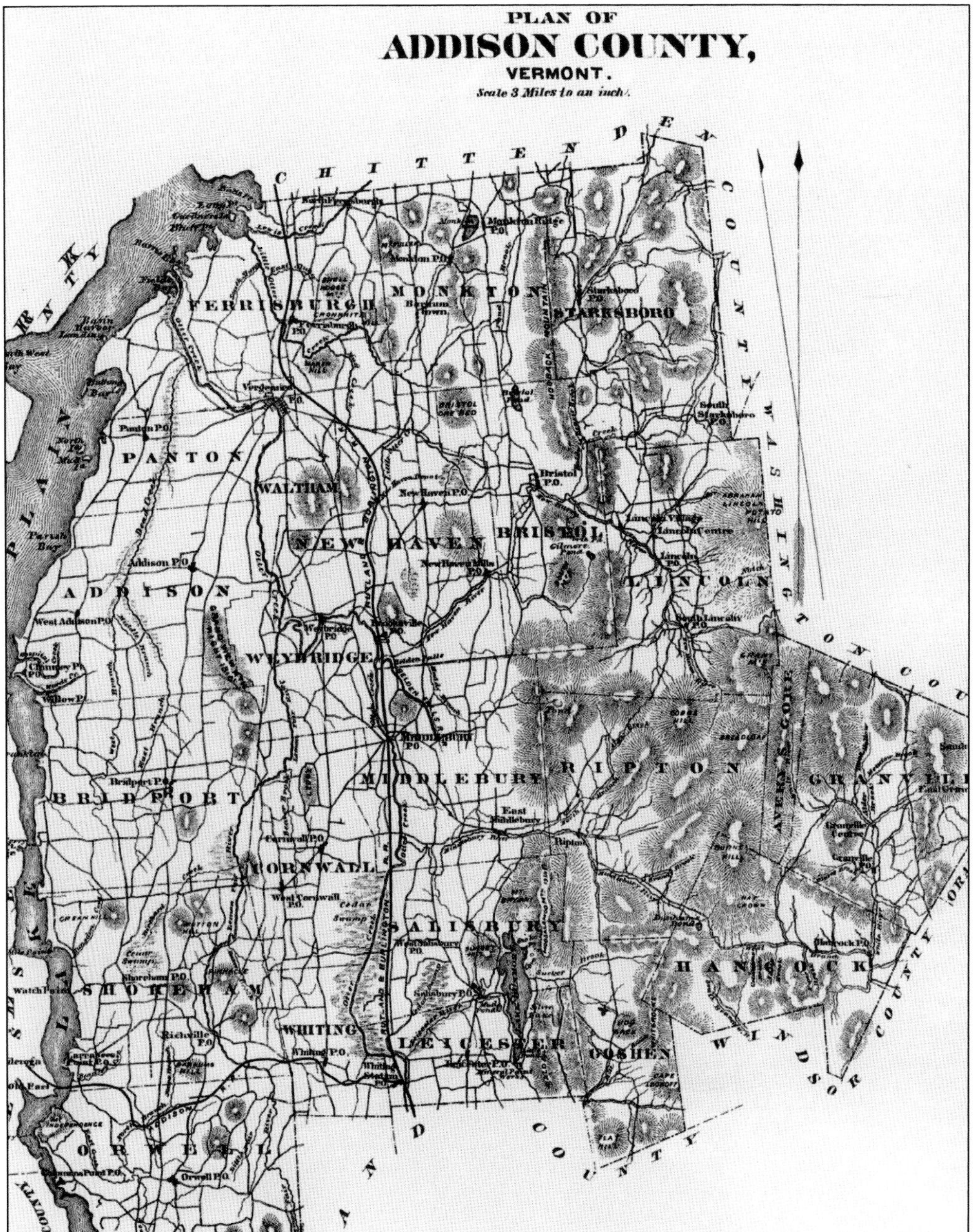

The 1871 *Beers Atlas of Addison County* shows the intense development of the lowlands in the Lake Champlain Valley. The Rutland–Burlington Railroad and shipping along Lake Champlain connected the county to distant points. Today's major roads, Routes 7, 30, and 22A, closely follow the old stage routes connecting the main villages shown on this map. Addison County has been spared the development of the interstate highway system, with its attendant malls and commercial districts, and has remained a location that requires a little extra effort to reach from major cities. This map shows the new railroad connection made in 1869 from Leicester Junction to New York, crossing Lake Champlain on a floating bridge at Larrabee's Point.

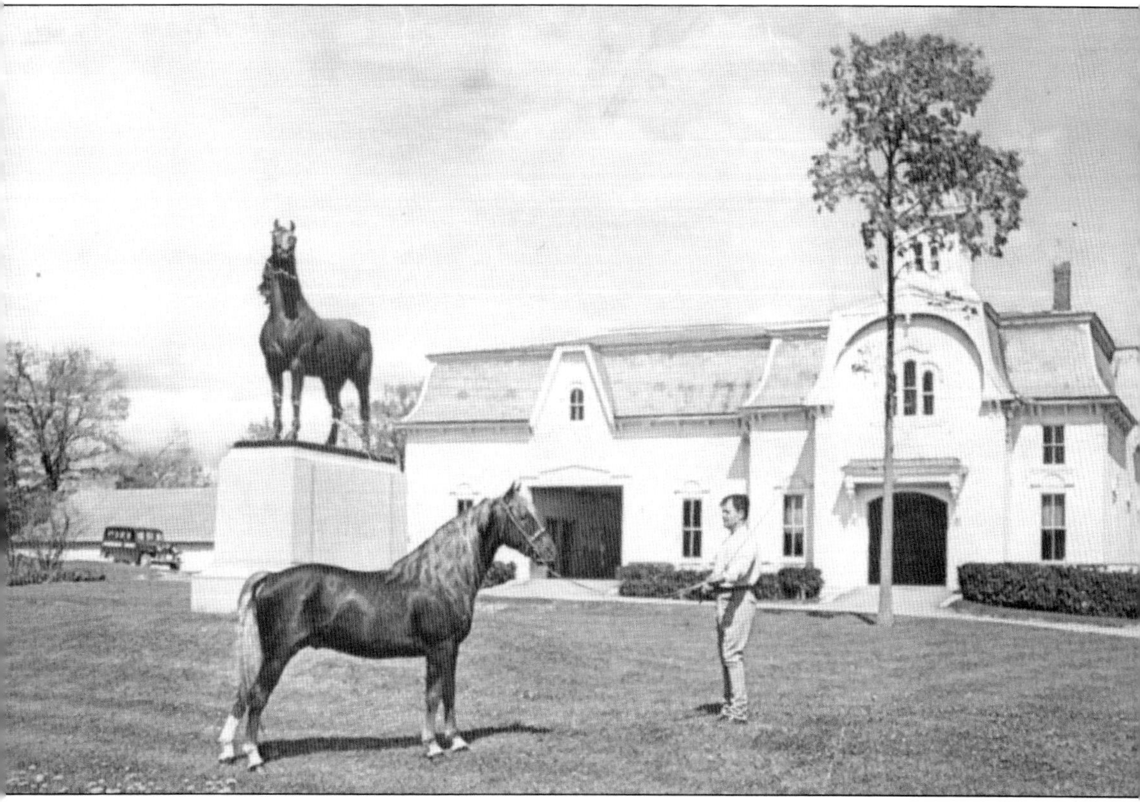

Joseph Battell, owner of the *Middlebury Register,* was a Morgan horse enthusiast. An opponent of the use of automobiles, Battell weekly published news of all automobile-related accidents and travesties. He collected and bred Morgan horses, made famous by local teacher Justin Morgan nearly 100 years earlier. Battell developed a farm in Weybridge to breed Morgans. The main barn of the Morgan Horse Farm was constructed in French Empire style and had elaborate interior appointments for the prized horses. The heavily built Morgan was ideal for farm and military use. The breeding of Morgans continues at Battell's country farm, now owned by the University of Vermont.

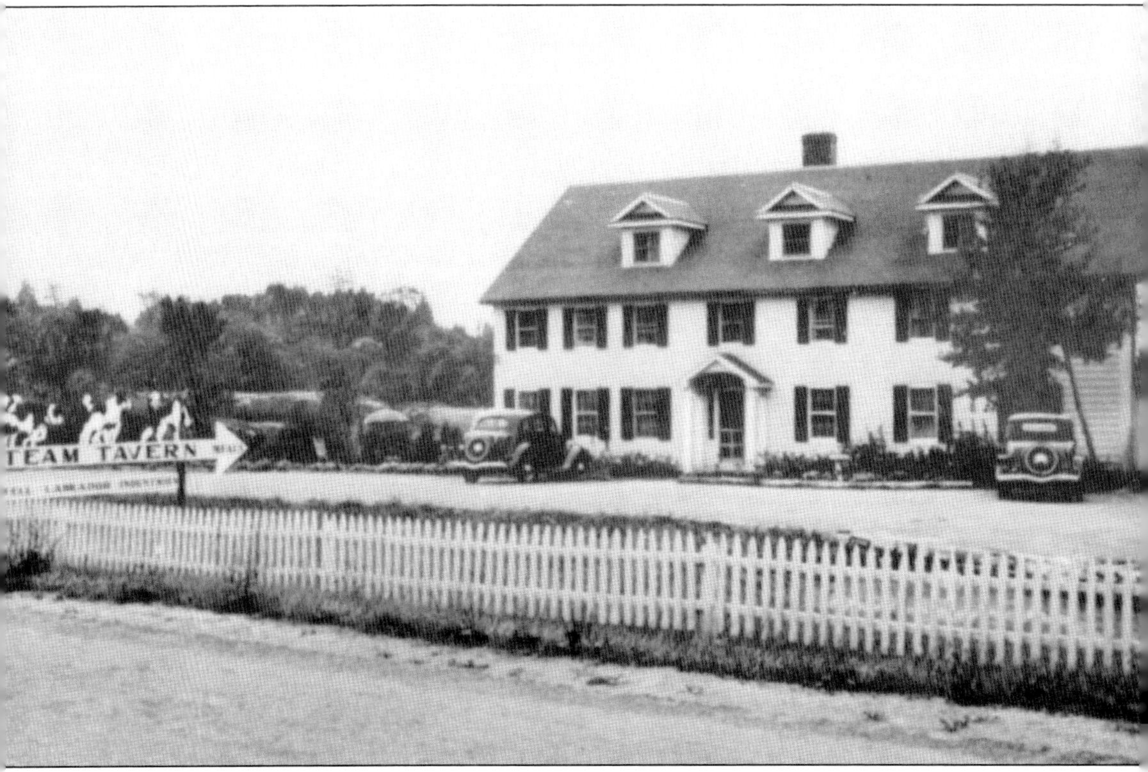

Over the years, the Dog Team Tavern has been the subject of numerous postcards. The restaurant was started in an old farmhouse by Sir Wilfred Grenfell, a British doctor who worked at a mission serving the native people of Labrador. The Dog Team Tavern was supported by volunteers, who served light meals, benefiting the Labrador mission. Later, owner Eban Joy expanded the menu, remodeled the house, and added decorations with a Gulf Coast shell theme from his winter home in Sanibel, Florida.

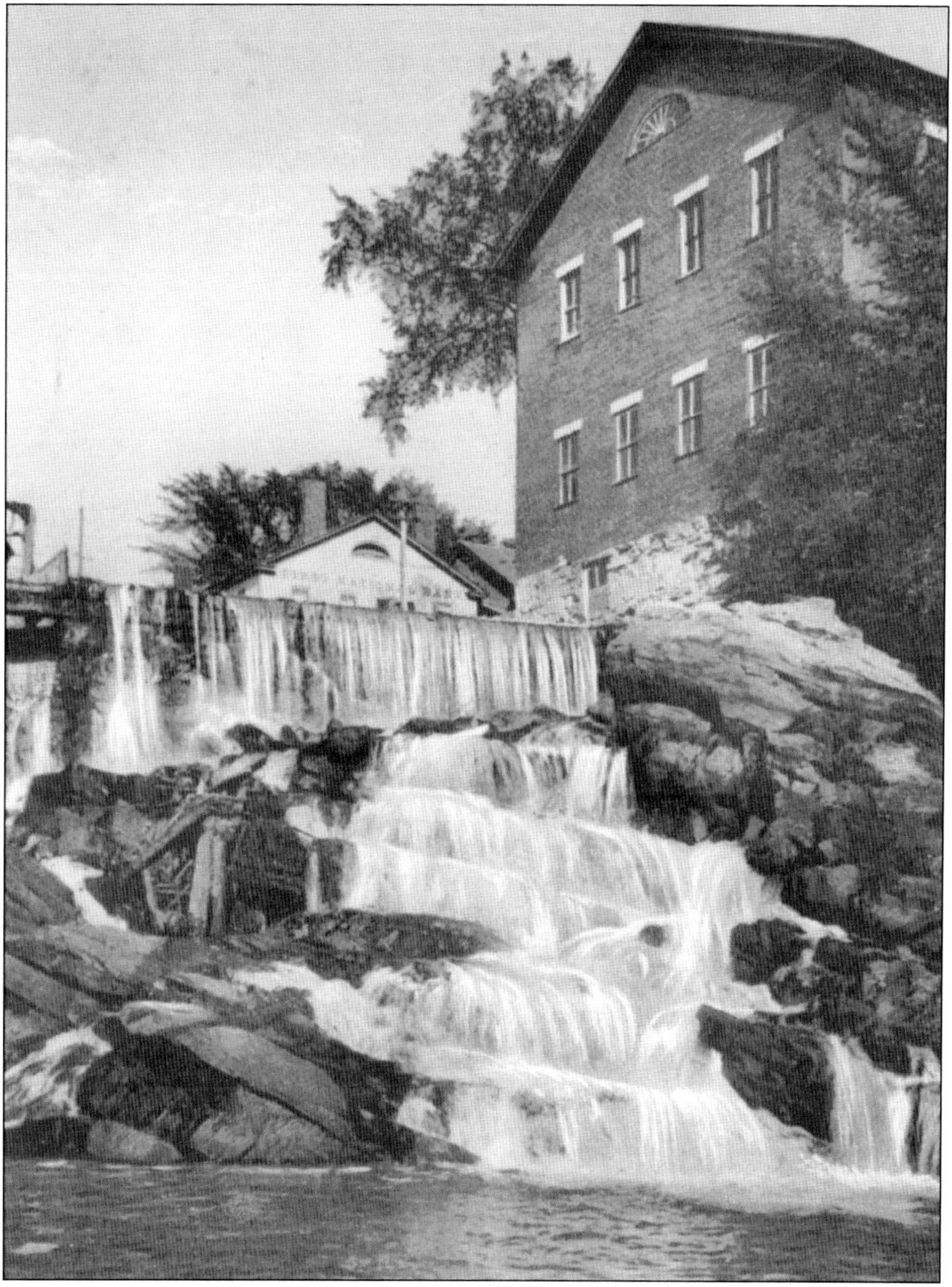

The village of Brandon began at approximately the same time as Middlebury, centered around Neshobe Falls on a tributary of Otter Creek. The waterfalls provided power for early sawmills and gristmills. Today, the falls remains at the center of Brandon, although not a prominent feature for visitors who drive between sections of the falls and see little. There are currently efforts in the village to reconfigure the area around the falls to make it a more integral part of the downtown landscape.

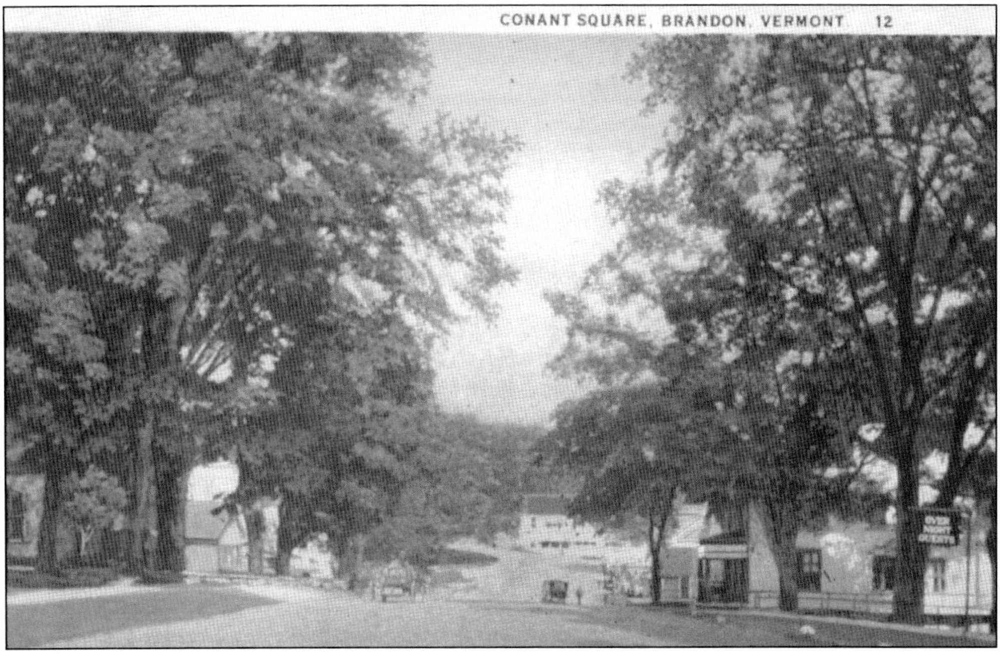

Conant Square is named for John Conant, who came to Brandon in 1796 and developed a series of mills and foundries along the borders of Neshobe Falls. Iron ore from Forestdale was mined and brought by wagon to the Conant furnaces, which were fired by charcoal produced in nearby Goshen. For the next 54 years, the Conant family dominated the commercial and social life of Brandon.

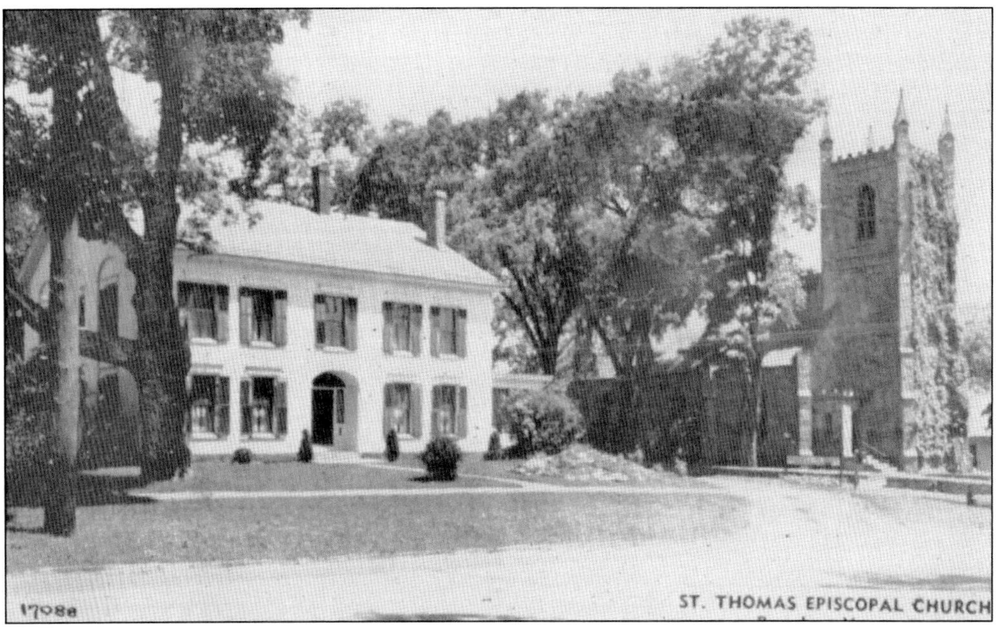

The house to the left of the St. Thomas Episcopal Church was built by John Conant in 1802 and still remains a major feature on Conant Square.

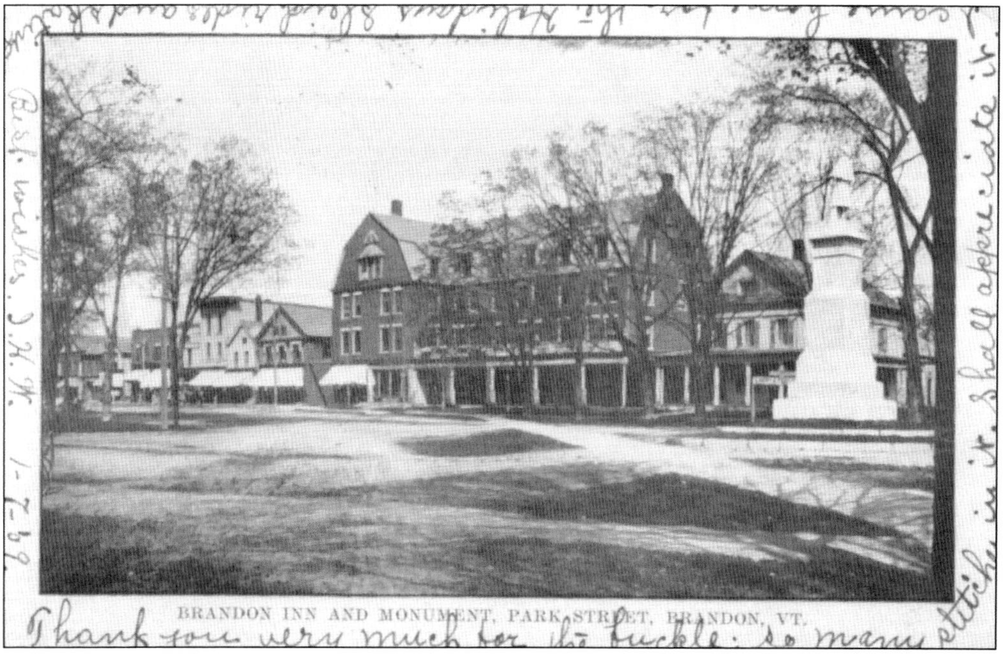

The Brandon Inn was built in 1892, replacing the Brandon House, which burned two years earlier on the same site. The Brandon Inn has been a major social feature in midtown Brandon for more than 100 years.

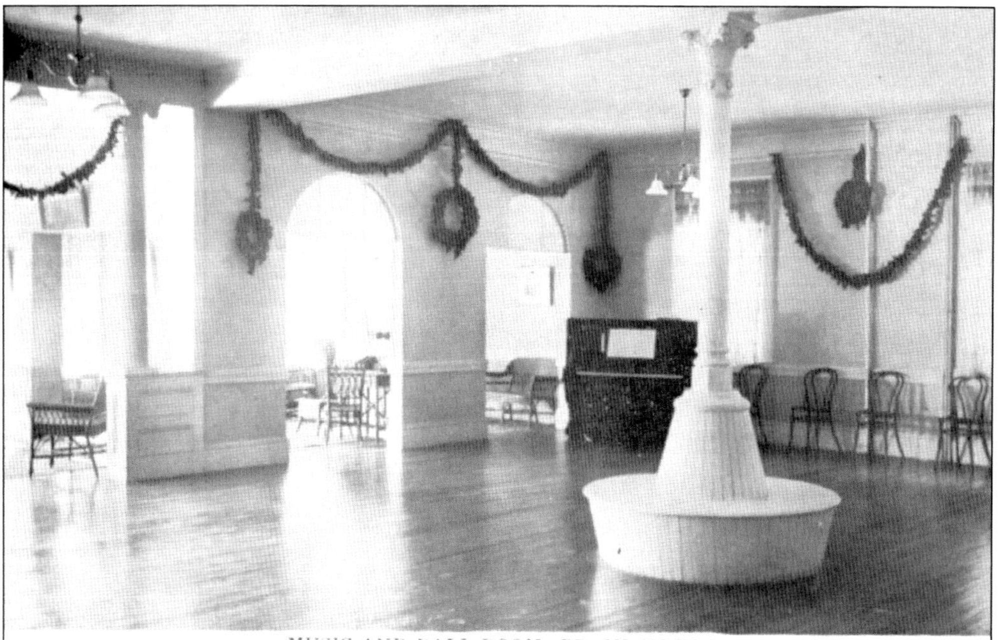

The interior of the Brandon Inn included a large restaurant and ballroom for dances, wedding receptions, and other events. Postcards were used to advertise the restaurant's menu and to show details of the features of the inn.

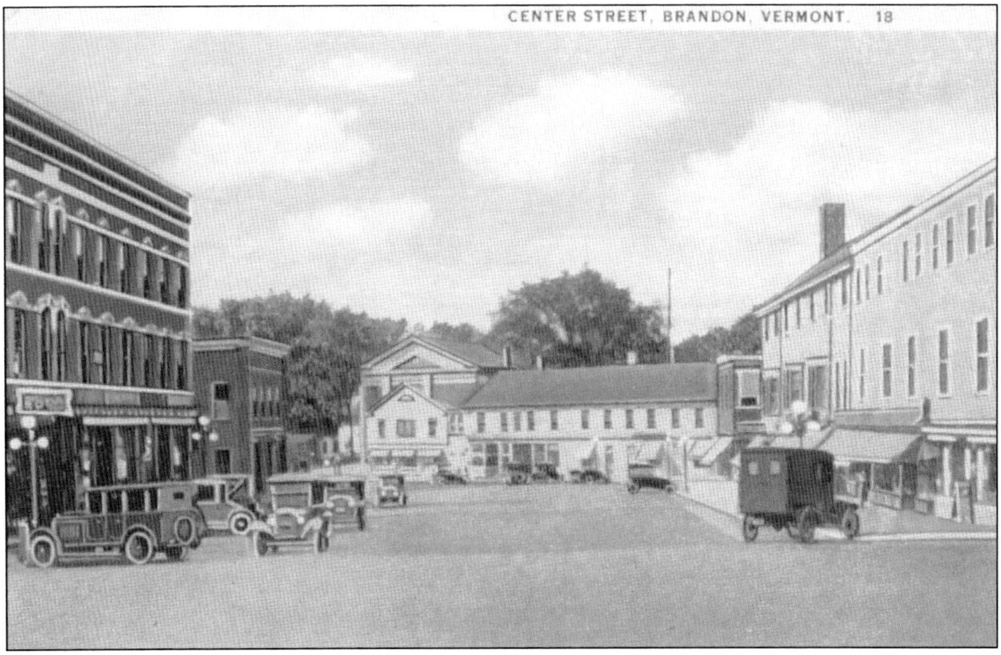

Center Street extends from Park Street to Conant Square and includes the major commercial section of town. Many of the buildings shown in the 1905 postcard are still present today.

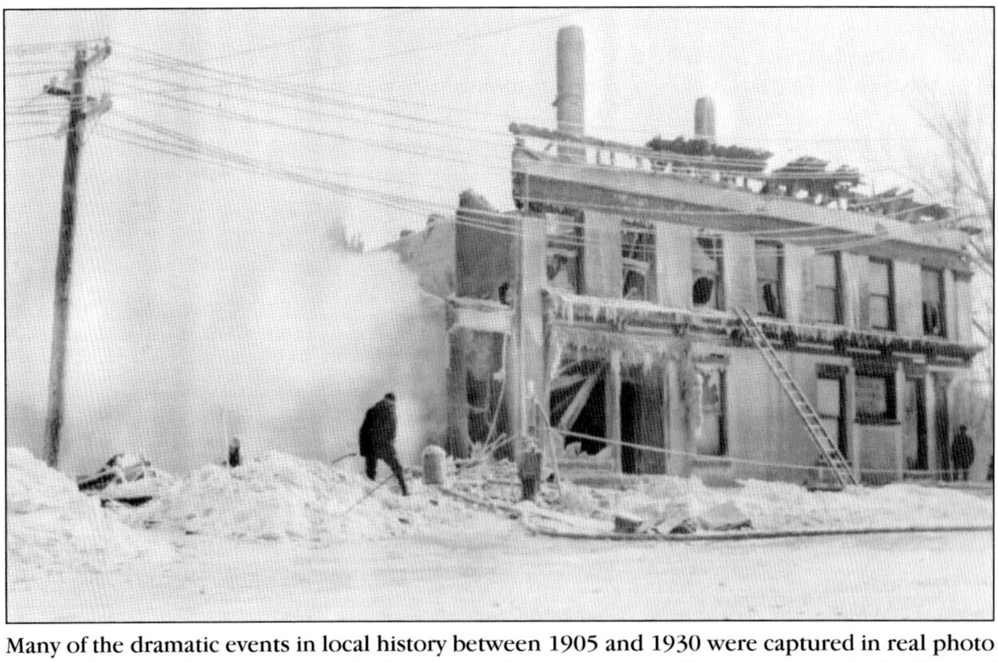

Many of the dramatic events in local history between 1905 and 1930 were captured in real photo postcards. An unfortunate type of urban renewal came to many Vermont towns in the form of disastrous fires that burned the wooden buildings in the commercial districts. By the late 1900s, however, most village downtowns were constructed of brick and stone. This postcard from February 1918 shows the fire that destroyed a major section of Park Street.

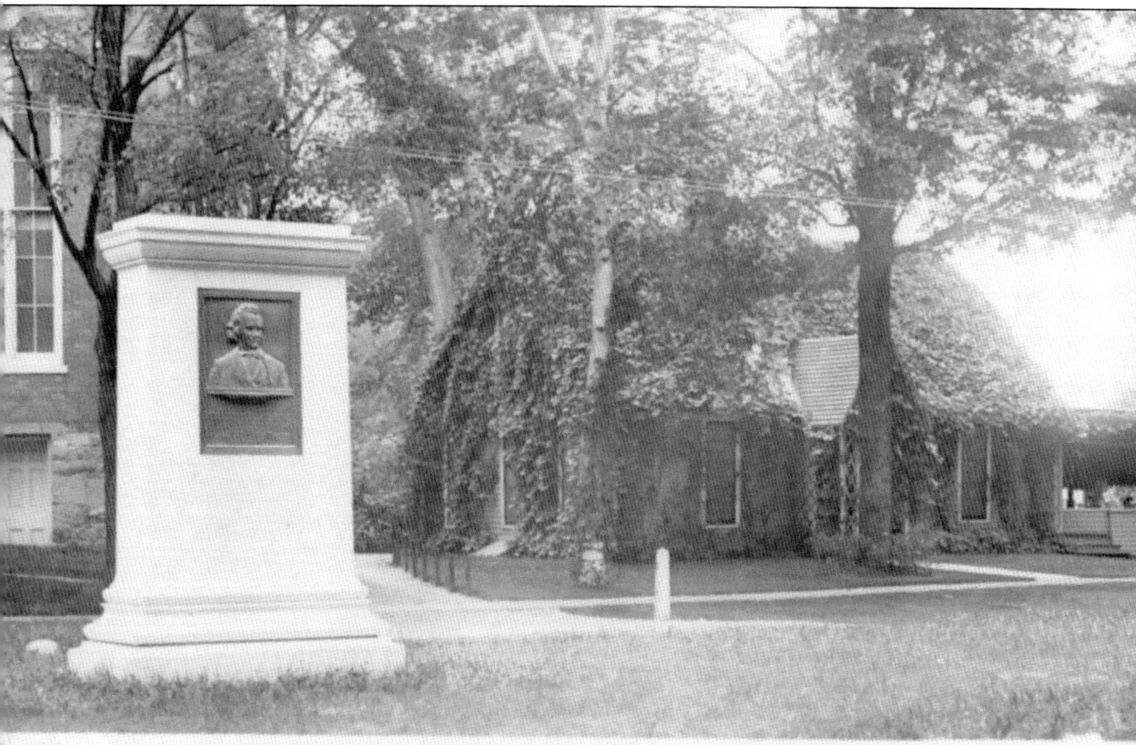

'8626 Birthplace and Memorial, Stephen A. Douglass
Brandon, Vt.

One of the most famous residents of Brandon was Stephen A. Douglas, born in 1813 in the small cottage next to the Baptist church. Douglas was trained as a cabinetmaker in Middlebury, before he went on to study law and become a politician. He was elected to the Senate from Illinois and ran against Abraham Lincoln in the 1860 election. A small and fragile man, Douglas died in 1863. His connection to Brandon is commemorated by a marble monument with a bronze plaque on Park Street in front of his childhood home.

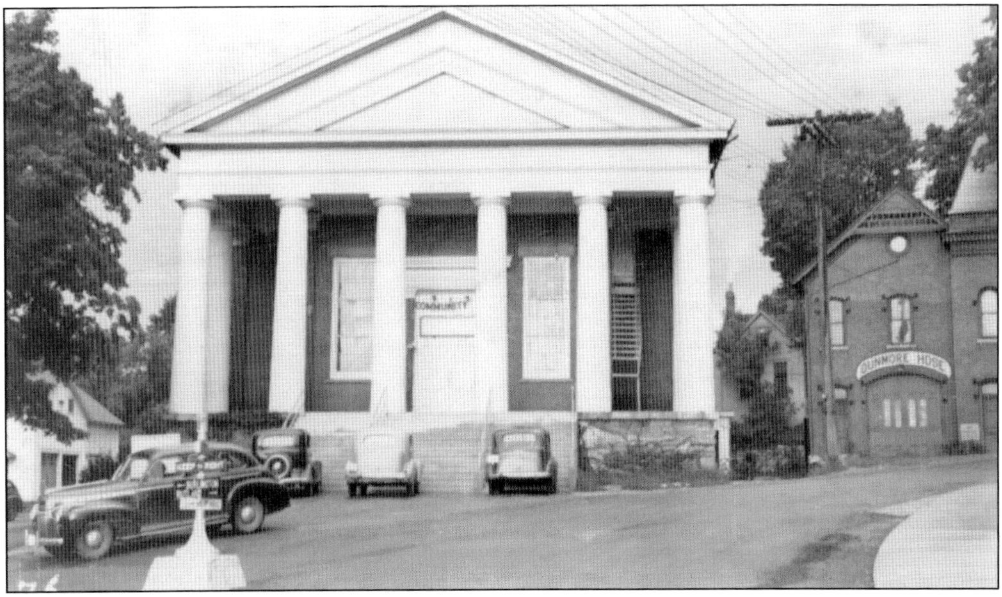

One of the most imposing buildings in western Vermont is the Brandon Town Hall. With its six grand pillars and huge pediment, the town hall is a distinctive landmark at the junction of Conant Square and Seminary Street.

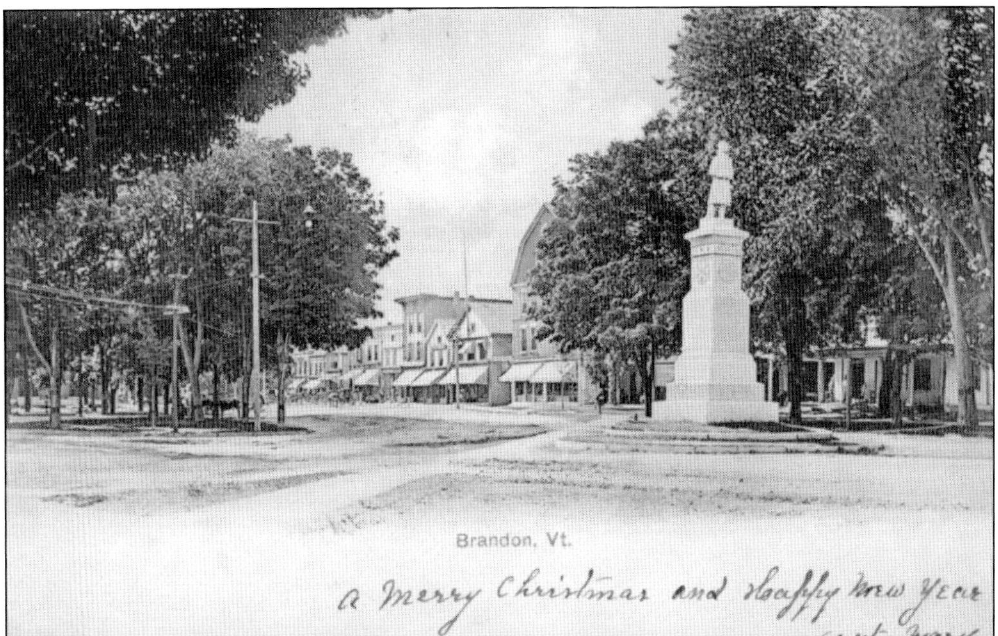

Brandon is distinctive among Vermont villages for its wide streets and public monuments. One of the most dramatic of these features is the Soldiers' Monument on Park Street, built 20 years before the Middlebury Civil War monument. Numerous postcards feature this statue.

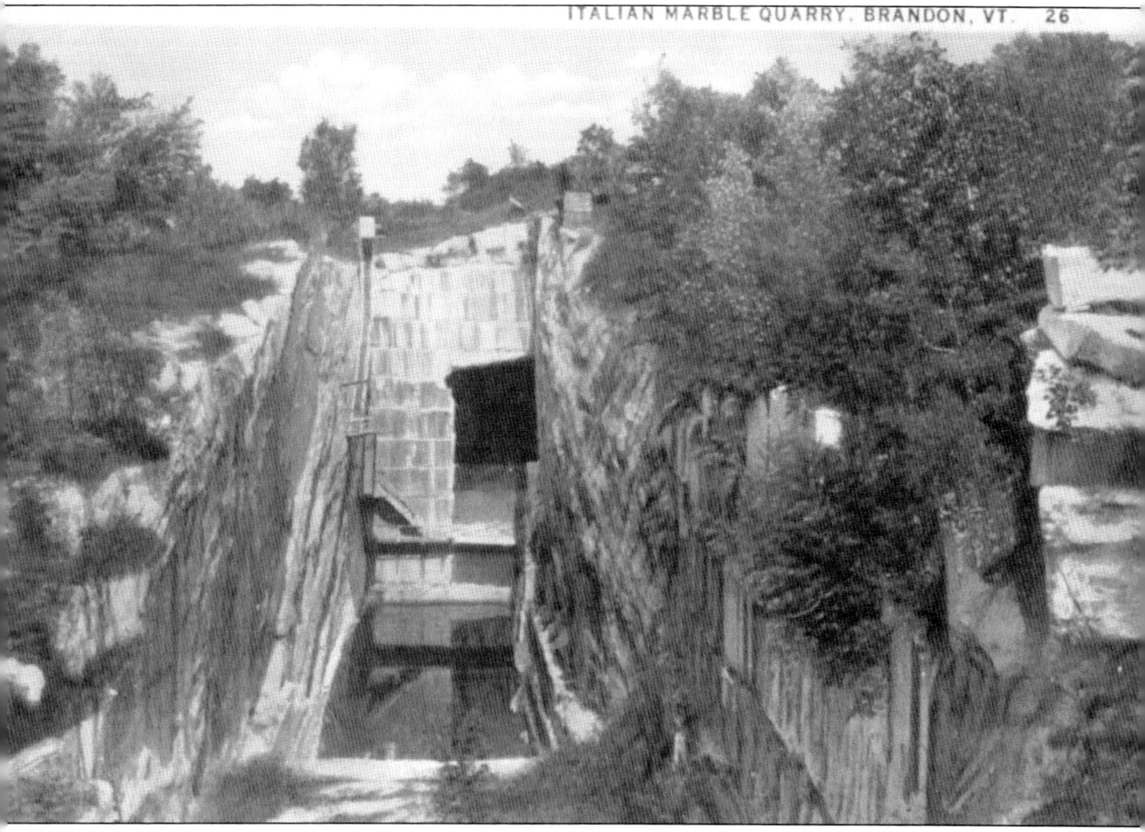

One of the most important industries in Brandon was the quarrying and cutting of marble. Brandon was famous for its white marble, which is valued for statuary and cemetery monuments. Blue Brandon marble was used in St. Mary's Church and the Baptist church, both located in Middlebury. The Vermont Italian Marble Factory was an important Brandon employer until the factory burned in 1896. The company subsequently relocated to Middlebury.

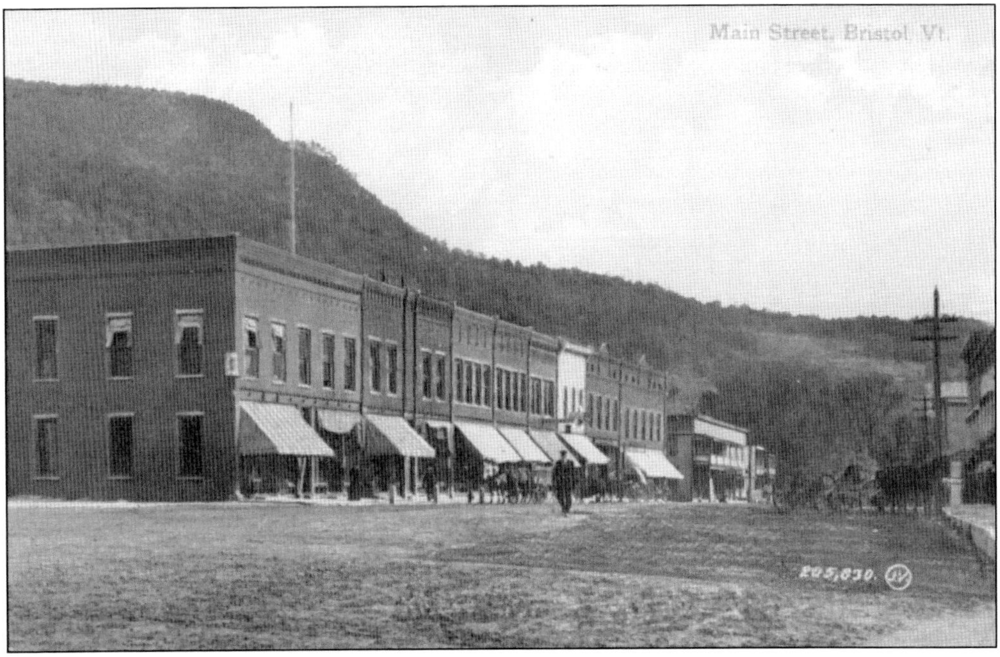

Set in the hills approaching Bristol Gap, the village of Bristol was an important logging community in its early days.

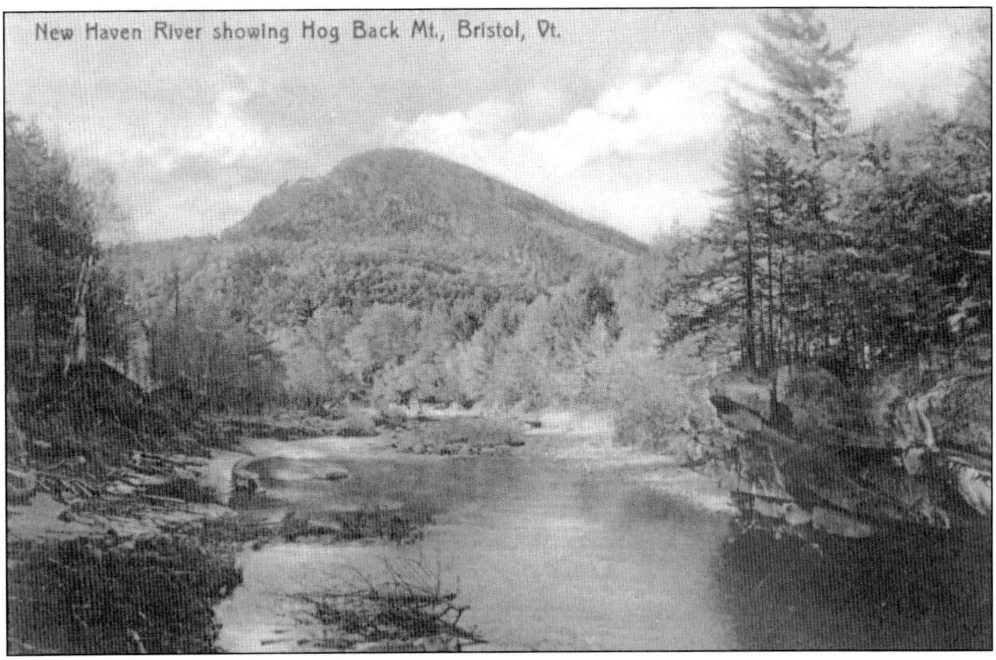

Abundant timber from the Green Mountains was transported through Bristol and milled into boards and wood products, using waterpower.

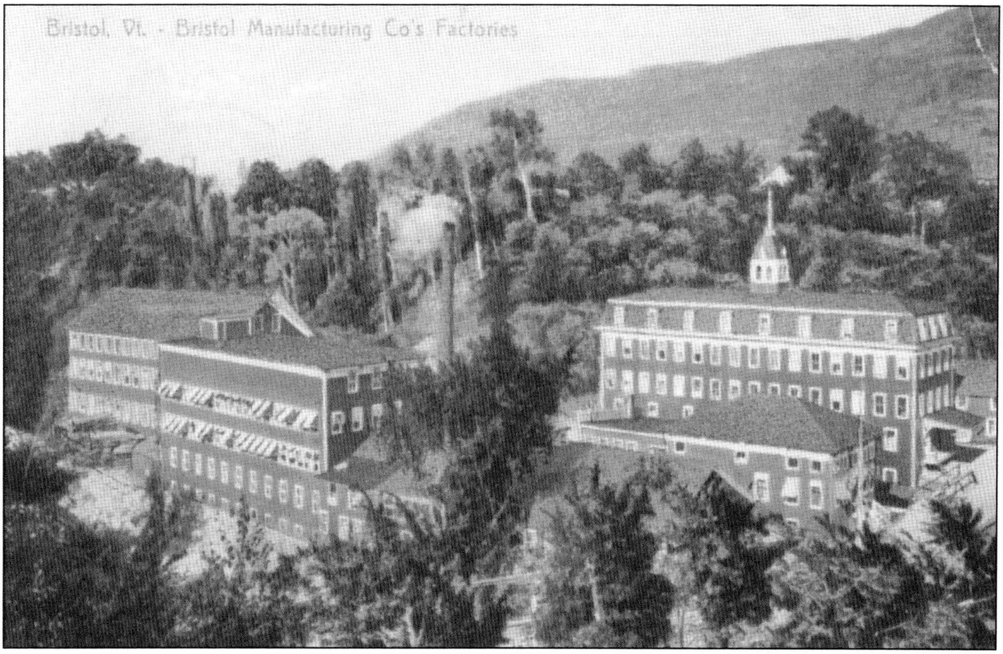

Over time, the Bristol Manufacturing Company expanded, using ample waterpower to make a wide range of wood products, including caskets.

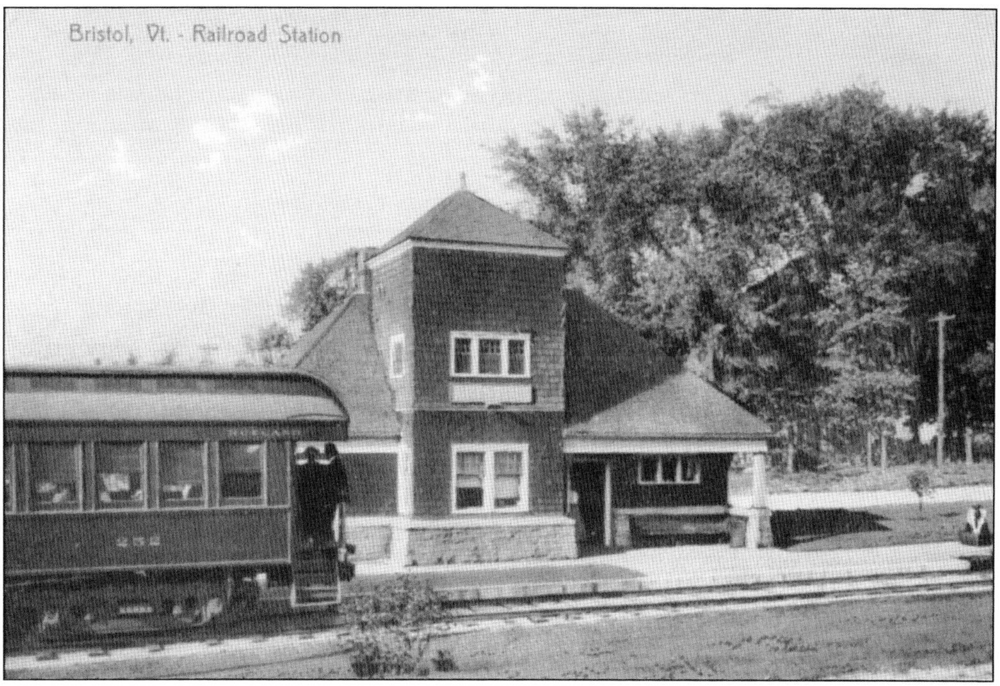

In 1896, a railroad spur extended to Bristol, increasing the efficiency of the transport of manufactured goods to distant markets.

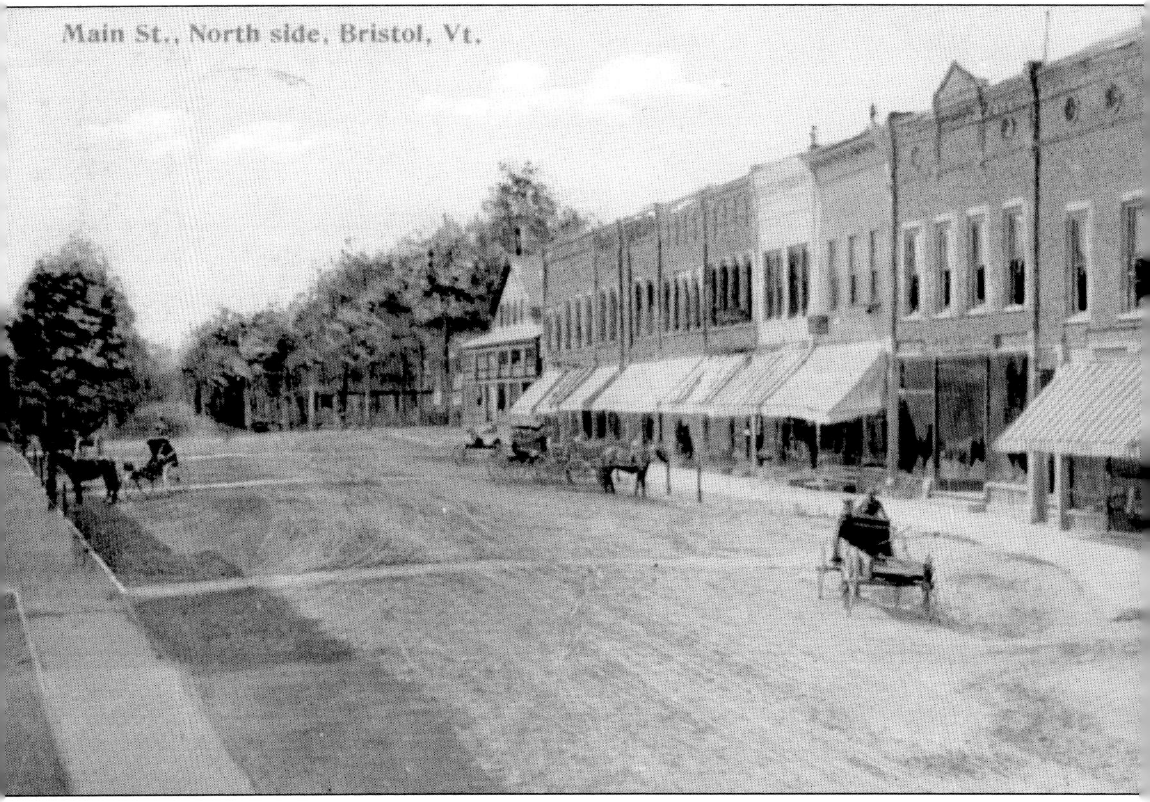

Like other Vermont towns, Bristol by the late 1800s had developed a densely packed series of attached commercial buildings, following major fires. These brick buildings with similar heights on the broad main street still dominate the business center of Bristol. The wooden building to the left is the Bristol House, built in 1810. In 1931, the Bristol House, then called the Bristol Inn, was developed into the German School at Middlebury College.

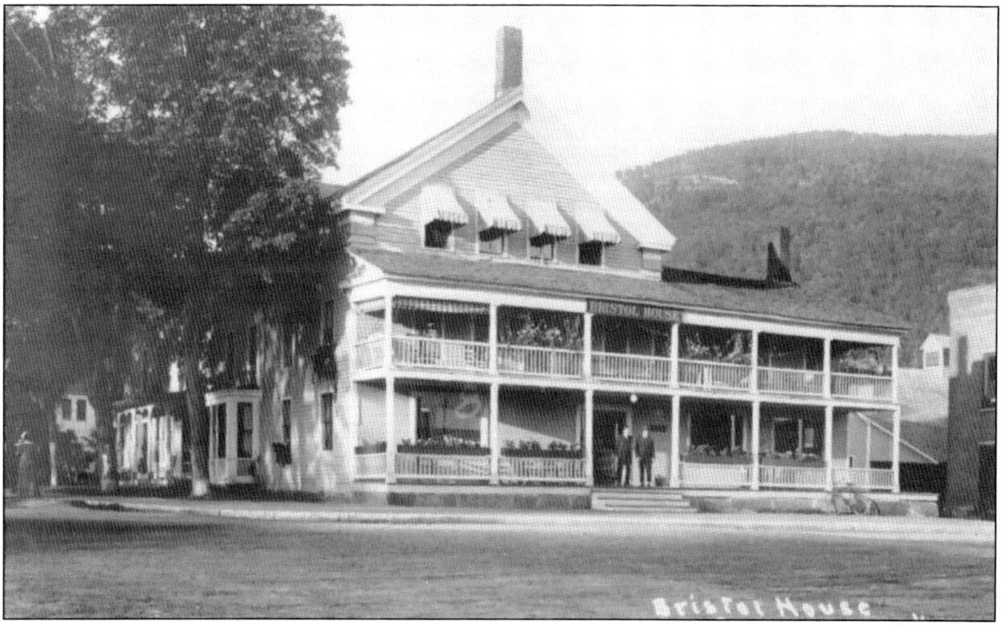

During World War II, the German School was discontinued because of American distaste for anything German. In 1961, the Bristol Inn was demolished to make room for the parking lot for the Grand Union Grocery Store. The loss of this significant Main Street historical building resulted in a new effort to preserve the historical character of Bristol.

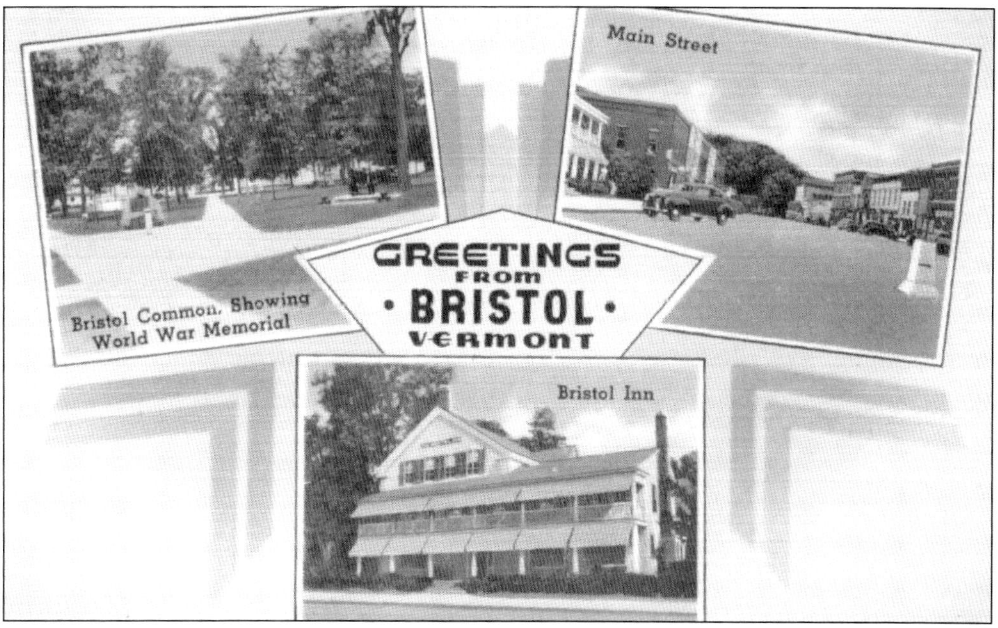

Even a small village like Bristol had sufficient civic pride to justify the production of postcards specifically to promote the village setting. This 1940s card shows three scenes of life in Bristol.

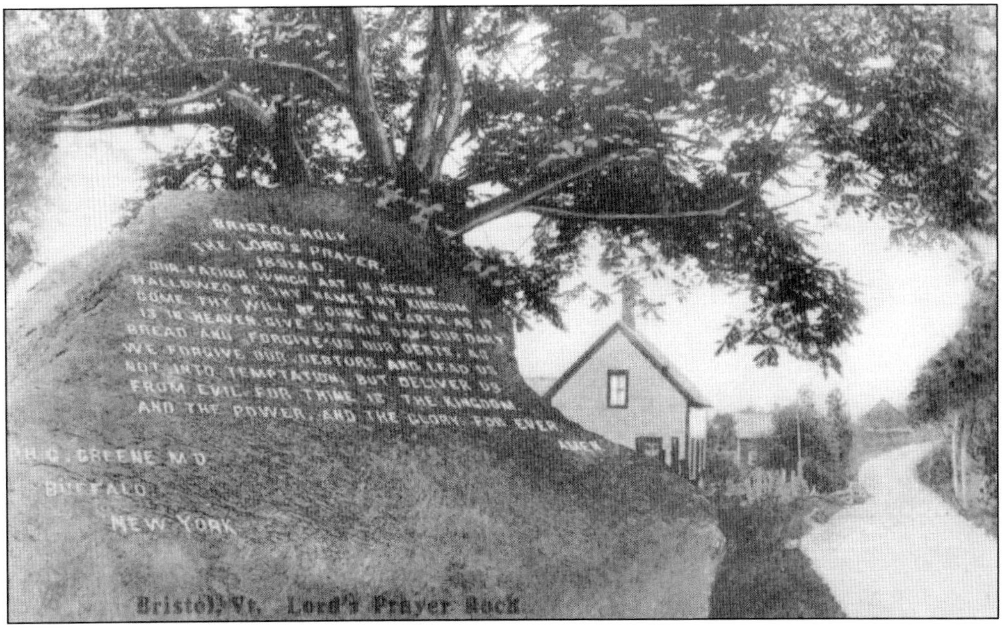

One of the major features east of Bristol is the Lord's Prayer Rock. Commissioned by Dr. Joseph Greene, the rock was inscribed in 1891. One story has it that workmen driving teams of horses frequently swore as they descended the steep road into Bristol and the reverent Dr. Greene was intent of reminding them of their godly duties.

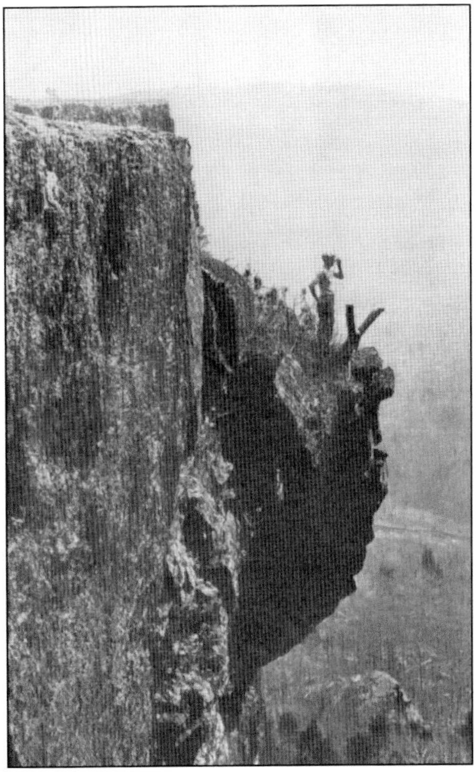

North of the village of Bristol is the dramatic rock outcrop Deer Leap, shown here with an intrepid hiker.

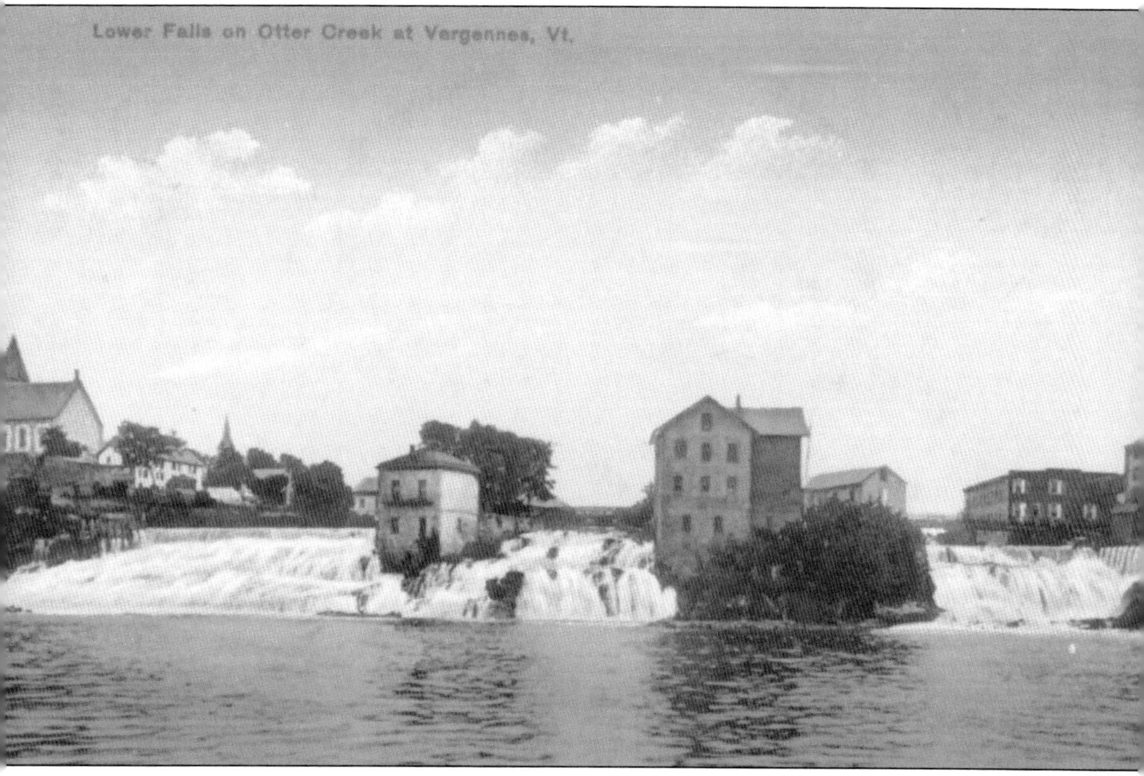

One of the most important early sites in western Vermont was the dramatic falls at Vergennes, where Otter Creek plunges a final 33 feet to its gradual descent into Lake Champlain. A major source of hydropower, the Vergennes Falls has a long and colorful history, including the location of the first town settlement, early iron foundries, sawmills, and clothing factories.

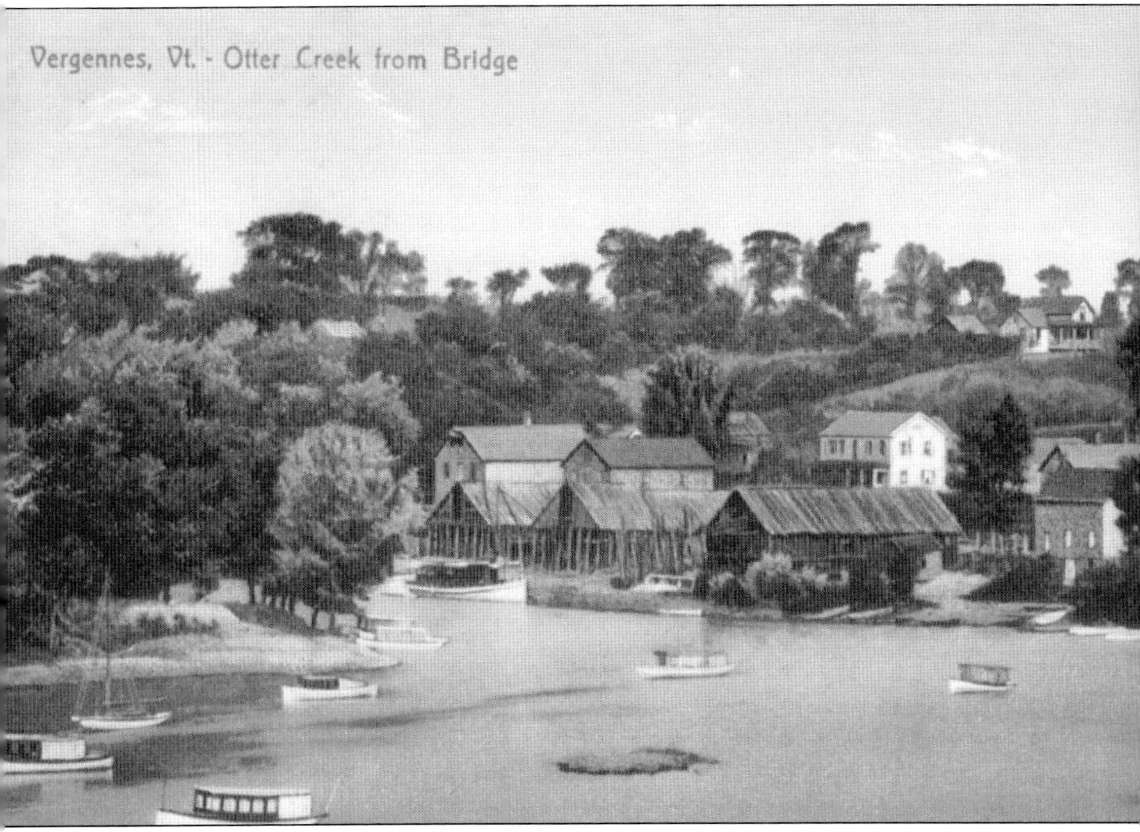

Otter Creek extends for 7 additional miles from the falls to Lake Champlain, offering a quiet refuge from the lake. In 1815, Commo. Thomas MacDonough built a fleet of seven boats for battle against the British at Plattsburgh. Throughout the winter of 1814–1815, construction continued at Vergennes. The successful naval battle at Plattsburgh was a decisive victory for the American Navy.

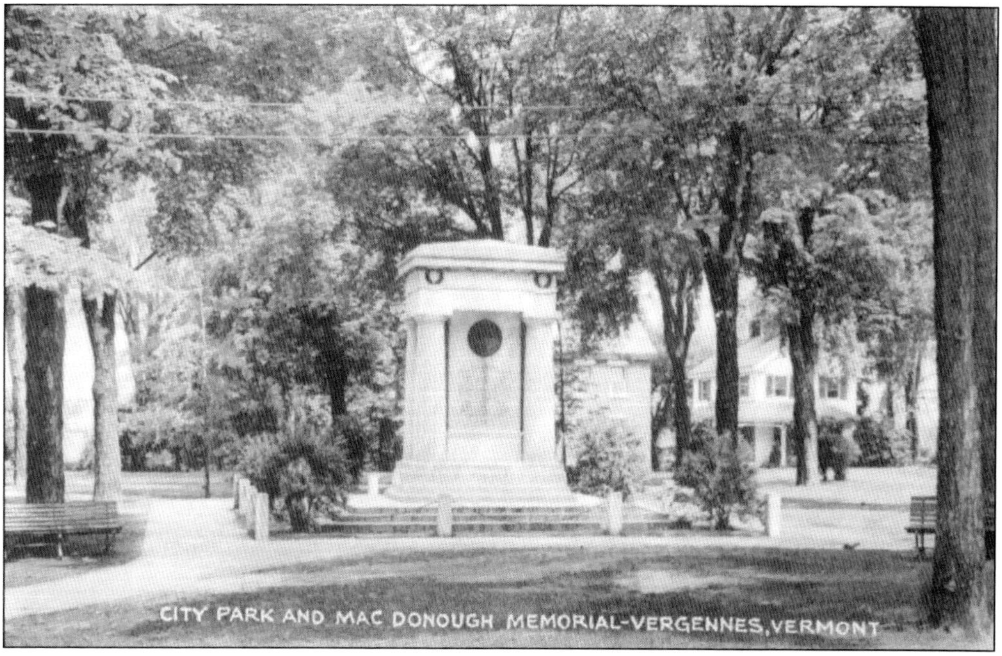

The MacDonough Memorial in City Park commemorates the roles of Commo. Thomas MacDonough, who was only 28 in 1814, and the local shipbuilders in the War of 1812.

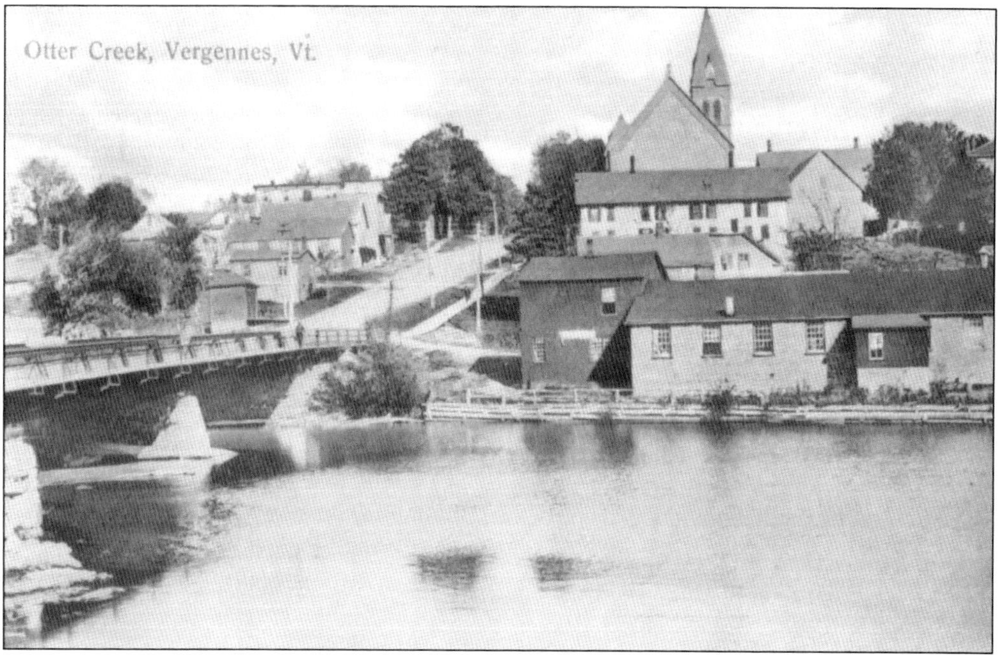

The village of Vergennes extended primarily from the falls and bridge that crossed Otter Creek above the falls along the road toward Burlington. In 1800, Vergennes was one of the largest towns on Lake Champlain, grown rich from the timber trade with Canada and, after the 1823 opening of the Champlain Canal, with Troy and New York City. At one time, Vergennes was the smallest incorporated city in the United States.

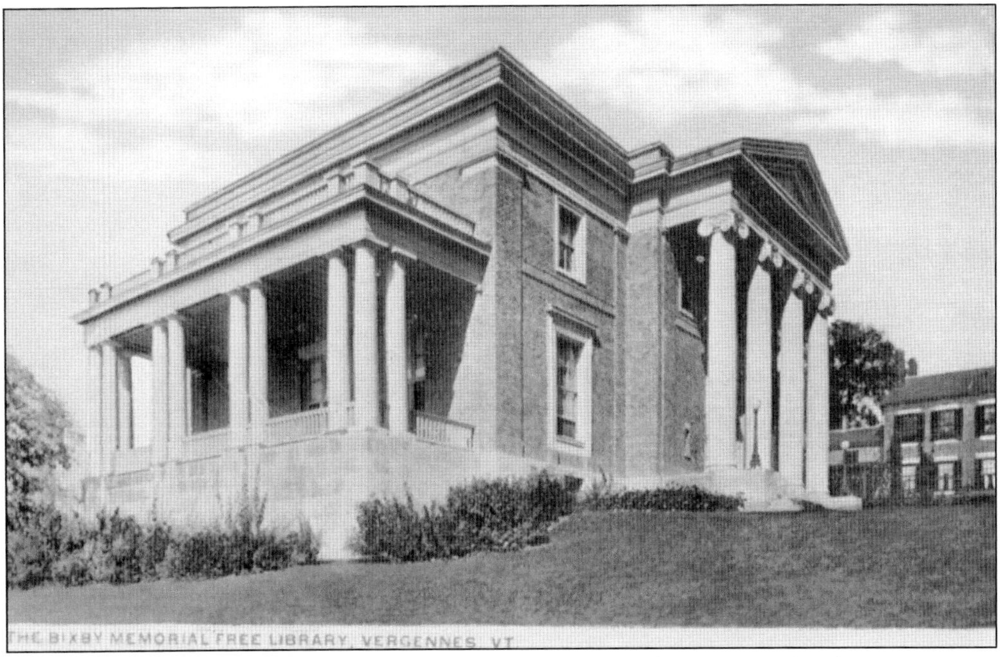

In 1907, William Bixby died, leaving $300,000 to the town of Vergennes for the construction of a public library. The imposing sandstone and brick Bixby Memorial Free Library was built in 1912.

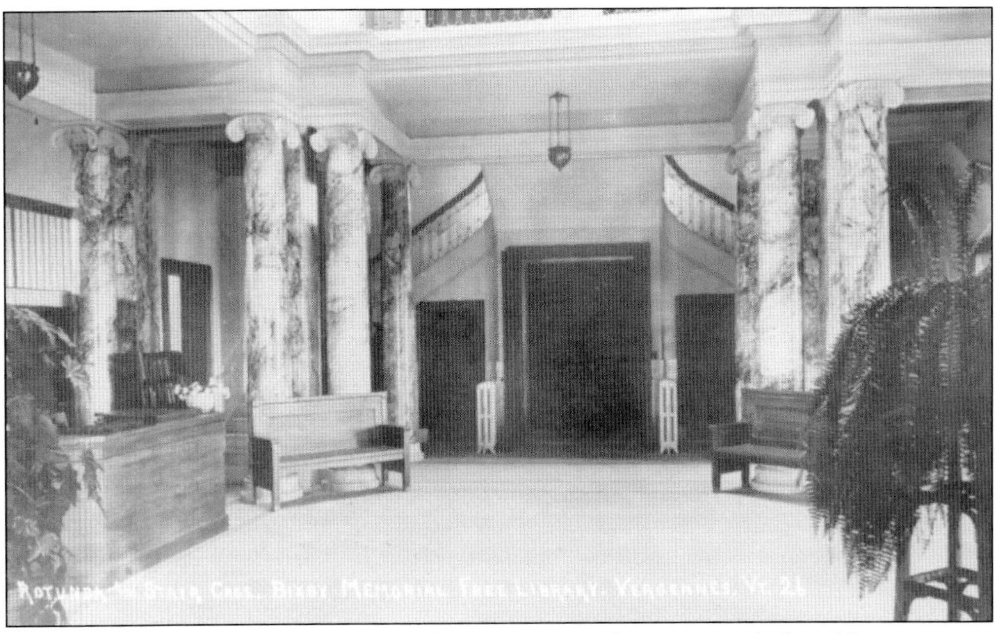

The dramatic interior of the Bixby Free Library was primarily constructed of marble.

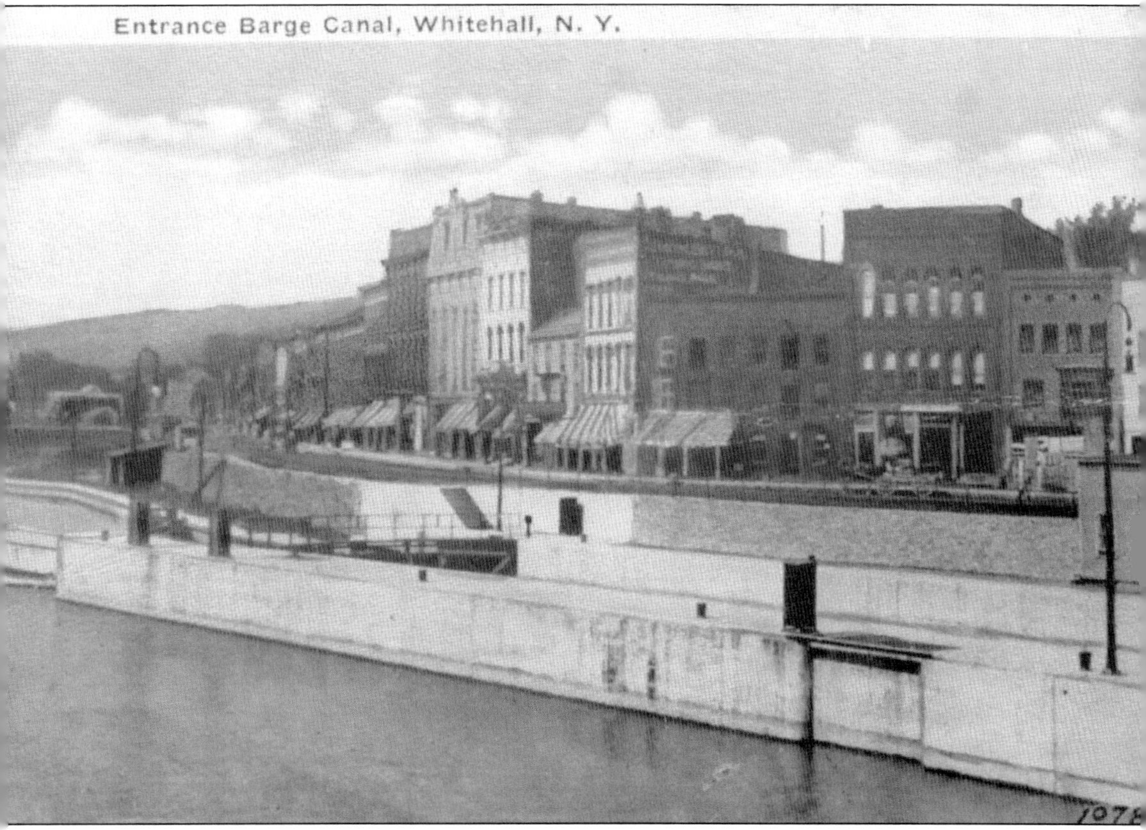

The Champlain Canal opened in 1823, connecting Lake Champlain and Canada with Troy, New York, and the Hudson River. This view of Whitehall shows the first in a series of locks that carried boats vertically the 95 feet from Lake Champlain to sea level at the Hudson River.

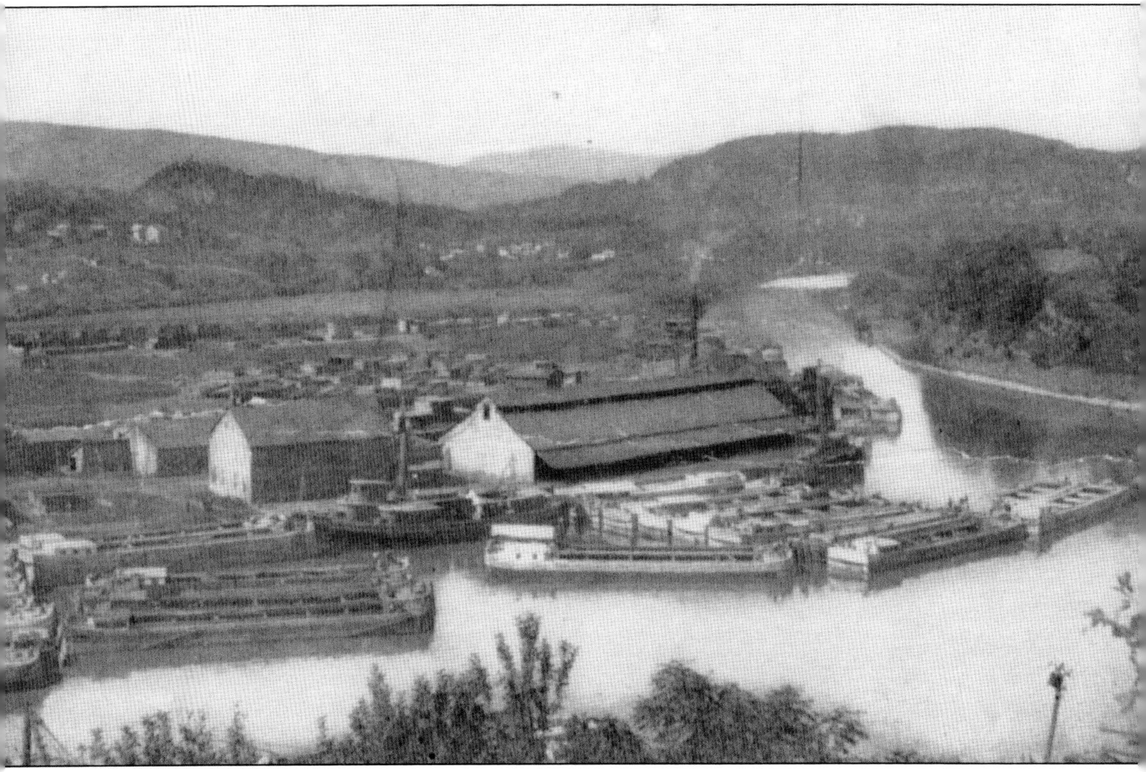

For many years, barges were the major means of transporting manufactured goods and raw materials from Vermont and upstate New York to points south. Dozens of barges would accumulate north of the canal entrance, waiting for space into the first lock.

In 1869, the Rutland Railroad constructed a branch from Leicester Junction to Ticonderoga. In Shoreham, a small covered railroad bridge crossed Lemon Fair, a tributary of Otter Creek. This 1950s view shows the covered bridge, which is still standing today.

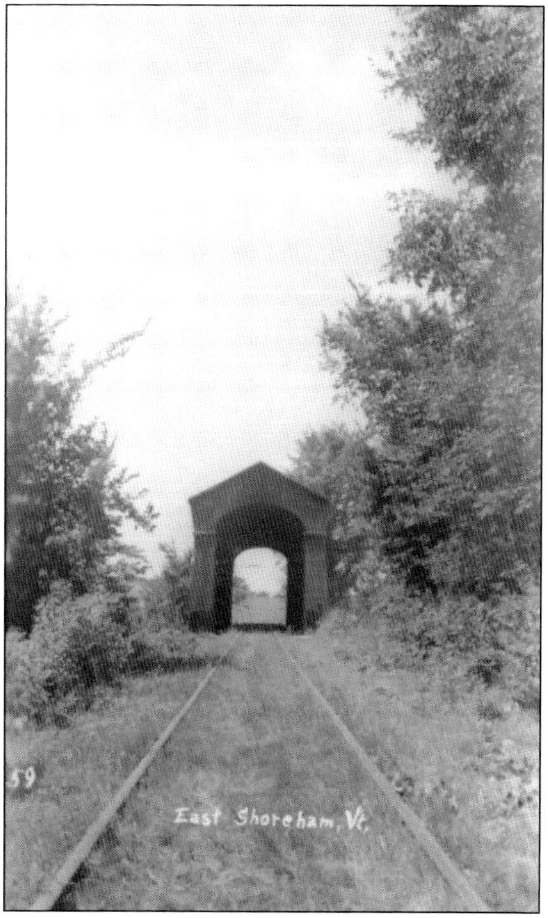

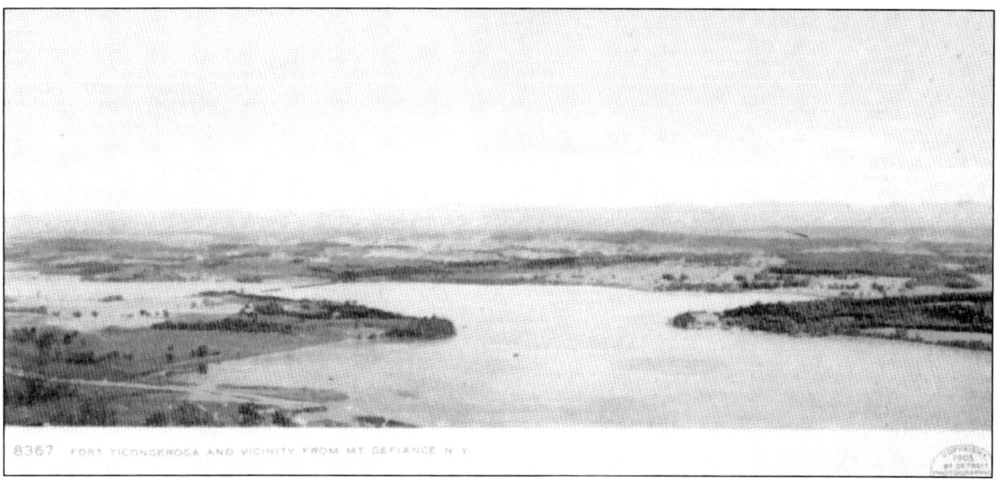

This view from Mount Defiance in New York, looking northeast, shows Mount Independence to the right and Fort Ticonderoga on the point to the left. There is a faint line crossing the lake, which was the floating railroad bridge of the Rutland Railroad, connecting Larrabee's Point to Ticonderoga.

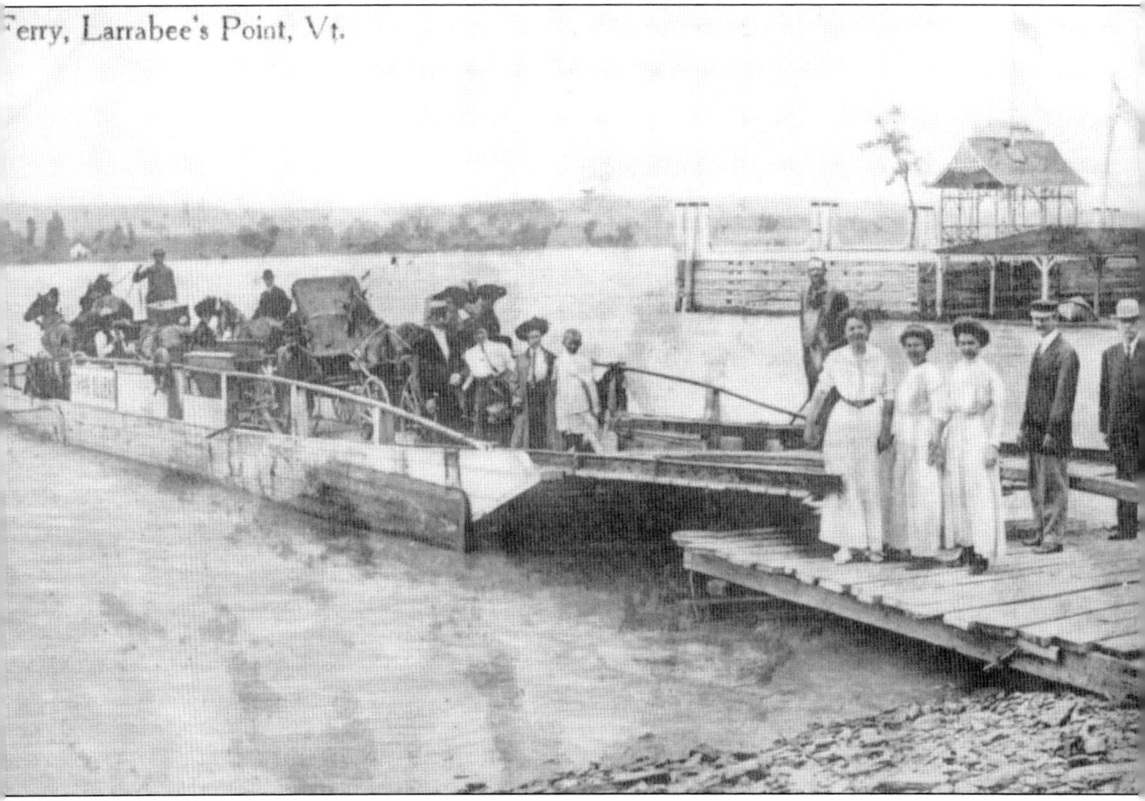

Since 1796, the Larrabee's Point ferry has carried passengers and freight across the Lake. In the right background is the steamboat dock where Lake Champlain steamboats anchored, discharging passengers and cargo.

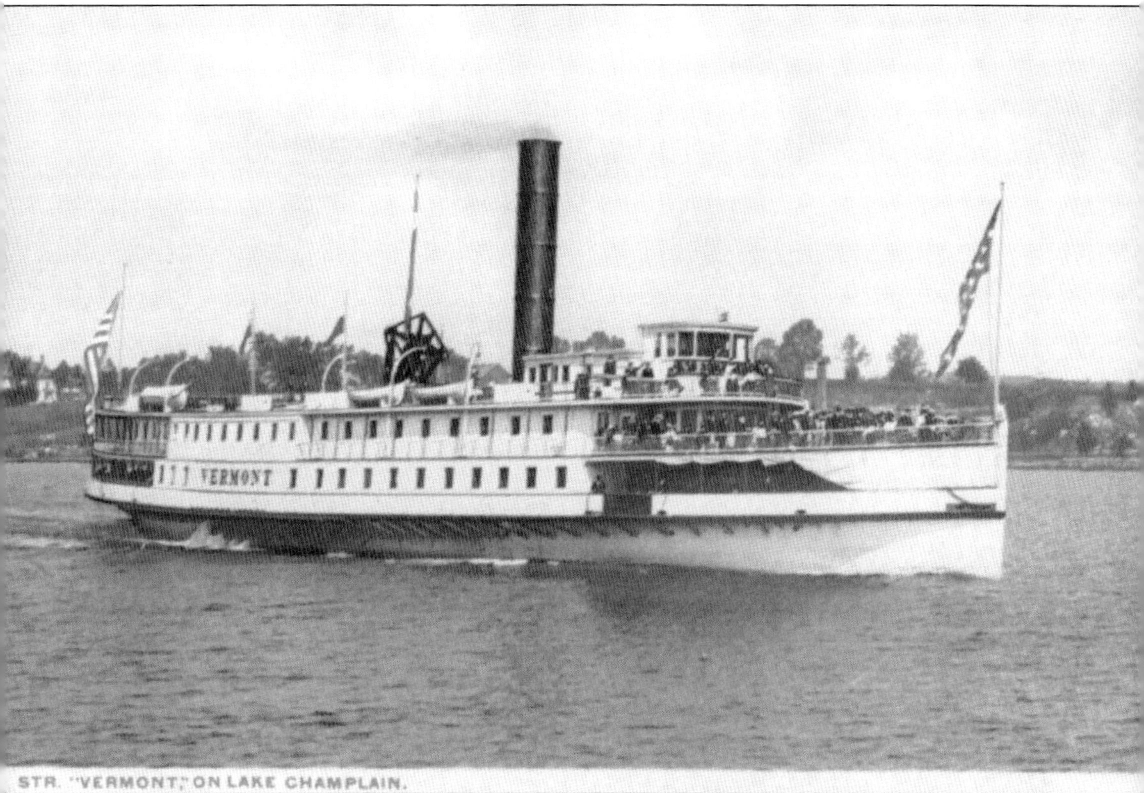

Steamboat travel on Lake Champlain began in the 1830s and continued into the 1940s, carrying businessmen, tourists, and freight between the prosperous lakeshore communities.

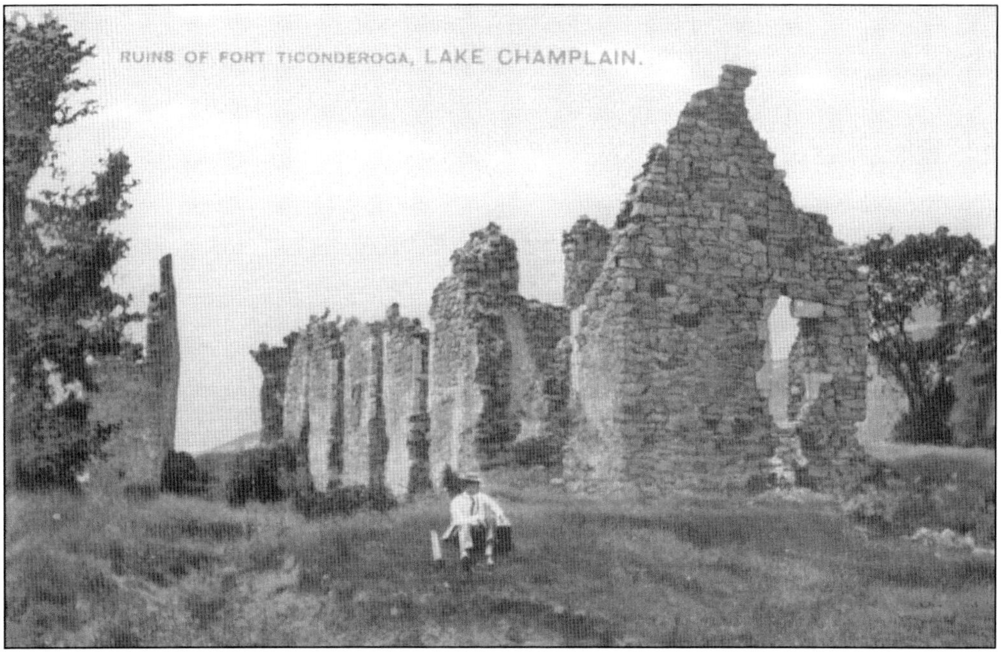

In 1905, at the time of the first local postcards, Fort Ticonderoga consisted of only a fragment of a stone building set in a cow pasture. Easily accessible from the nearby train station, the fort was a popular tourist destination and the subject of numerous romantic cards of the mysterious ruin in the beautiful lake landscape.

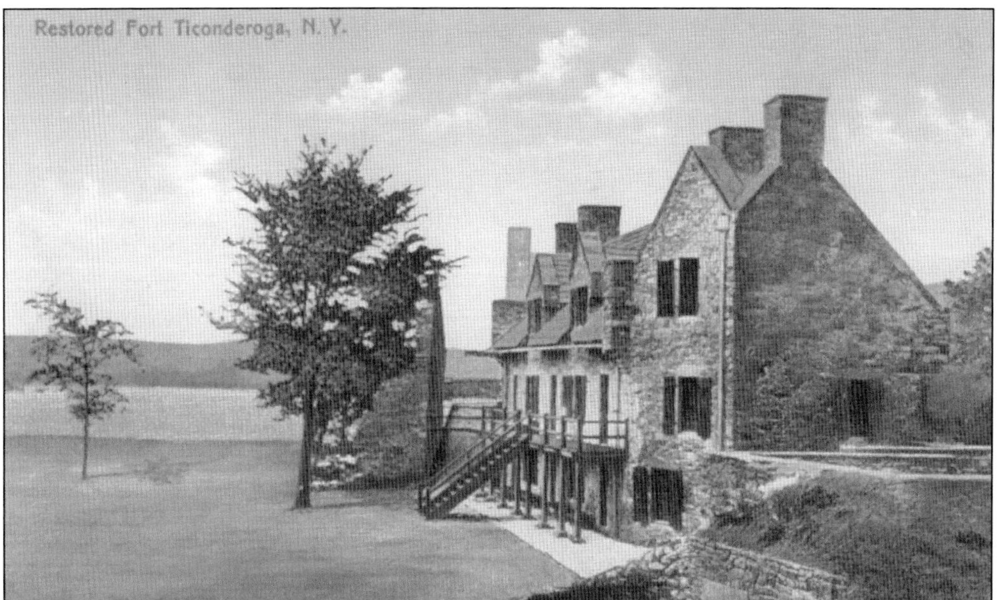

Over the years, the Pell family coordinated the reconstruction of Fort Ticonderoga. The progress of reassembling the major features of what is the fort today is well documented in hundreds of postcards.

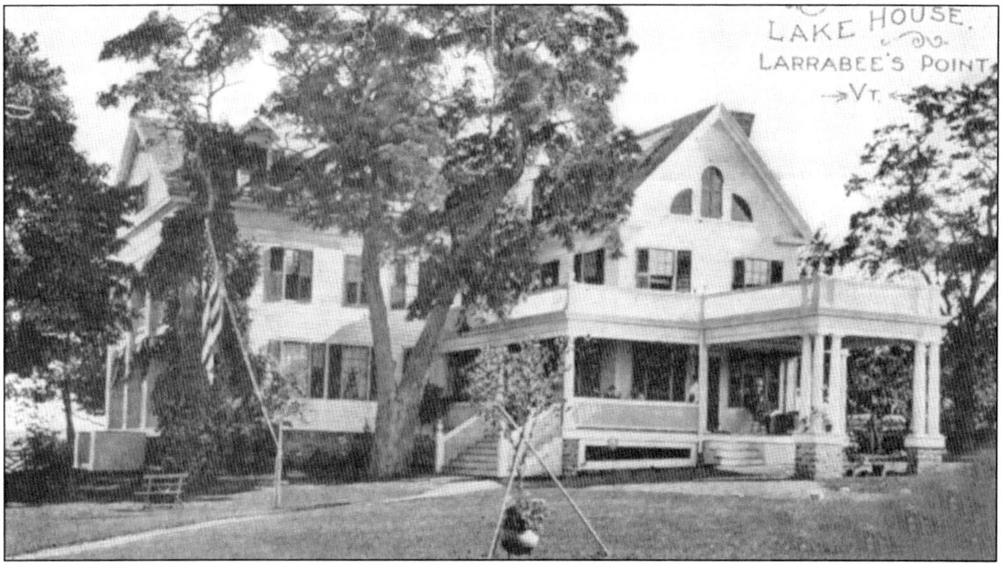

The Lakehouse at Larrabee's Point, also called the United States Hotel, was built in 1847 and provided a full range of services with guest cottages and an elegant restaurant. It was located in a prime spot, with easy access by stagecoach, railroad, and steamboat. The inn burned in 1917.

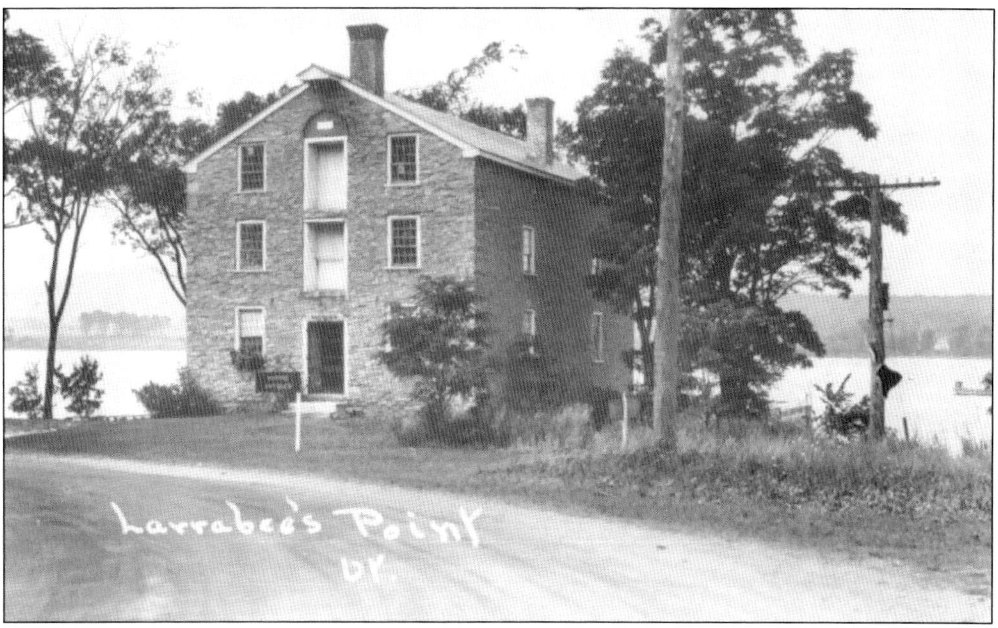

The stone building on the lake at Larrabee's Point was built in 1823 from material scavenged from the Fort Ticonderoga ruins. Originally a warehouse used at one time to stockpile wool, the building is now the Teachout Store.

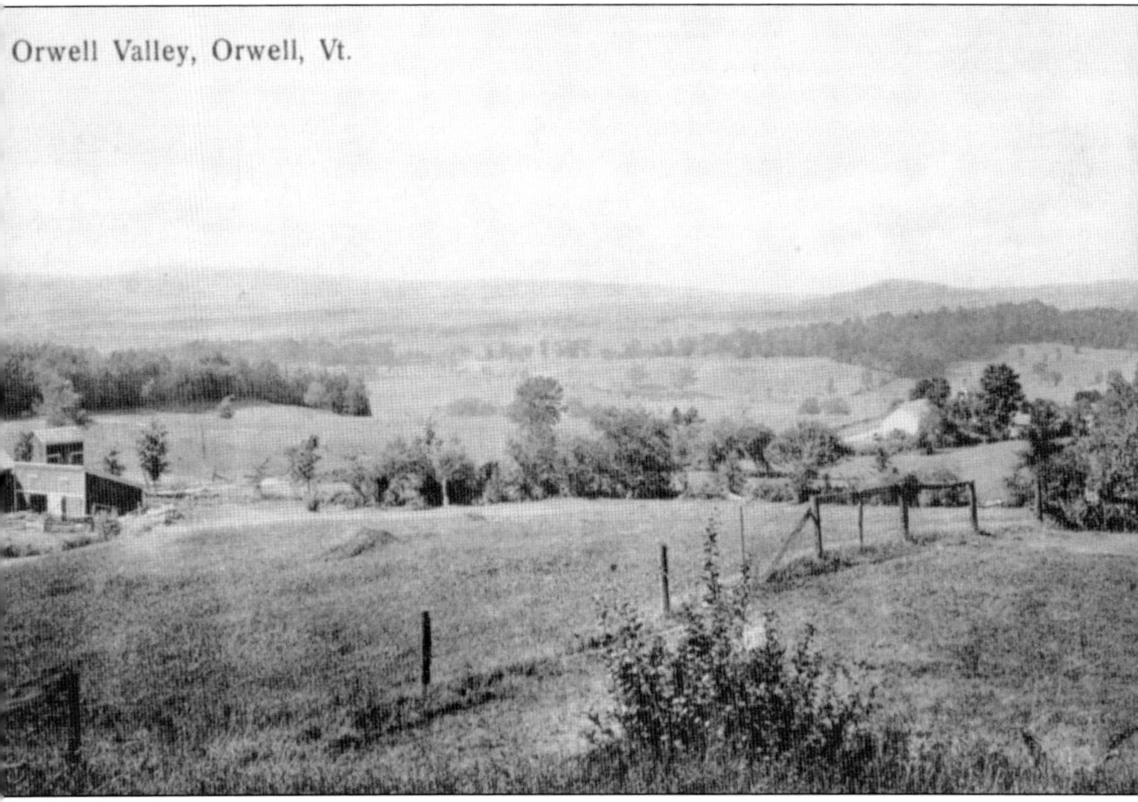

Many of the small farms in Addison County were consolidated into larger holdings over time and have shifted from tilled crops to sheep and finally to dairy farming. Addison County remains one of the most productive dairy regions of the Northeast.

Six

Lake Dunmore

A short distance from Middlebury is Lake Dunmore, a scenic retreat from the hot agricultural lowlands and village life. Early events around the lake included a major logging operation and the first glass factory in Vermont. By the mid-1800s, trains brought visitors from far-off places to the three large hotels: the Lake Dunmore House, the Mountain Spring House, and the Silver Lake Hotel, nearby in the hills above Lake Dunmore. A series of less formal guesthouses, seasonal dance pavilions, and, later, cottage complexes brought an even broader range of visitors to the lake. In the 1920s and 1930s, people from Middlebury, Brandon, and other nearby towns built cottages along the lakeshore and brought a new character to the mountain lake. Postcards documented it all. The hotels are particularly well represented, as are general lake scenes, the pavilions, and summer camps.

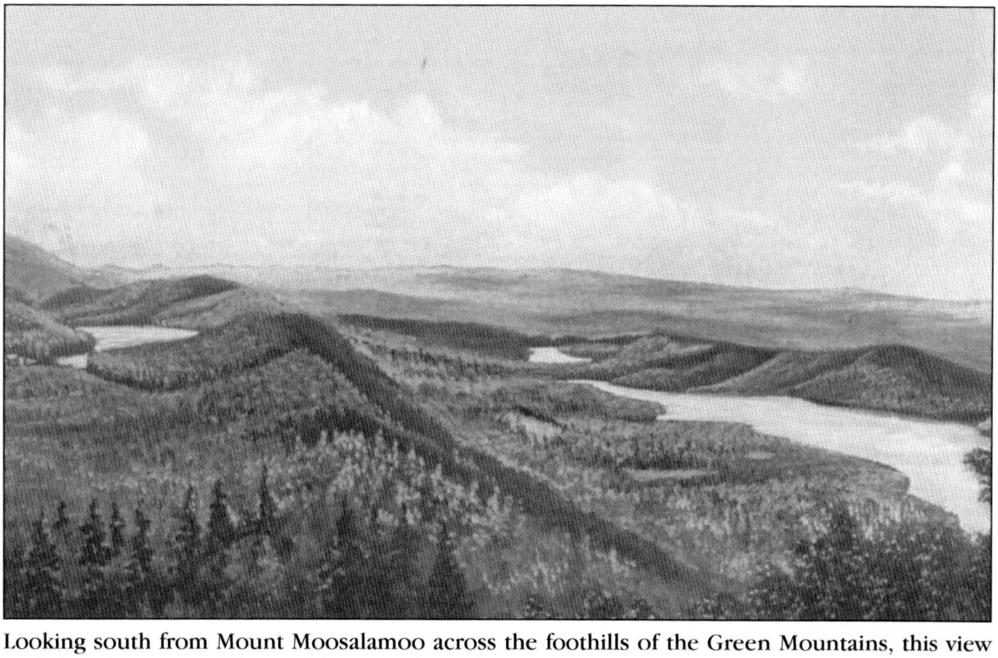

Looking south from Mount Moosalamoo across the foothills of the Green Mountains, this view includes three very different lakes. To the right is Lake Dunmore, which has a long and varied history. It was named in 1773 for Lord Dunmore, who had claimed ownership of the area when he was governor of New York. To the left is Silver Lake, high upon Chandler Ridge. In the distance is Fern Lake, which, even today, has only limited development along its shores.

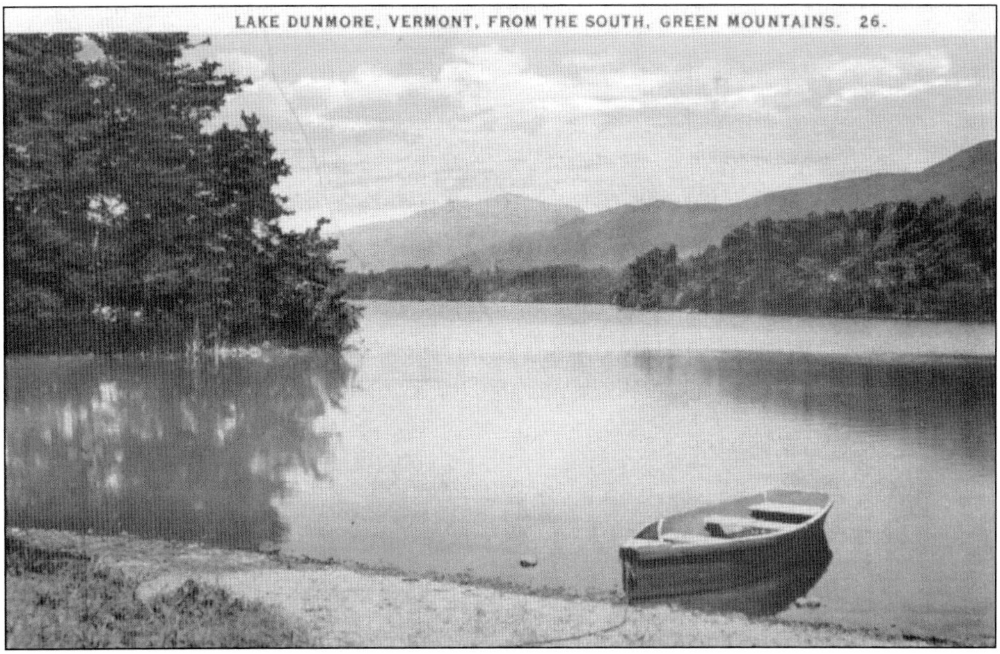

More than 100 postcard views feature Lake Dunmore in its setting among the rounded mountains of Vermont. Most of these scenes include boats, suggesting recreation, but few actually show people.

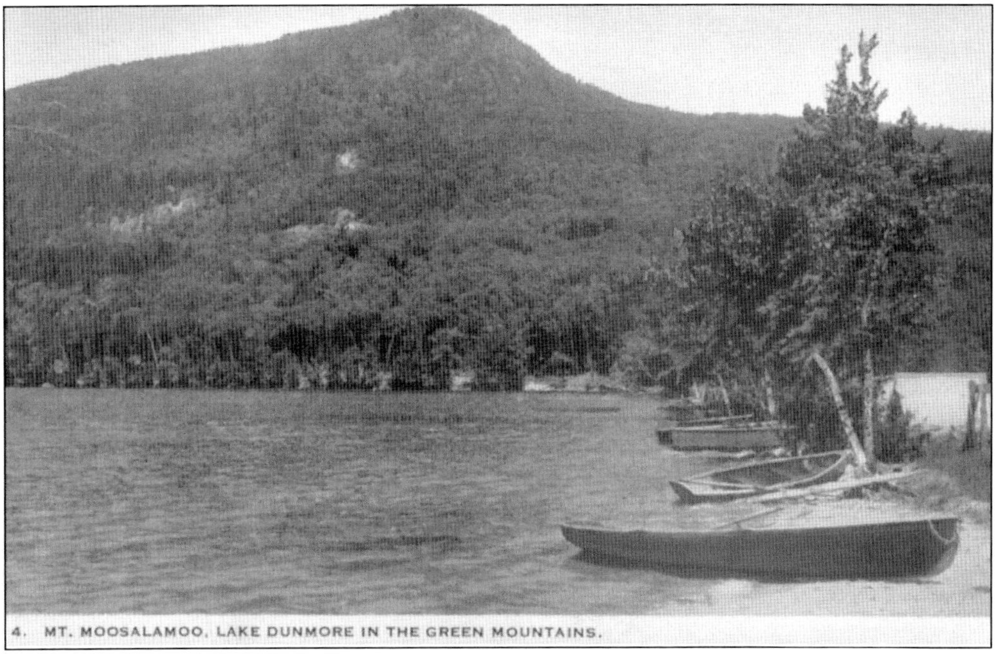

The mountains near Lake Dunmore were a major source of timber in the late 1700s and throughout the 1800s. By the 1840s, the virgin timber along the west face of the Green Mountains was nearly gone. Logging operations included the Newton and Thompson Sawmill, from 1864 to the 1930s, and A. Johnson's Sawmill at the north end of the lake in the 1920s.

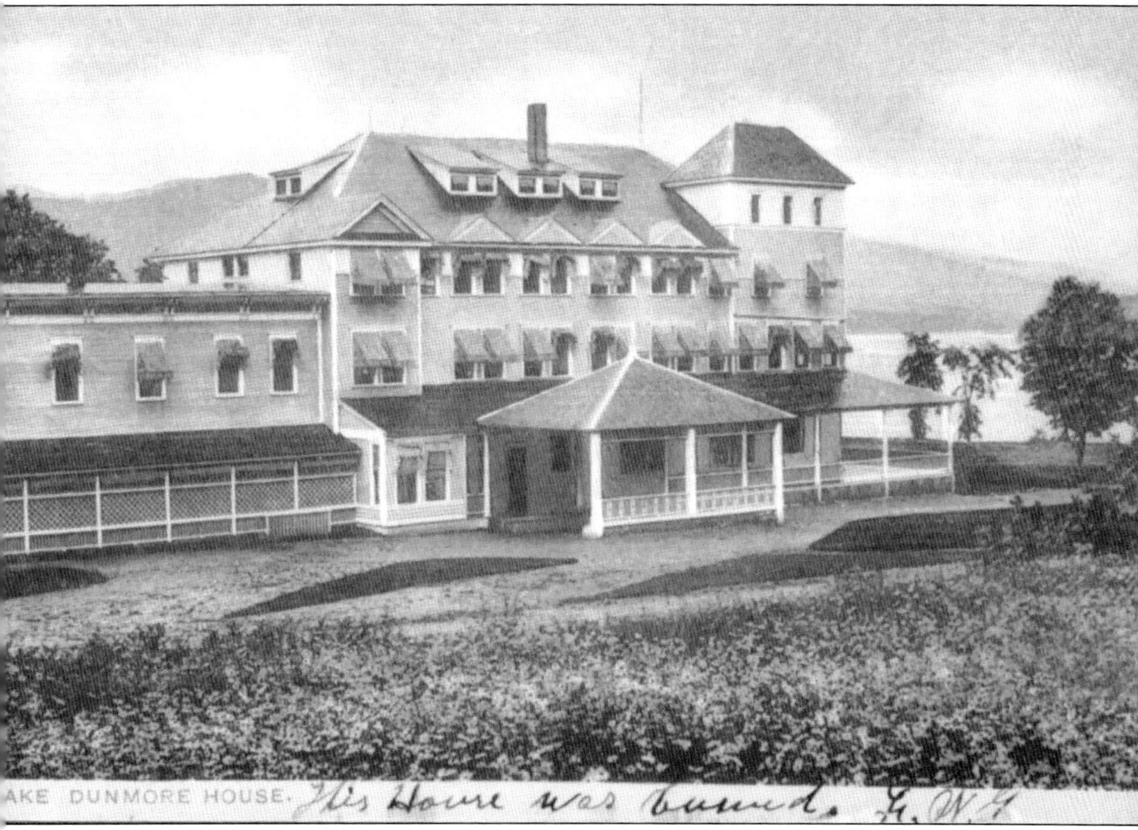

The Lake Dunmore House was built *c.* 1854 near the location of the old Vermont Glass Factory, with dramatic views looking south down the lake. The first Lake Dunmore House burned in 1877 and was quickly replaced by a larger, more modern hotel. Over time, the facility expanded and included a series of cottages, tennis courts, a lakeside dance pavilion, and boathouses. The hotel was a self-contained resort. It burned again in 1906 and was never rebuilt.

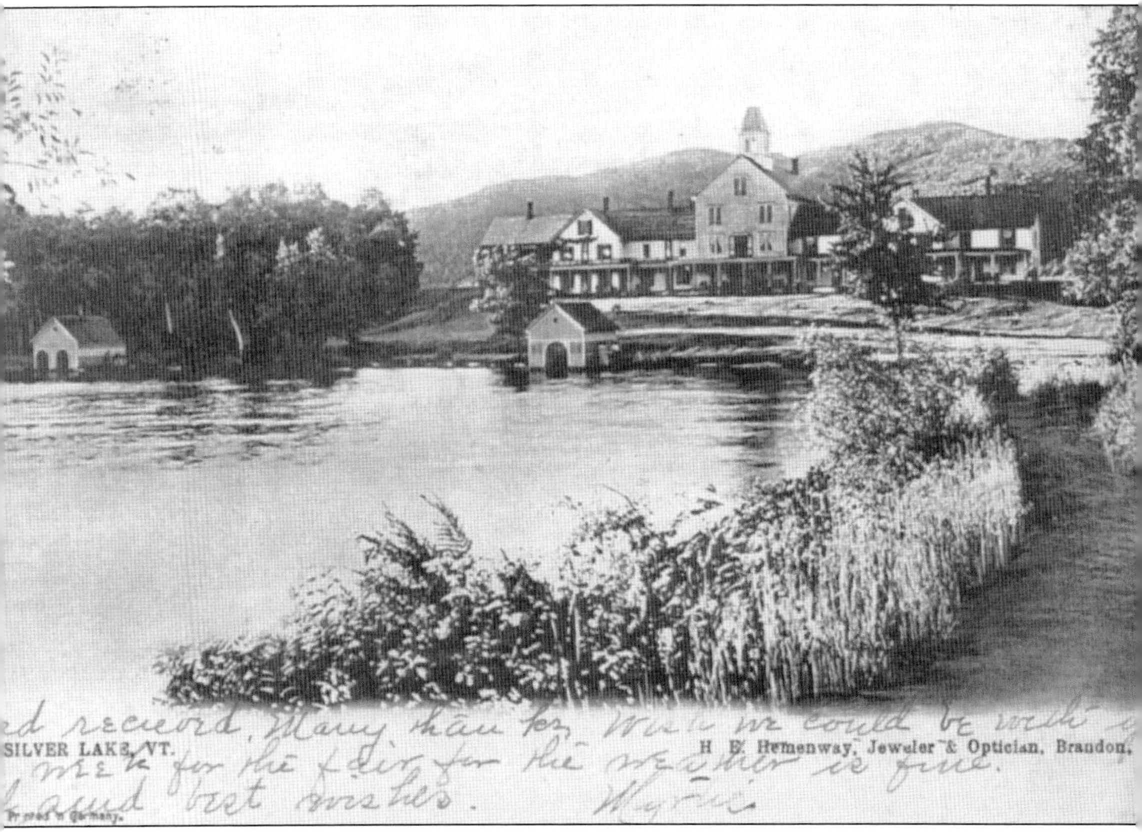

Frank Chandler, a local evangelist farmer, established a commercial hotel at Silver Lake in the late 1870s. During the hotel's 40-plus years of operation, Chandler set aside several weeks each year to host religious camp meetings. These meetings were free of charge and open to all denominations. The center section of the hotel was constructed in 1885 and included a chapel. After Chandler's death in 1927, the hotel fell into disuse. Rumors say that Middlebury College fraternities held blindfolded, naked hazings there at night. The hotel burned to the ground in 1942.

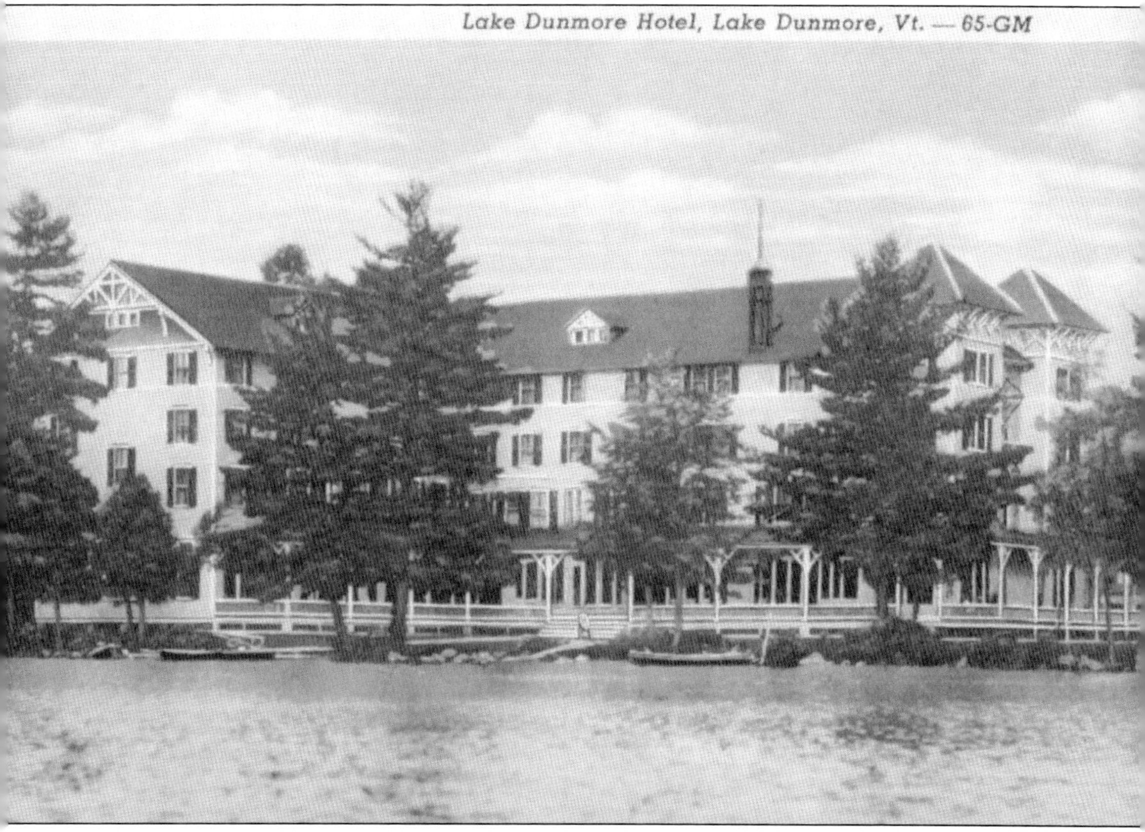

The Mountain Spring House was built in 1892 and competed with the nearby Lake Dunmore House. With similar facilities, the Mountain Spring House was a more modern version of the aging inn. After the loss of the Lake Dunmore House in 1906, the Mountain Spring House changed its name to the Lake Dunmore Hotel. The last large inn on Lake Dunmore was condemned by the State of Vermont as unsafe in 1957. The derelict hotel building burned in 1979.

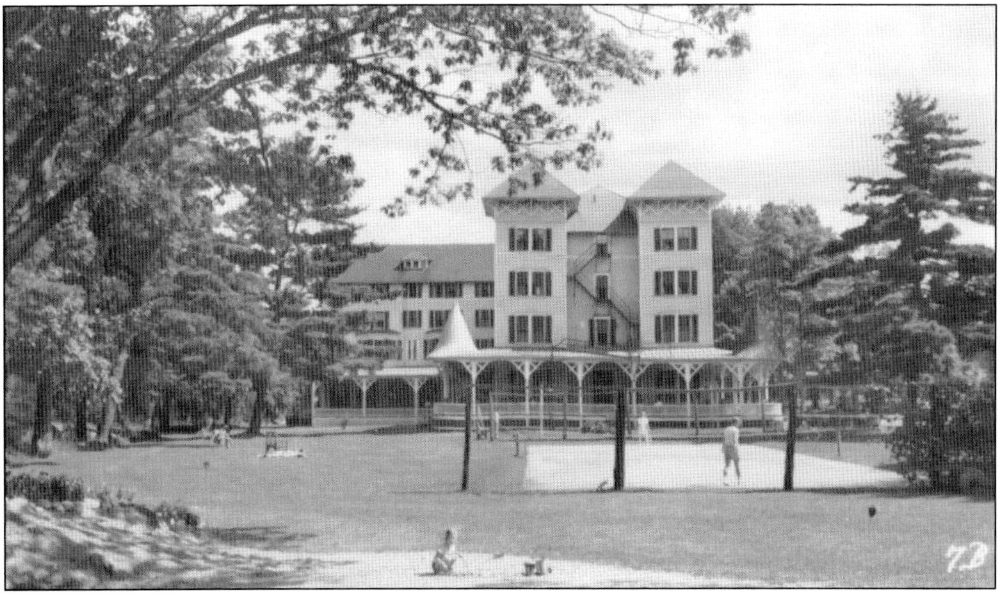

Like most late-19th-century country inns, the Lake Dunmore Hotel included guest cottages and a full range of entertainment facilities, including tennis courts, docks, and a boathouse. Although the hotel is gone, several of the cottages are still in use.

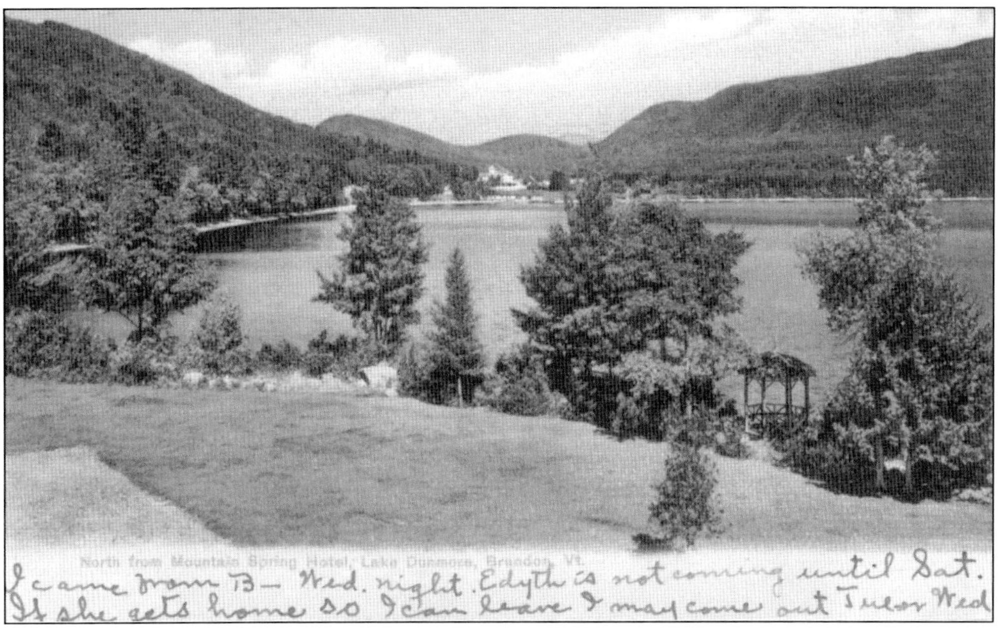

For many visitors, the view from the shoreline in front of the Lake Dunmore Hotel is the most distinctive on the lake. This postcard from 1905 shows the Lake Dunmore House in the distance in its last year of operation. Keewaydin Girls' Camp now occupies this choice location. The profile of the hills, including Moosalamoo to the right, is easily recognizable to those who know the lake.

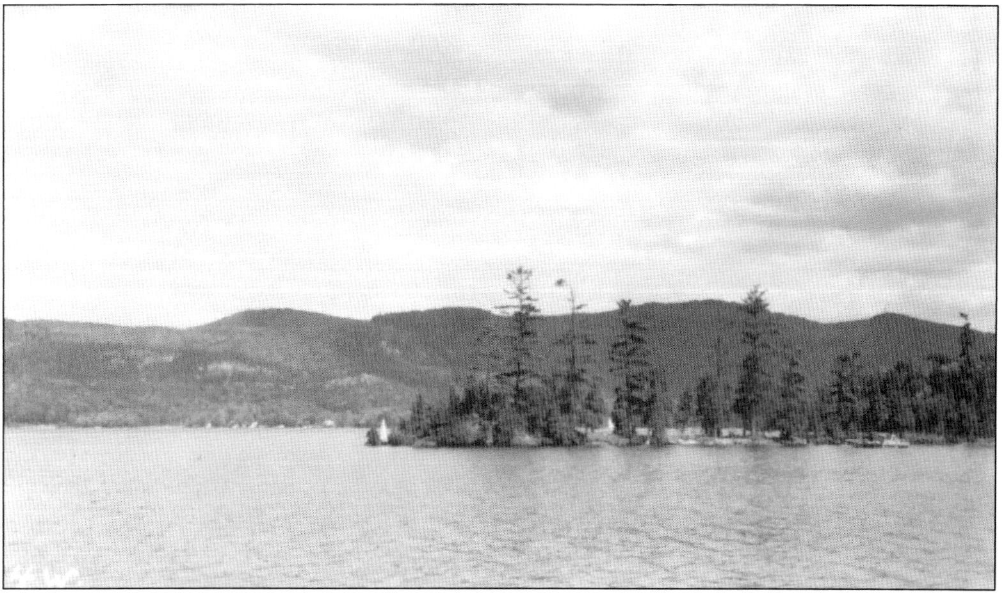

Waterhouse's began in 1887 as a boat excursion facility just south of the Lake Dunmore Hotel. Over time, the complex was developed as a popular beach and picnic area. A dance pavilion was added later. The view from Waterhouse's, as shown in this real photo postcard, included a small lighthouse on the point of the peninsula in front of the facility. Many college parties and family outings have taken place at Waterhouse's, which is today the oldest business in operation on the lake.

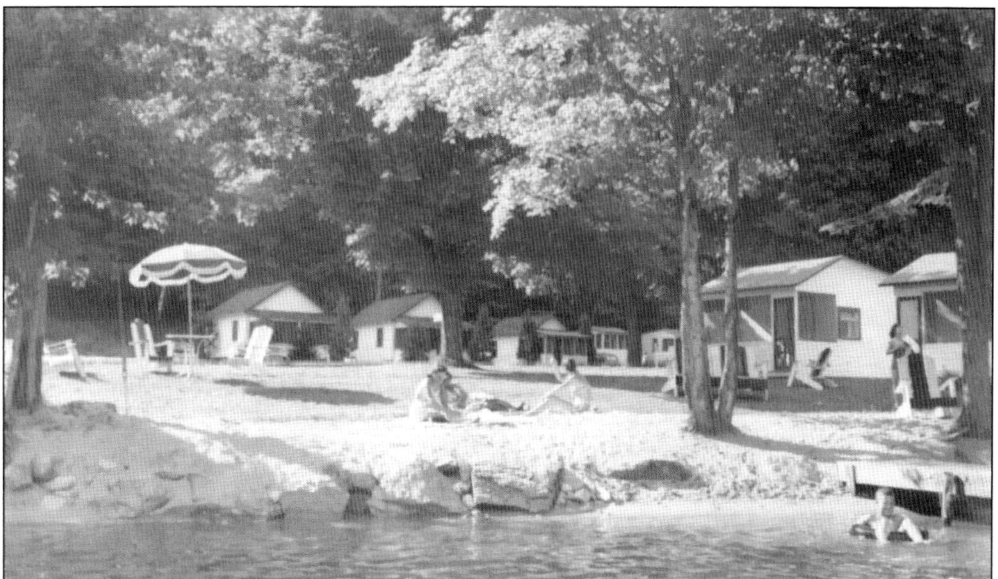

Hoffman's was located just south of Waterhouse's within the same small embayment protected by the peninsula. Hoffman's was started in the 1930s by William Hoffman, who built small rental cottages and charged a day-use fee for the beach. Hoffman's widow sold the property in 1963 to the State of Vermont, which developed a boat launch and associated parking lot, increasing access to the lake for boaters.

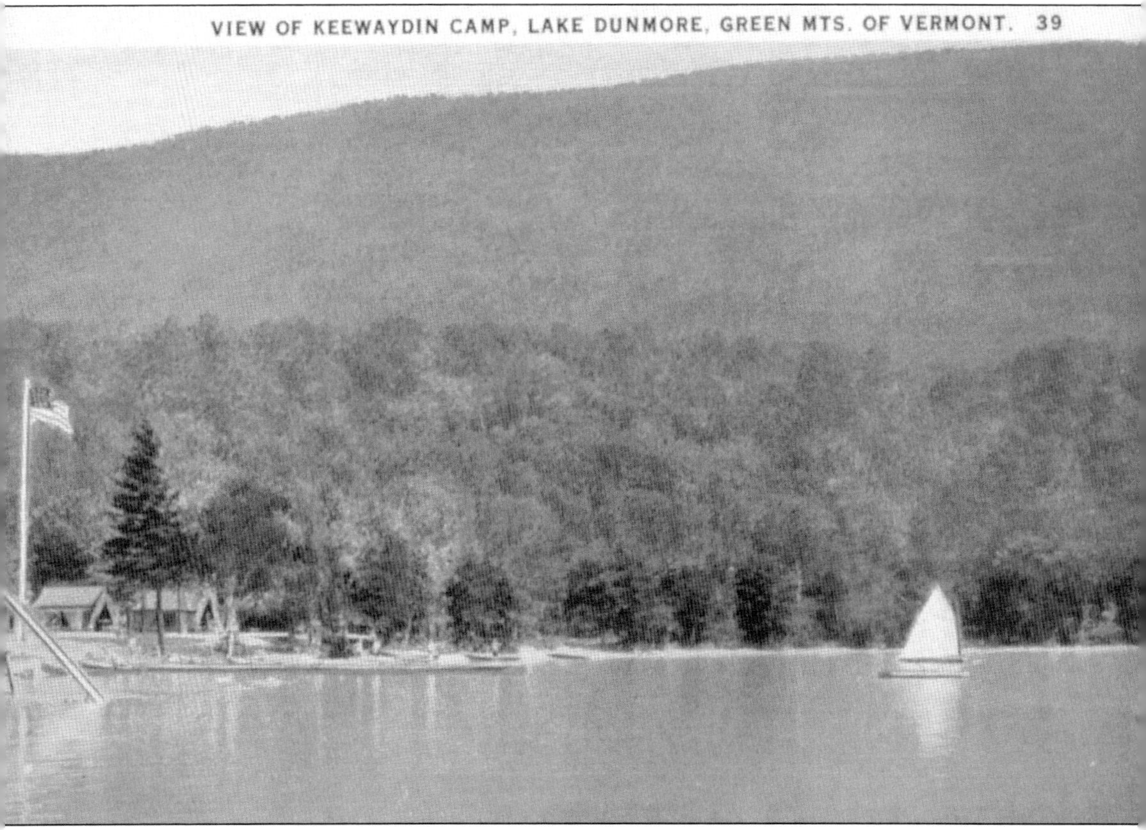

Camp Keewaydin is the oldest camp for boys on the lake and the fifth oldest in the United States. Beginning in 1910, Keewaydin was, at one time, the last point of access along the north shore of the lake. Today, the facility serves approximately 200 boys each summer and also provides an environmental education program for local schools.

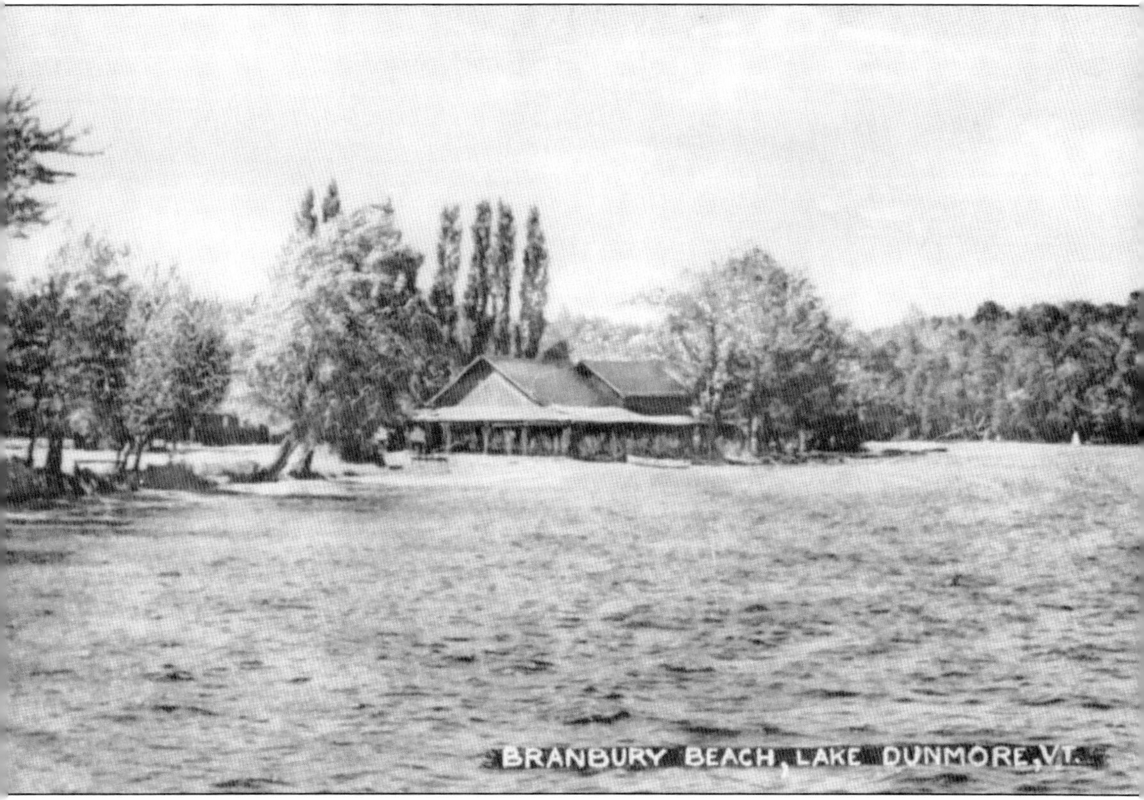

This early view of Banbury State Park shows the old clubhouse of a popular waterside dance pavilion in the 1920s. This location, which was at the end of the road from the south until 1913, was the site of an early hotel, a boys' camp, and a commercial beach. Owner Shirley Farr gave the property to the State of Vermont in 1945. The facility became the popular Banbury State Park, providing, for the first time, general public access to the clean water of Lake Dunmore.

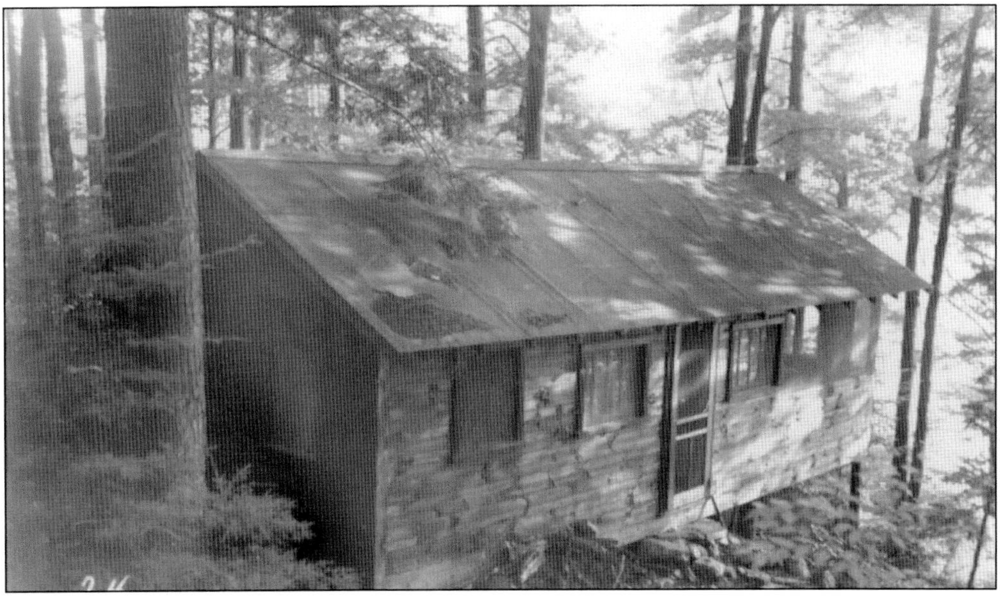

In the 1920s and 1930s, local families began to build small camps along the lakeshore for summer use. Numerous cottages were built along the north shore, where many families have now, for several generations, spent their entire summers. Some of these camps were documented in real photo postcards.

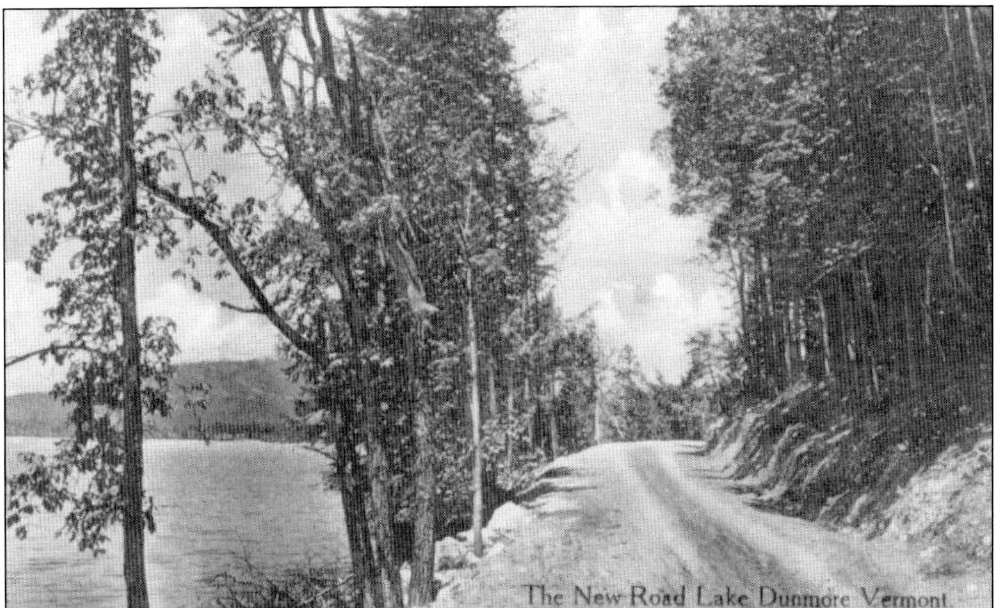

For many years, the east side of the lake was inaccessible because of the steep ascent of the Green Mountains to the lakeshore. A new road was cut along the shore in 1913. Several postcards proudly show this new road. Numerous cottages were subsequently built along this road.

Lana Falls is located along Sucker Brook. For many years, its picturesque series of falls have been a frequent visitors' destination. It is said that Lana Falls, originally called Sucker Brook Falls, was renamed during a visit by Gen. John Wool, who served in the Mexican War in the 1840s. An aide suggested that, in honor of the general, the falls be called Lana Falls, as the Spanish word for wool is *lana*.

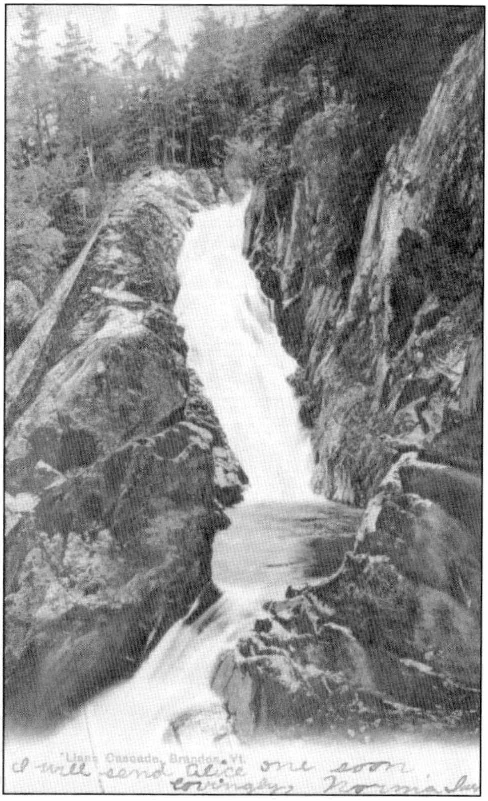

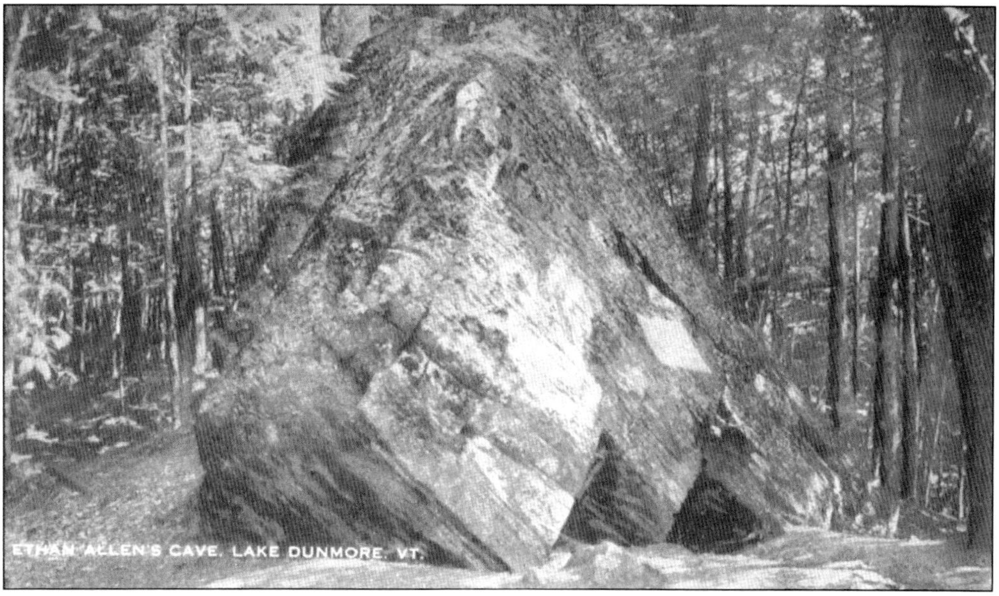

Another popular destination near Lake Dunmore was the Green Mountain Boys' Cave. A small cave part way up the slope above Lake Dunmore, it has provided shelter for hikers. There are local legends that it was used by Native Americans and as a hiding place for Ethan Allen and his supporters.

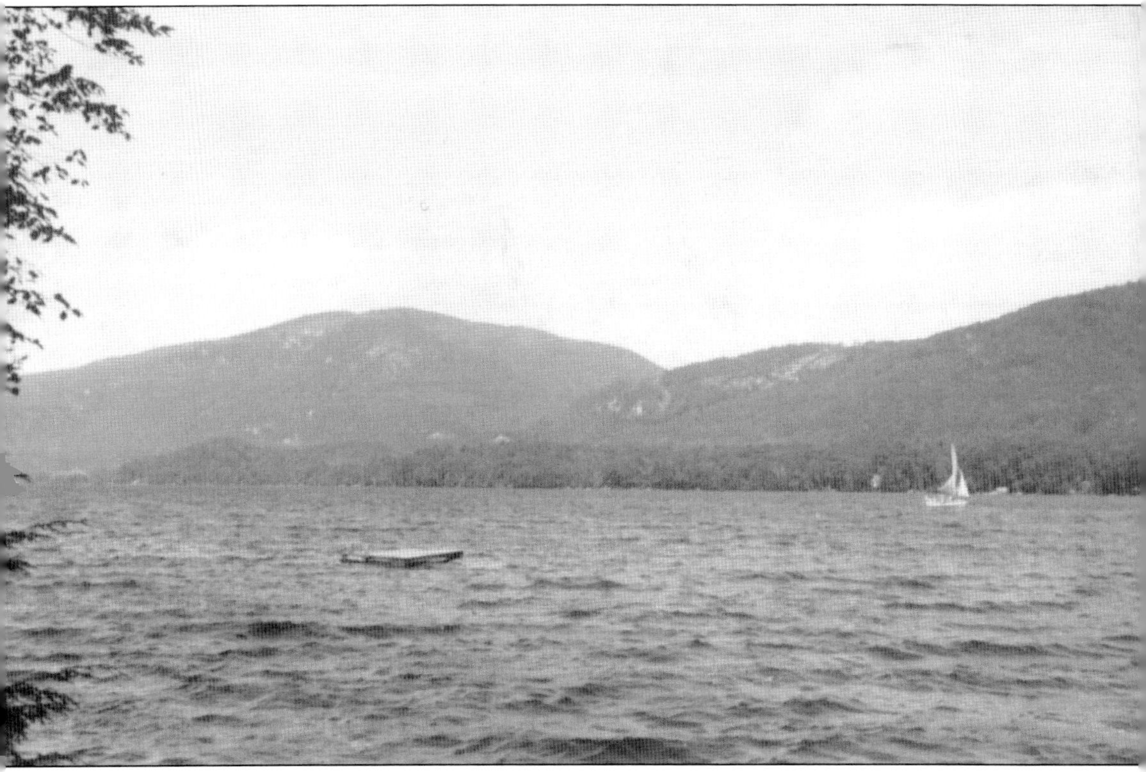

The lake and mountain scene at Dunmore has been the subject of postcards for nearly 100 years. Early visitors to the lake would easily recognize the landscape today. Dunmore continues to be a popular place for families.

Seven

AGRICULTURE AND INDUSTRY

The soils of Addison County and nearby sections of the Lake Champlain lowlands are extremely fertile and were cleared of trees very early after settlement. Today, there are few areas that support this former forest, the original composition of which is currently debated by Vermont ecologists. Following first clearing, the soils were successful for the growing of wheat, which made many farmers wealthy, although their crops had to be transported by wagon as far as Troy, New York. The year-round freezes of 1817 and subsequent wheat diseases and pest infestations put a rapid end to wheat prosperity. Farmers turned to other pursuits, quickly discovering new wealth in sheep, which thrived on the rich pastures of Addison County. In 1840, Addison County was the major sheep-farming center in the country. Competition from Midwest and Far West farms soon resulted in a rapid decline in demand for Vermont wool and mutton. The farmers shifted to breeding Merino sheep imported from Europe, and a new wave of prosperity swept across the valley towns. By the advent of postcards, sheep breeding was in serious decline and dairy and apple farming were dominant. The valley was also an important center for marble and slate, as well as manufactured products from wood, stone, iron, wool, and, later, cotton.

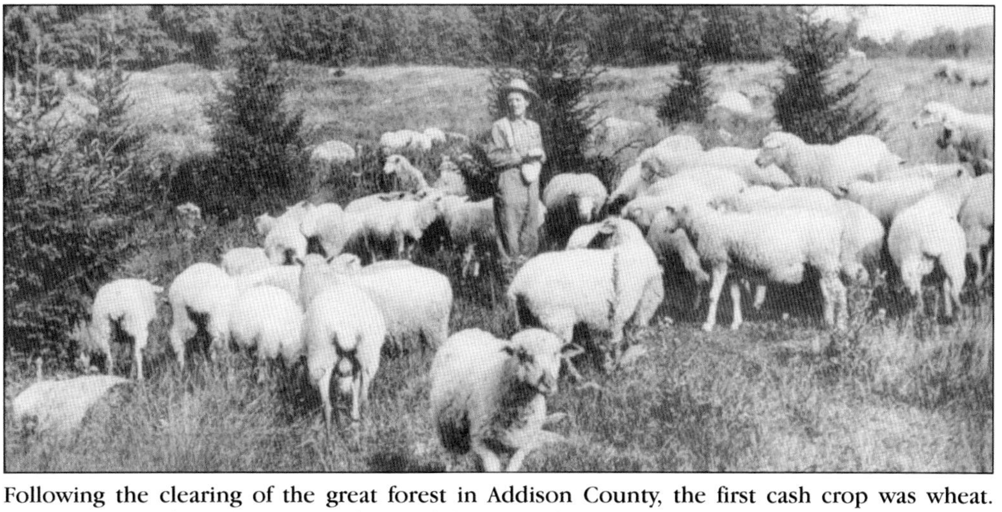

Following the clearing of the great forest in Addison County, the first cash crop was wheat. Initially successful, wheat soon depleted the soil of nutrients, and farmers turned to sheep. Between 1820 and 1850, Vermont was the major sheep-producing region of the country. Addison County supported more sheep in 1840 than did any other place in the United States.

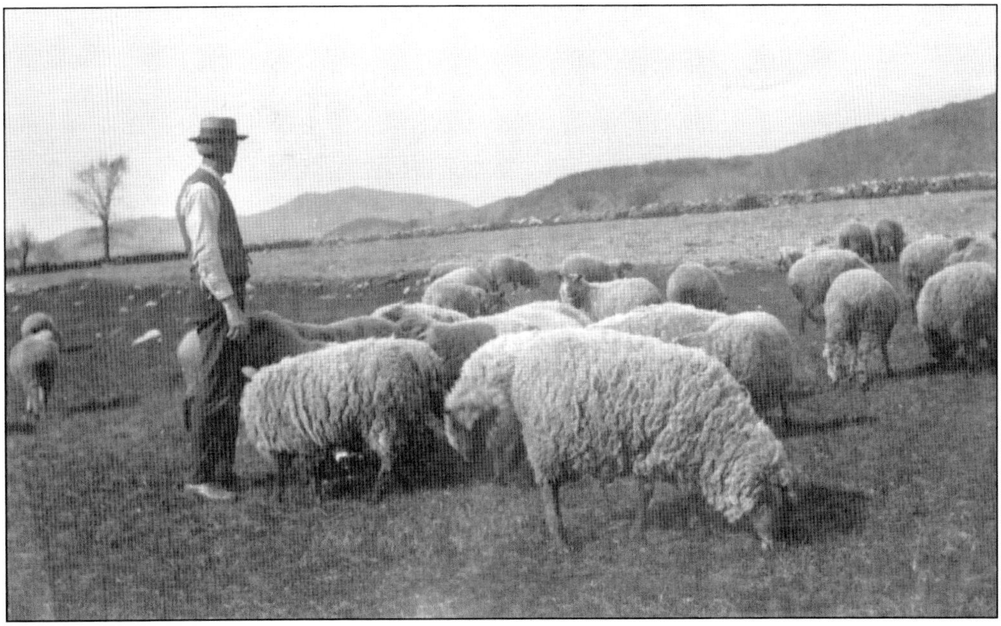

Settlement westward and more efficient transportation moved the sheep industry out of Vermont. By the period of early postcards, Vermont was still known for its sheep, but the days of huge herds, Merino sheep, and sheep breeding were over. Only a few remnant farms with sheep persisted, with the scattering of notable and beautiful homes built by the successful sheep farmers of the 19th century.

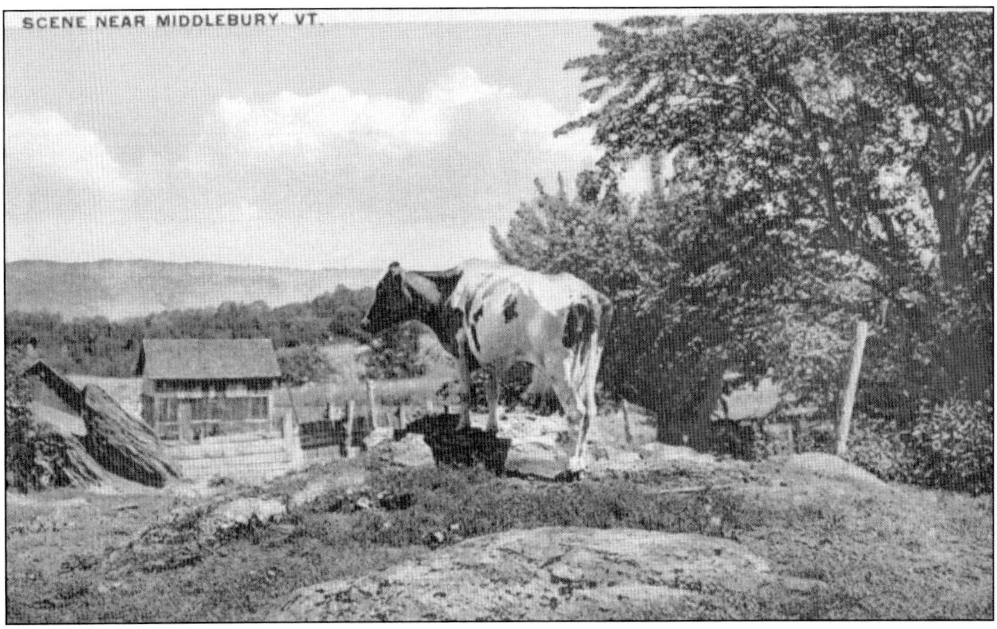

As sheep farming waned, dairy farming took its place. Smaller farms combined into larger operations. Addison County was well connected by train to all East Coast markets and produced high-quality milk and cheese.

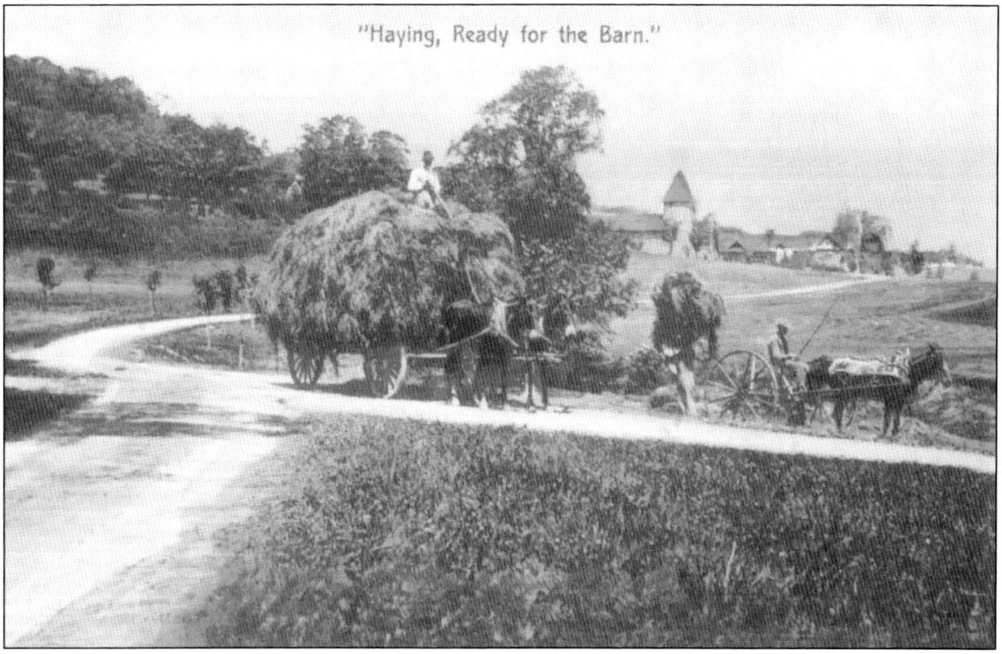

Dairy farming was successful in part because of the rich soils of Addison County that can grow three good crops of hay in a year with favorable weather.

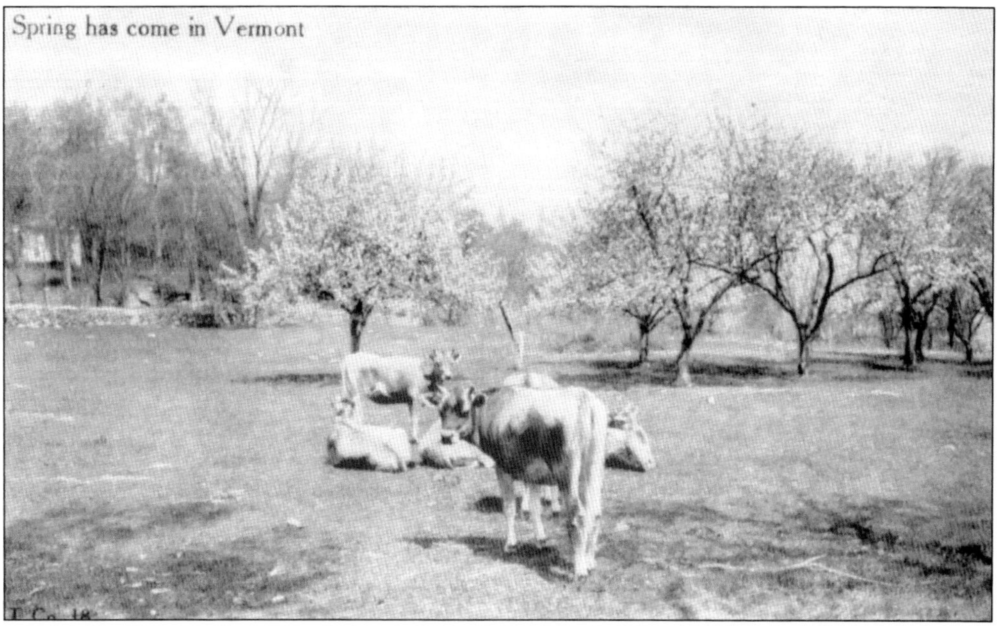

Country scenes with cows were made popular by photographer Wallace Nutting and other commercial artists near the beginning of the 20th century. Many postcards document the rural Vermont landscape that was admired by city-dwelling visitors.

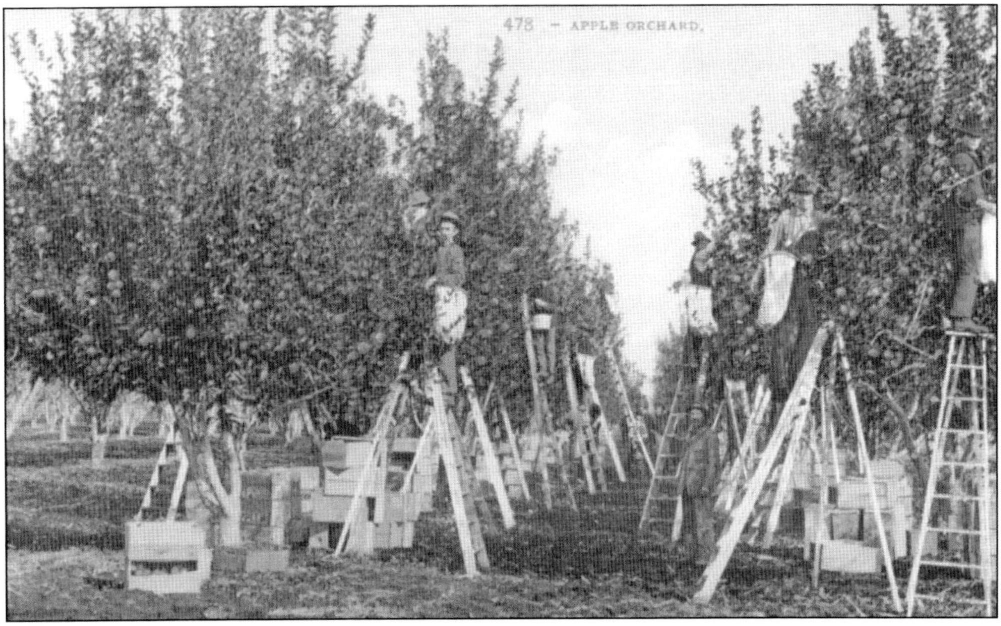

Addison County farmers were always seeking more effective ways to use their land. The rocky slopes along Lake Champlain were ideally suited for growing apples. Fruit trees were a part of all large farms in early colonial America. Apples were particularly successful on these farms. Following the reduction in sheep farming, many farmers began apple orchards, especially in Shoreham and Cornwall.

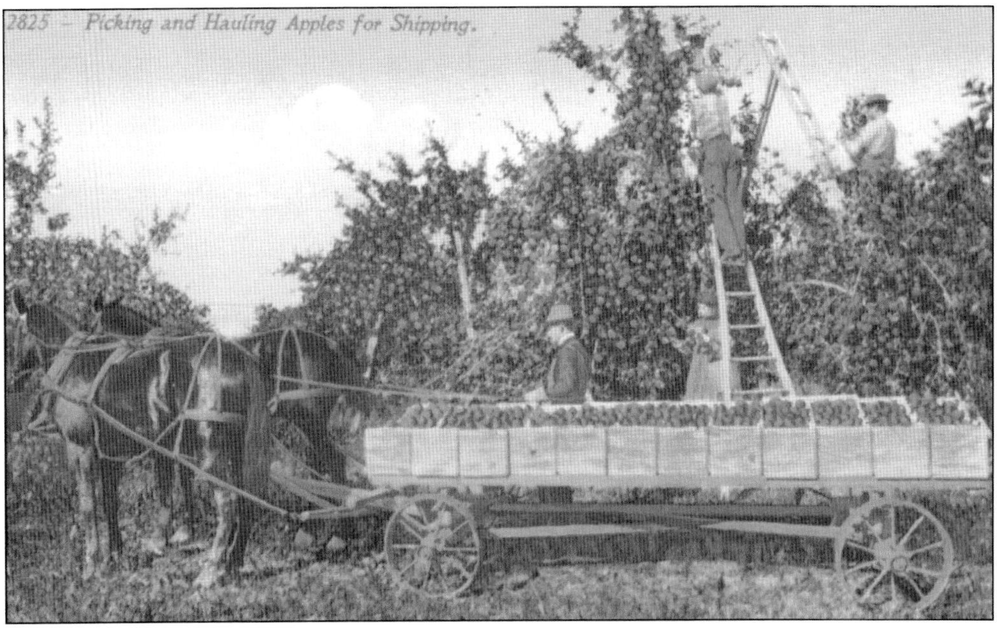

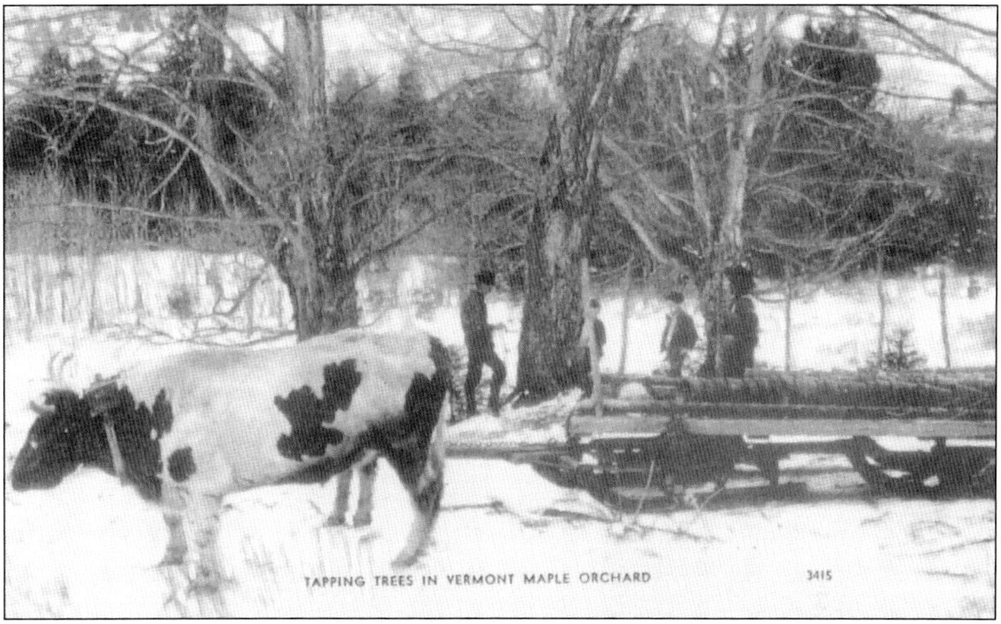

During the 19th century, most farmers tapped maple trees in early spring before mud season for the collection of sap to make maple syrup. By the time postcards were first produced, maple sugaring was a minor industry, which held an attraction for tourists who enjoyed seeing traditional farming practices still in use. Postcards documented the tapping of trees, the collection of sap, and the boiling of sap to concentrate sugars.

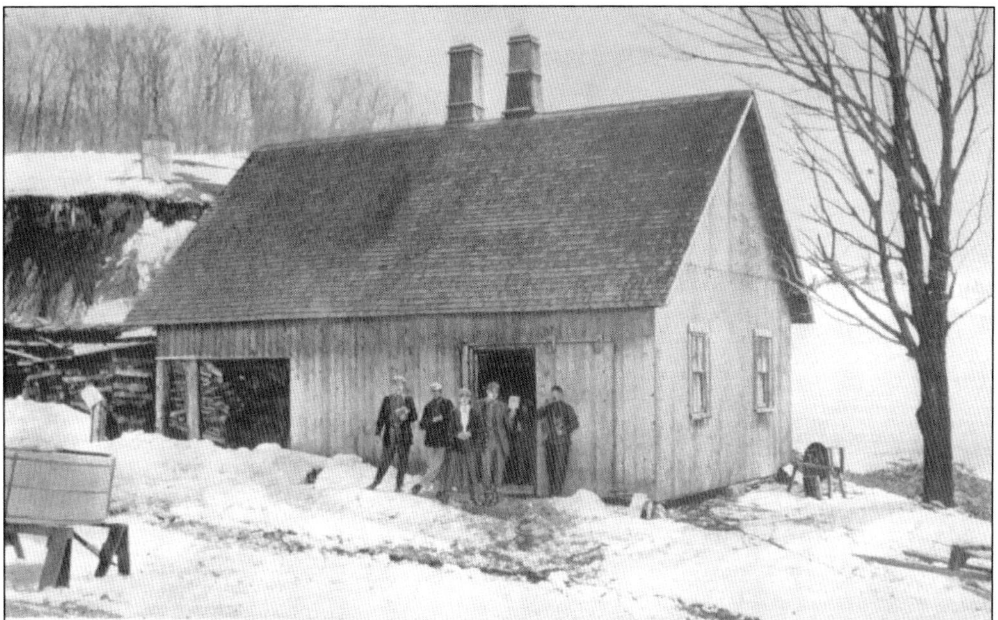

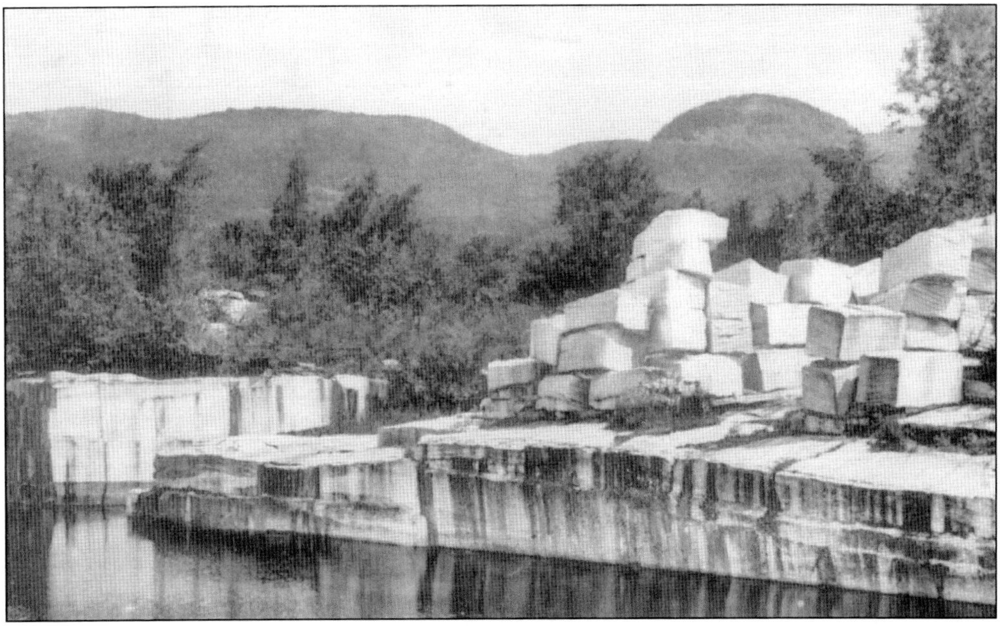

Large deposits of marble are found in the lowlands west of the Green Mountains. Middlebury, Brandon, and Proctor, to the south, all have extensive marble resources that were initially quarried for local use. Later, the railroad made it possible for the export of cut marble to distant markets.

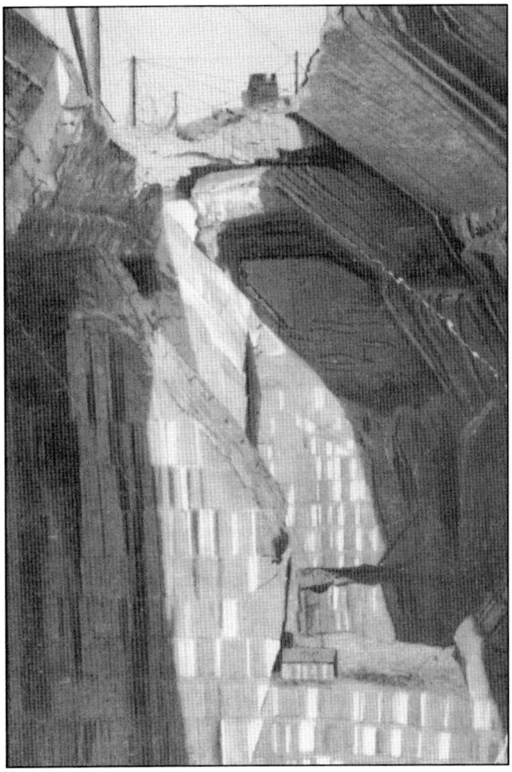

The Middlebury marble works was a major manufacturer on the north side of the falls that used waterpower to cut stone. Initially, stone was transported by wagon to Larrabee's Point or Vergennes for shipment along the lake. Later, railroads transported milled stone.

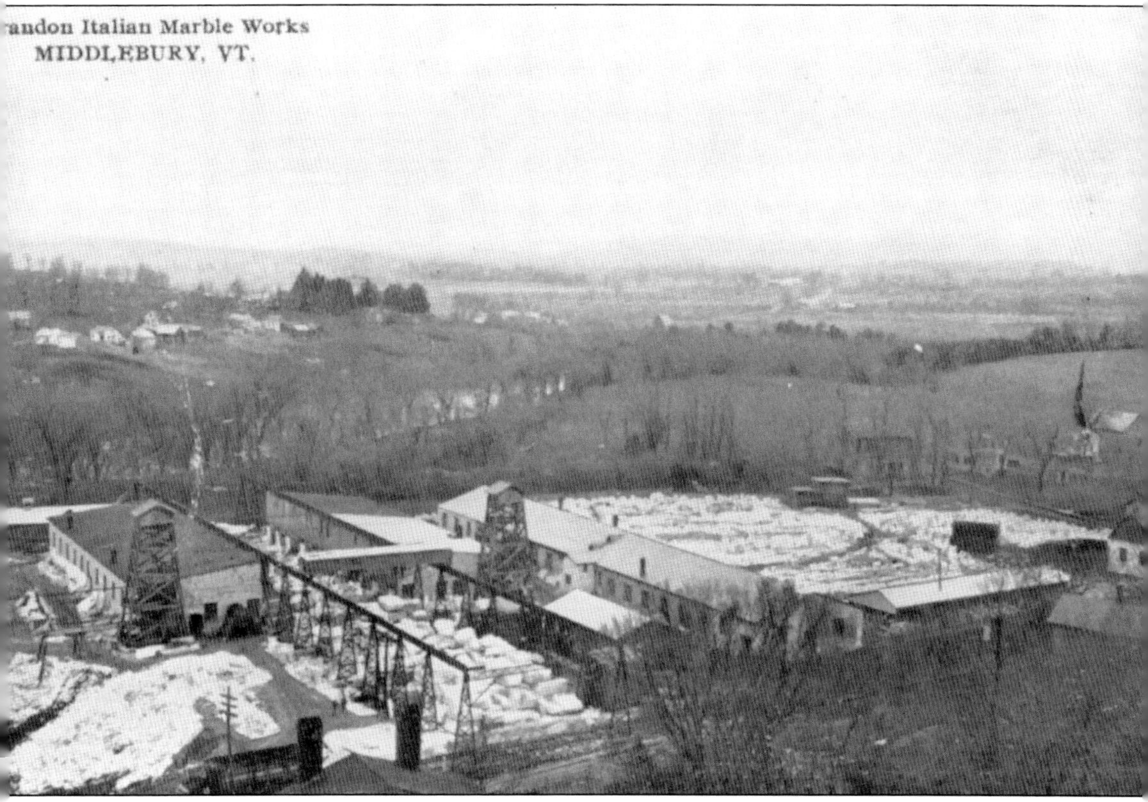

Several fires in the marble factory in Brandon shifted the milling operation to Middlebury, leading to the reconstruction of the Middlebury mills. Several of these buildings are still present today north of the falls.

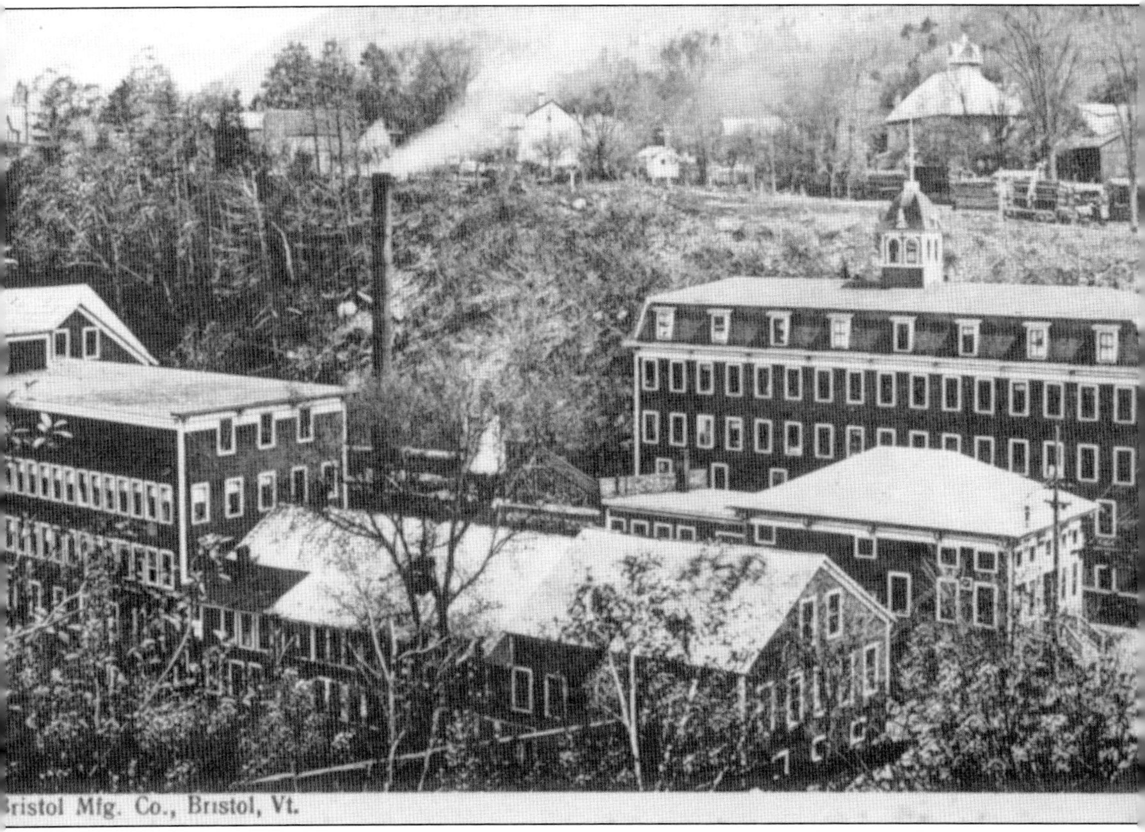

Throughout the 19th century, the industrial activity that was found scattered across Addison County related to power generated from waterfalls and the location of natural resources. Timber, iron, marble, and wool were all worked in large factories into goods for local use and for export. In later years, more efficient sources of power and the ability to transport raw material long distances drove all but a few remnant manufacturing operations out of Addison County.

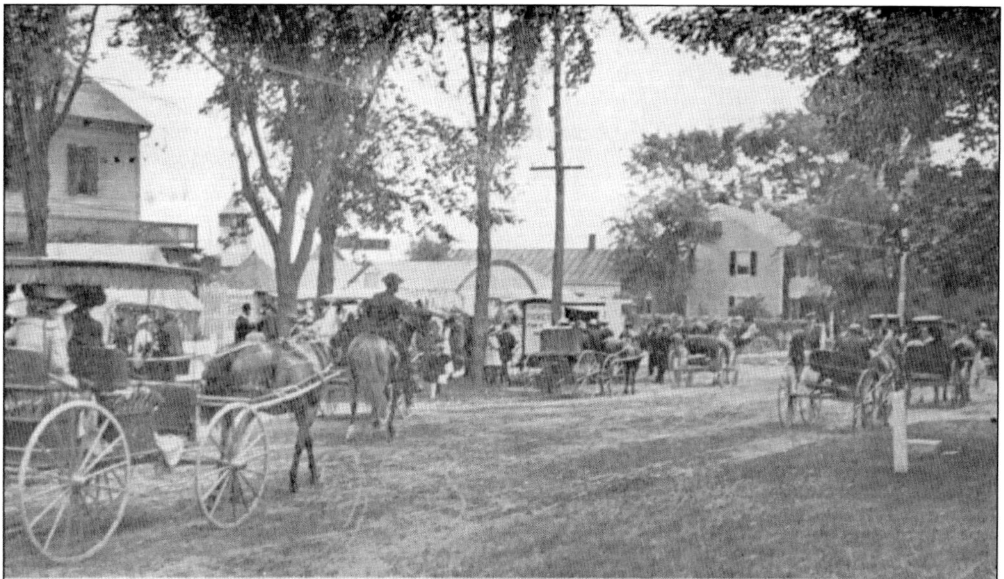

ENTRANCE TO MIDDLEBURY'S GREAT FAIR

The Addison County Agricultural Society Fairgrounds was located east of Court Street. The major entrance was under the arch, near the road to the Mary Hogan School. The building to the left is the south wing of the Sargeant Hotel, located where Milne Travel is today.

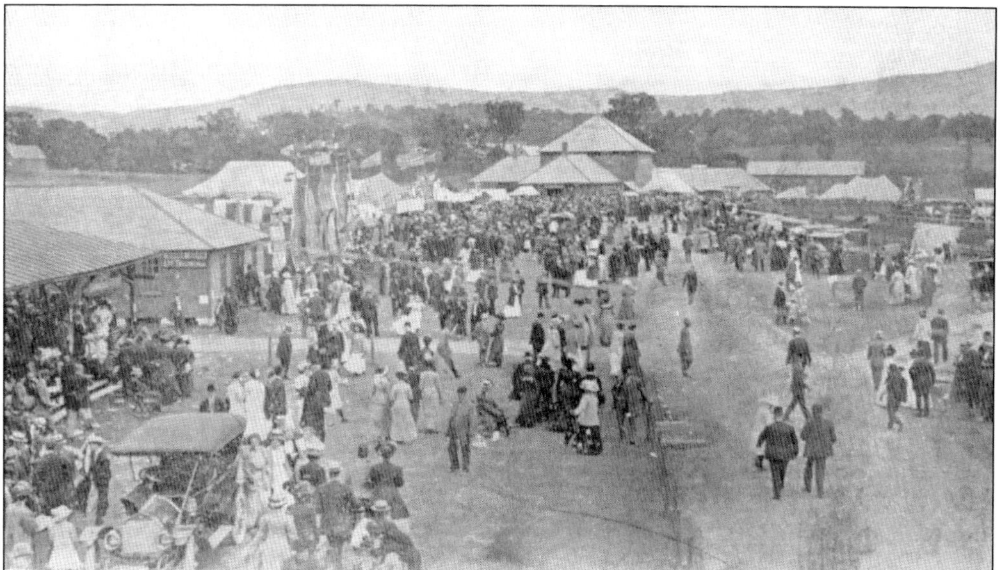

MIDWAY FROM BALCONY OF FLORAL HALL

The Great Addison County Fair was held in late August or early September each year and was the major social and commercial event of the year. The fairgrounds included animals and plant displays, food competitions, and examples of the latest inventions. Early airplane rides were offered at the fairgrounds to eager visitors.

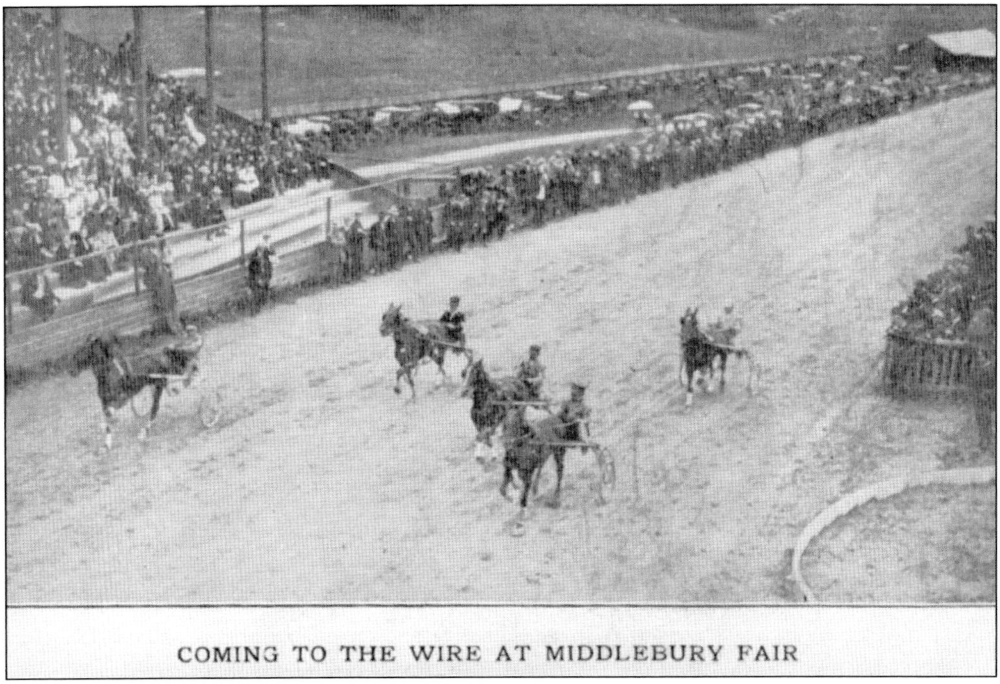

The Addison County Agricultural Society Fairgrounds was one of the largest and most popular in the Northeast, with a grandstand seating 5,000. Racing offered entertainment and an opportunity for horse owners to show off their competitive skills and talents as breeders.

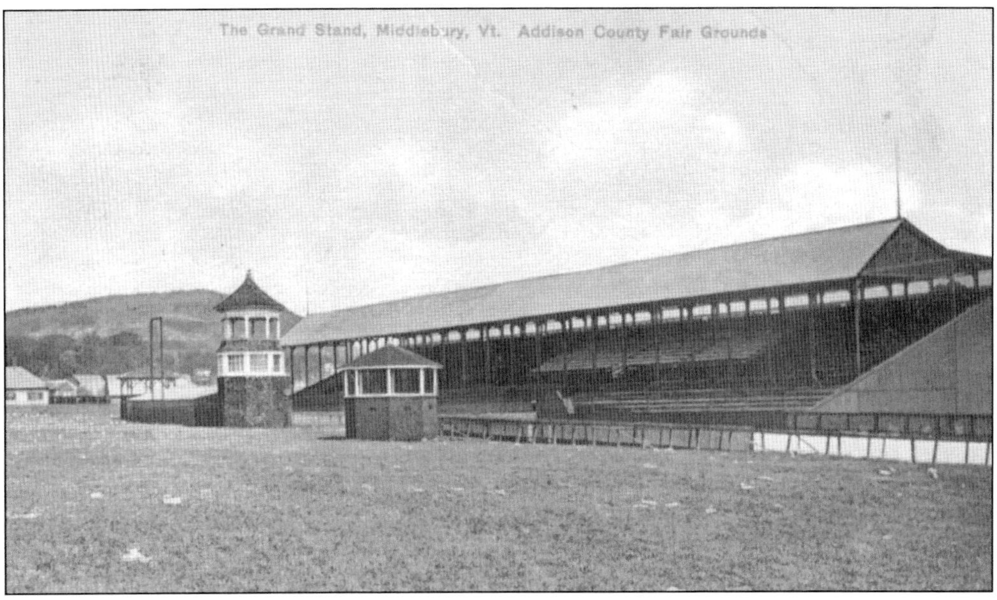

In the 1930s, the fairgrounds fell on hard times. The Depression slowed attendance, and larger fairs in Rutland and Burlington, held at the same time, drew away crowds, who could by then travel longer distances by car. The last fair was held in 1938. Many of the fairground buildings were torn down within only a few years. Today, the original fairground buildings are gone, replaced with modern buildings with year-round functions.

Eight

MESSAGES FROM AROUND MIDDLEBURY

Postcards (then called postals) played an important role in country social life. Mail delivery at the beginning of the 20th century was an efficient way to communicate, before telephones were universal. Cards were often sent with very brief messages. On early cards, only the recipient's address could appear on the back of the card. Any message had to be written on the front side with the image. Later cards had divided backs, with a section for the address and a section for a short message; more detailed information could be included. Postcards were used to announce events, send holiday greetings, advertise businesses, and, later, for correspondence between shortwave radio operators. There were a series of so-called stock cards produced, for which the name of any town could be written into the image. Postcards could reflect stereotypical images of country life. Some postcards were also very personal or humorous.

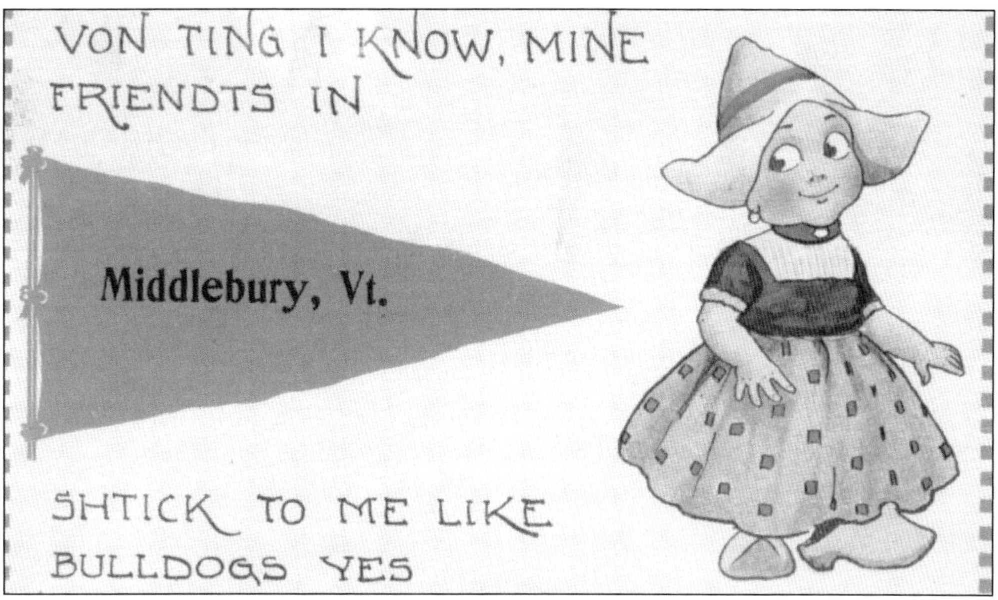

Some stock cards had a distinctive ethnic flare.

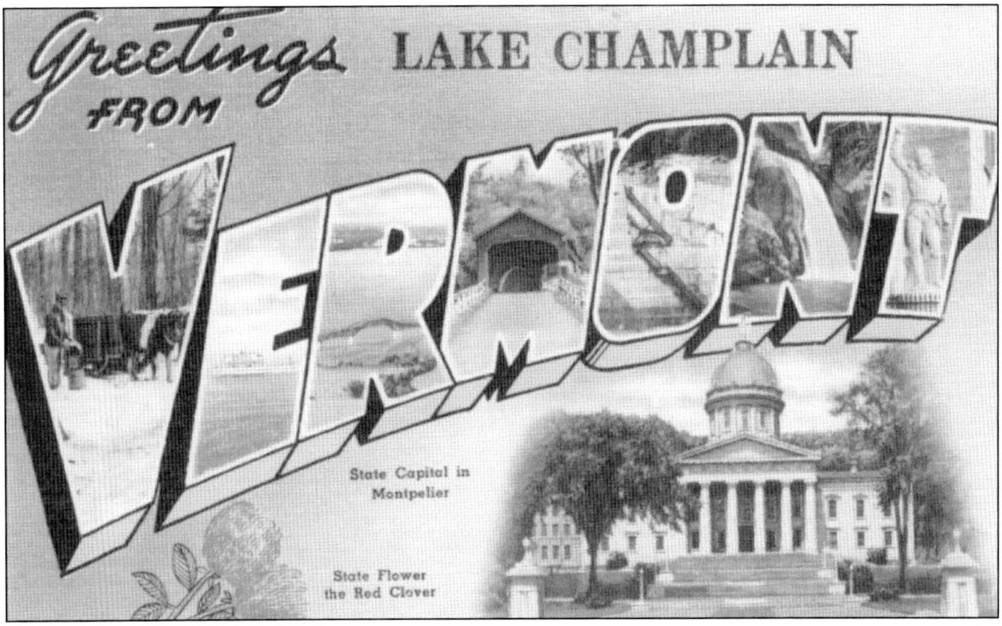

Large letter postcards were produced for many areas and included individual images for each letter.

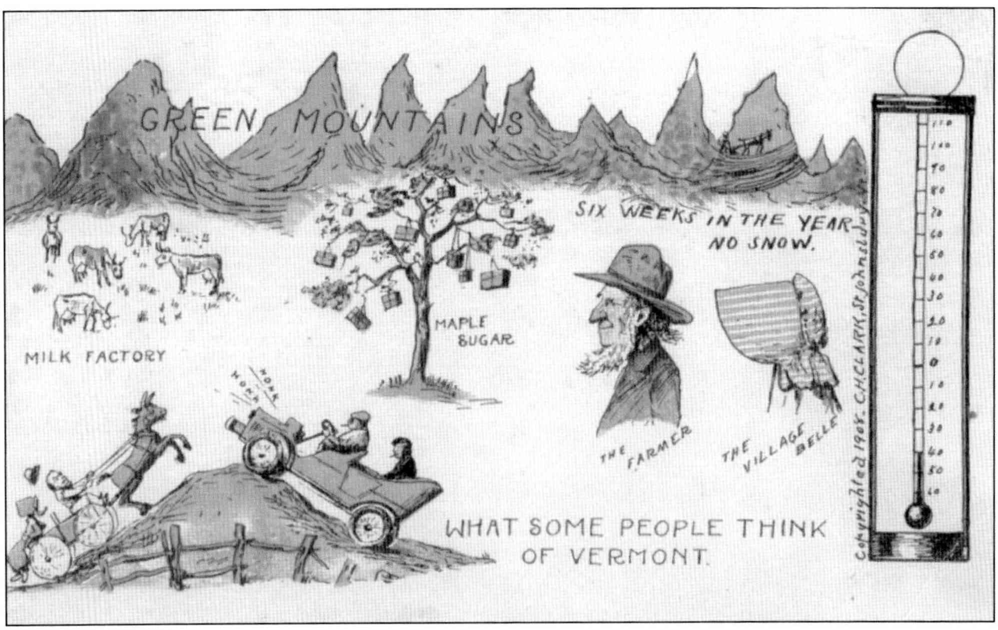

Cartoon postcards, usually purchased by visitors from out of state, made fun of Vermont images but defined the spirit of the tourists interacting with local people.

Another common form of postcard included poetry extolling the beauty of the hometown. A small image of Pearsons Hall at Middlebury College was pasted into a general opening in this stock card.

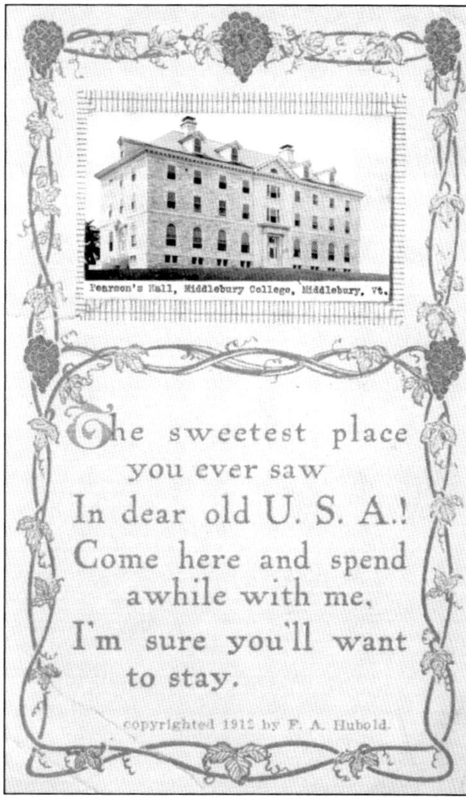

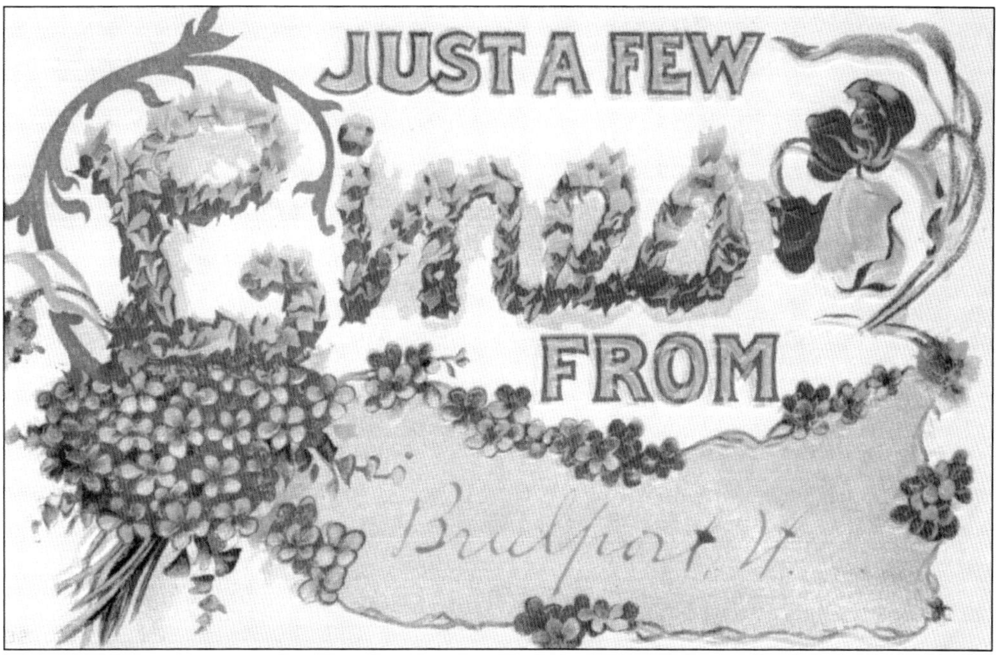

This floral card with words spelled out in violets is one of the few cards from the small town of Bridport.

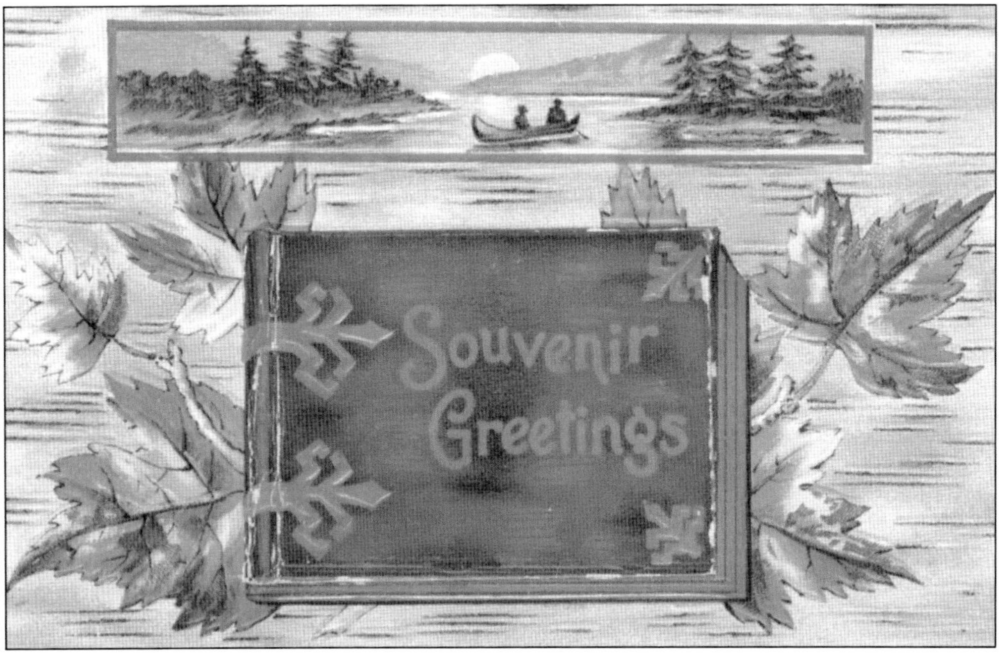

Another interesting form of postcard from the beginning of the 20th century was the accordion card, in which a string of small images pulled out from a flap of paper on the face of the card. This accordion card included a series of early black-and-white images of the town and college.

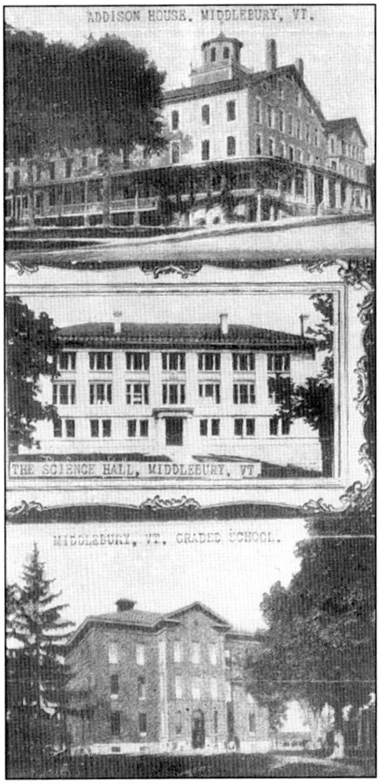

The buildings shown in this section of the accordian card foldout, from top to bottom, are the Addison House, the Science Hall at Middlebury College, and the Graded School.

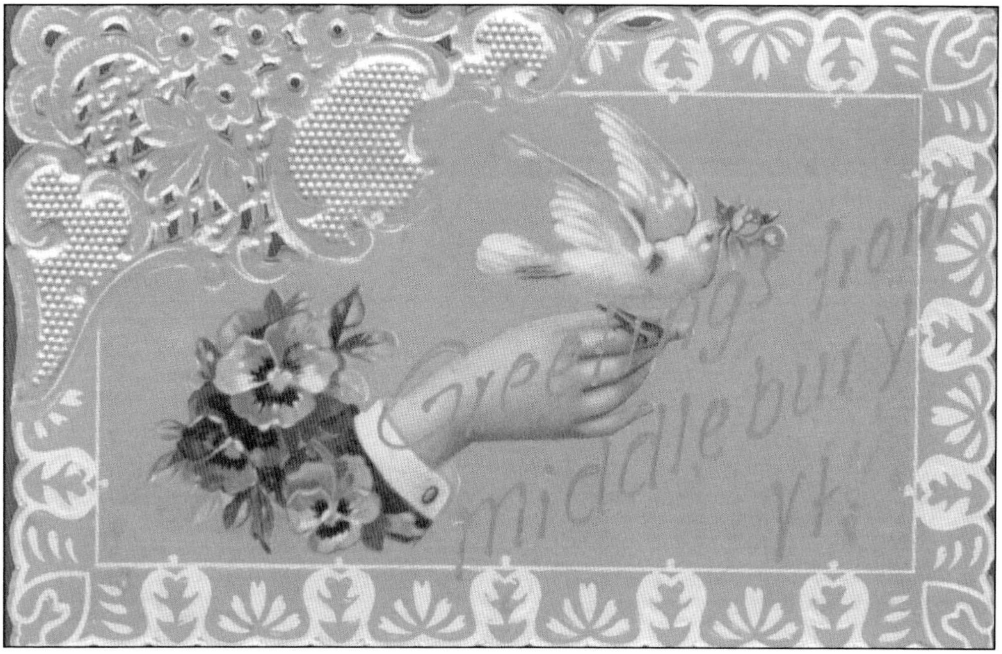

Another type of stock card included cutout sections, creating a lacy, doilylike effect. Again, the local town is written onto the card, in this case in gold letters.

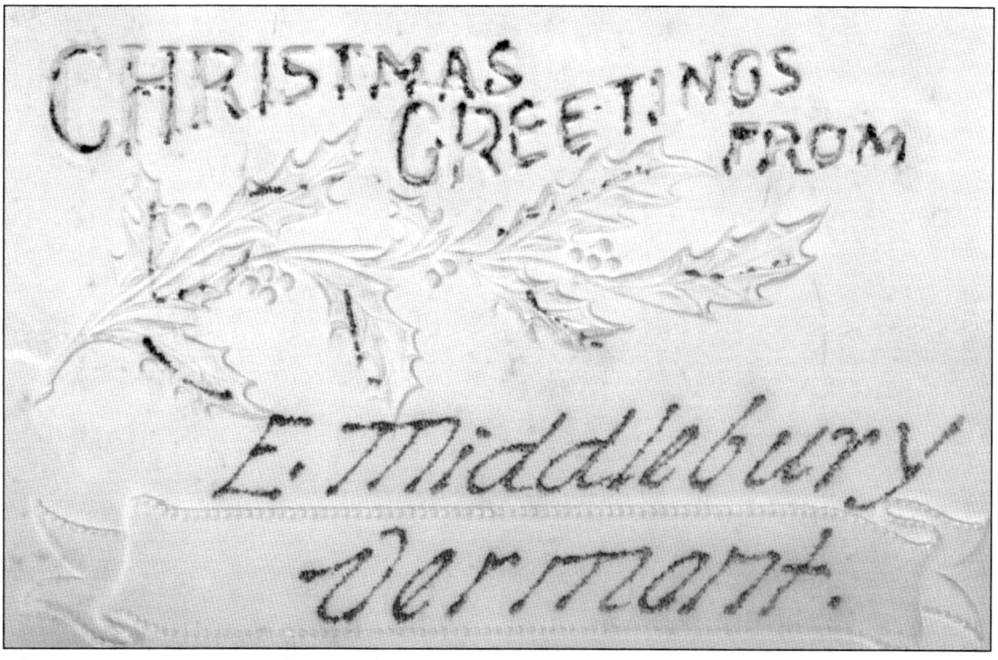

Christmas greetings were also sent by way of postcards. The words on this card are all written in glitter.

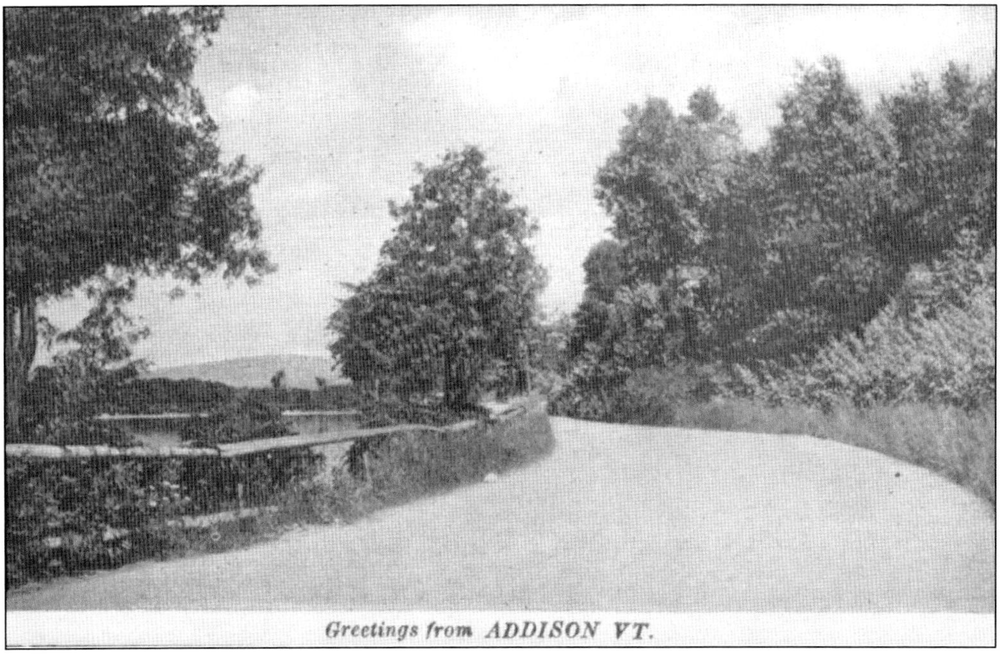

This stock card, labeled for Addison, was used for many areas throughout New England. The image of a general roadside with maple trees and grasses was equally useful in Vermont and Connecticut.

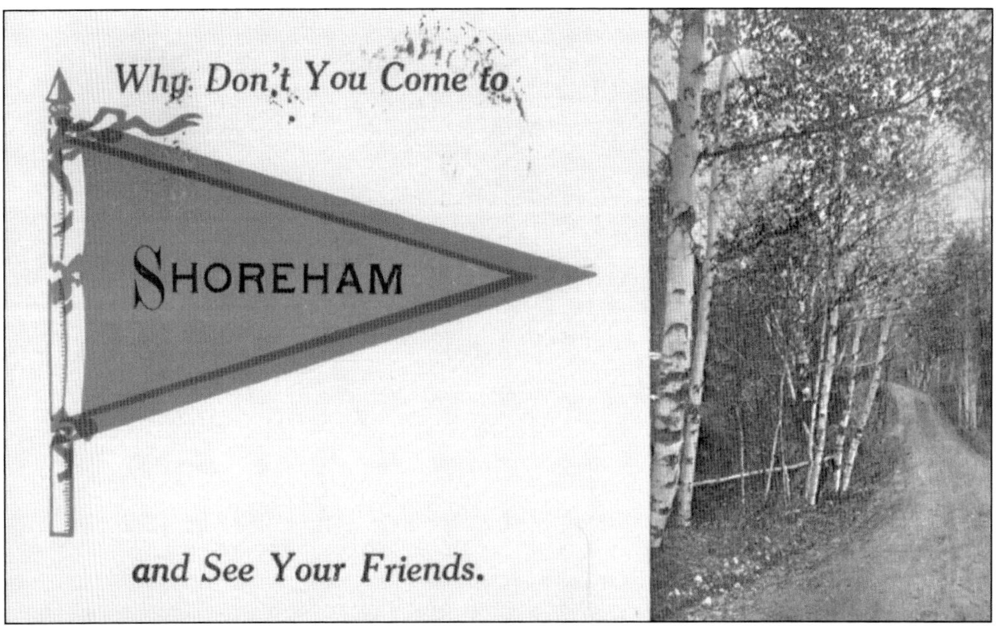

Personalized postcards were produced for even very small towns, such as Shoreham.

Certainly one of the most beautiful seasons in Vermont is winter. There are, however, a surprisingly small number of winter scene postcards among the early images of Middlebury. Perhaps the general inconvenience of winter reduced the appeal of snowy scenes to those who purchased postcards.

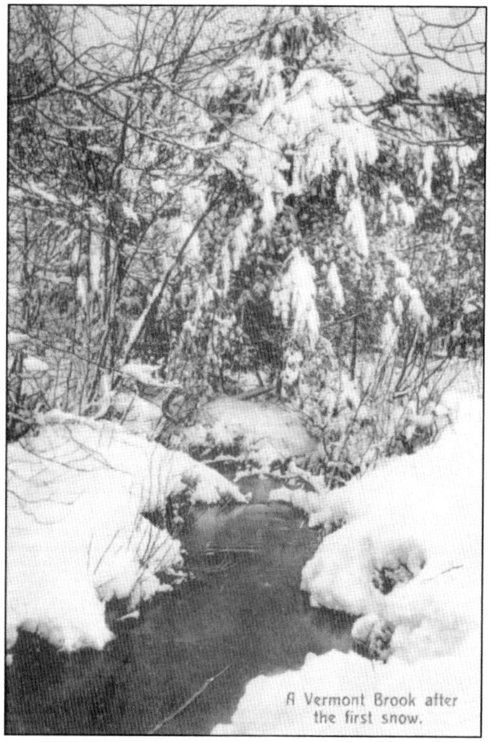

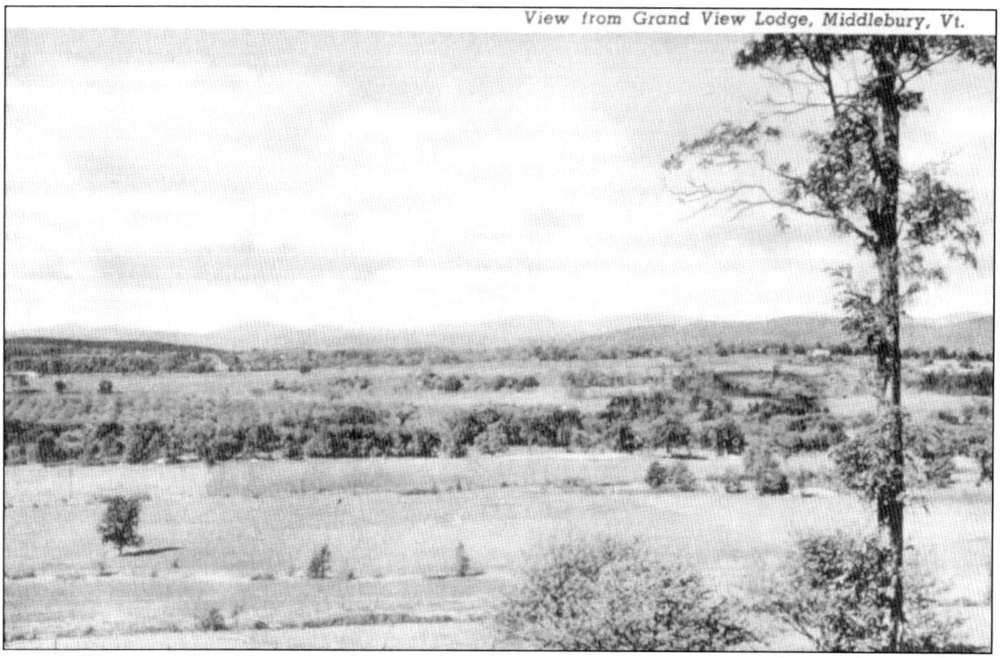

Many early postcards of Middlebury show the long views across the rolling foothills to Lake Champlain and the distant Adirondacks to the west. Few of these actually capture well the broad sweeping landscape around Middlebury. This view from Snake Mountain, northwest of Middlebury from the Grand View Lodge, looks westward across Bridport to the mountains.

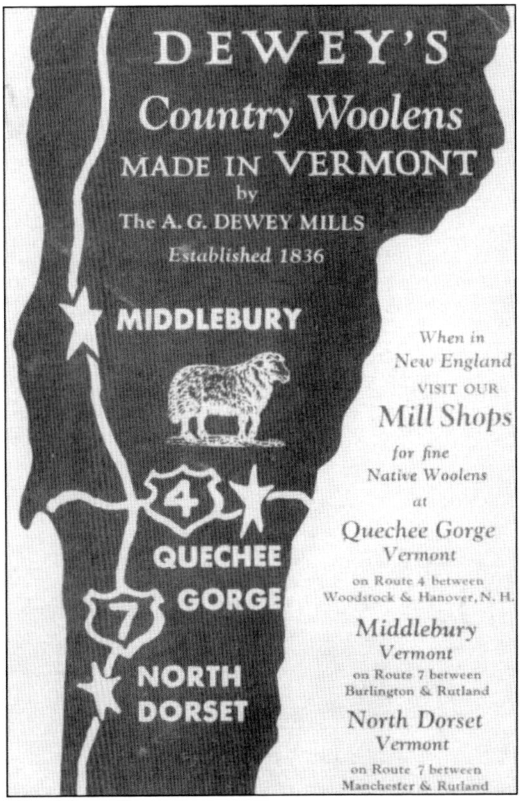

Postcards were also used as advertisements.

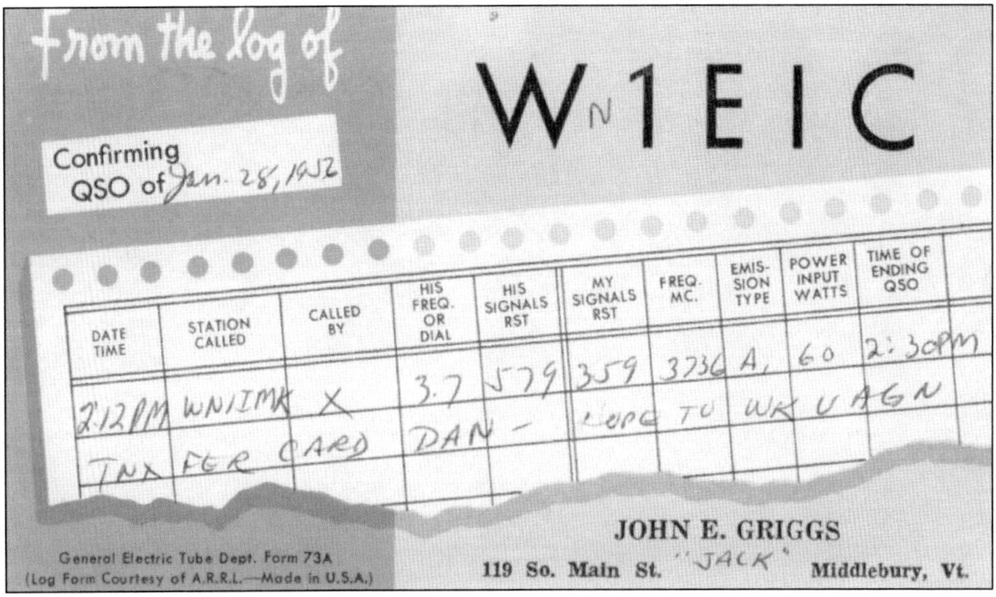

Postcards were popular among shortwave radio operators to document signals received from distant locations.

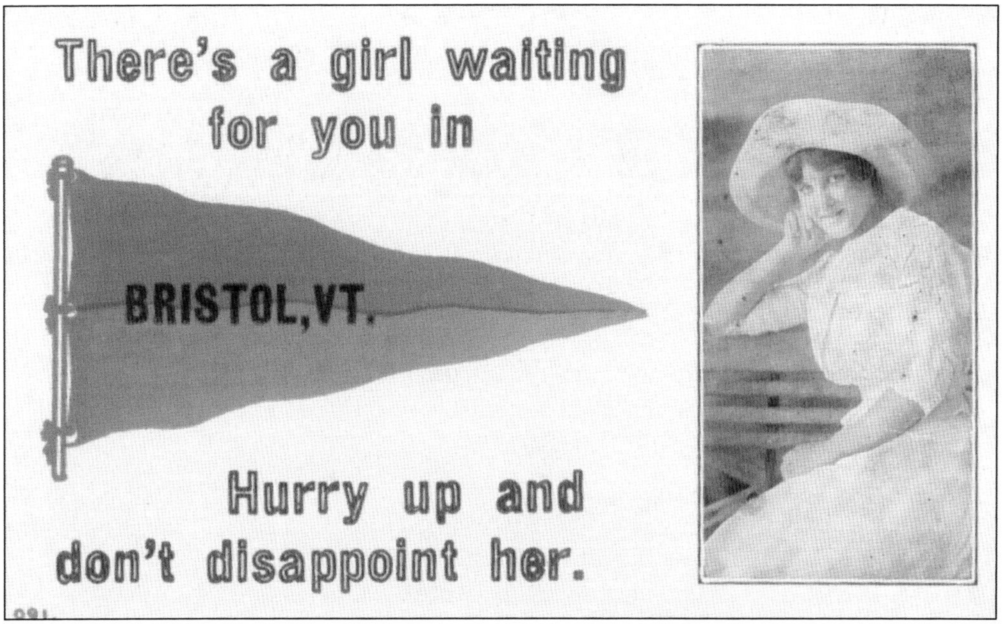

Some cards were a part of late Victorian courtship, showing beautiful girls and suggestions of eager contact.

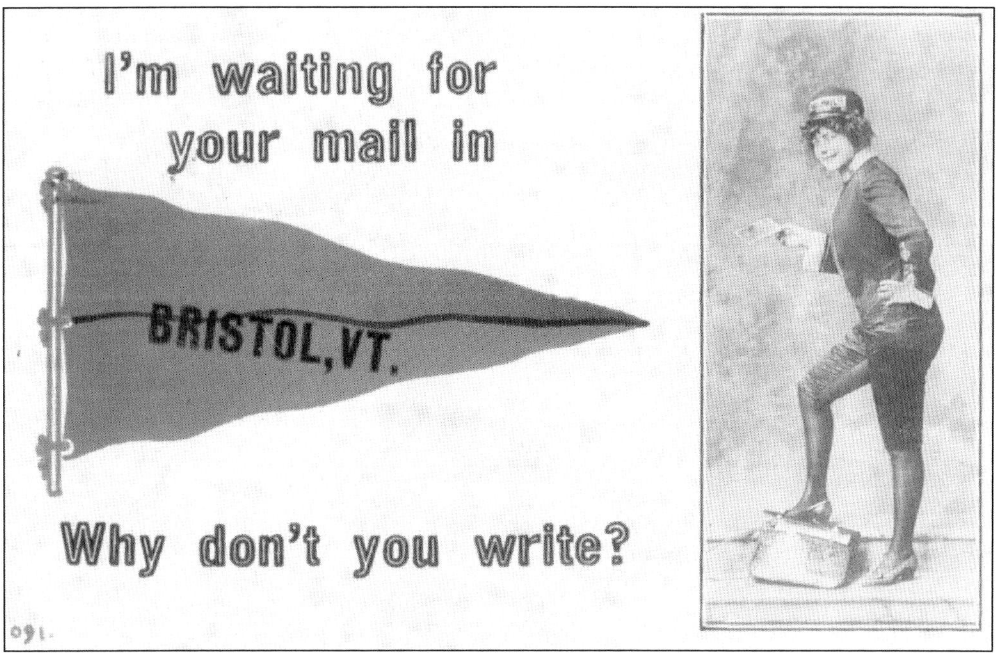

Apparently Bristol was a lonely place reaching out to the world for mail.

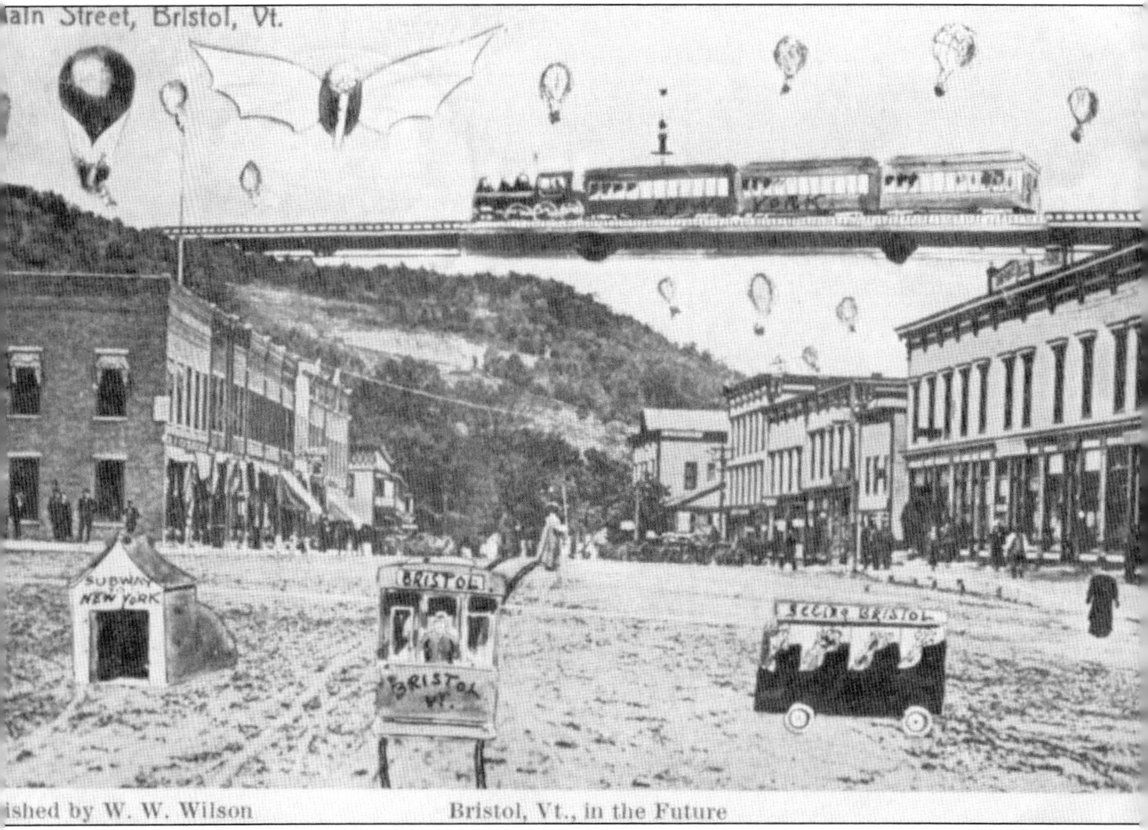

This "future card" from 1908 is typical of a series of postcards produced for many locations, using a recognizable town scene with added images of future urbanization. According to this card, the expansion of the New York City subway system would one day reach as far as Bristol.

BIBLIOGRAPHY

Anderson, George A. *Bread Loaf School of English: The First Fifty Years.* Middlebury, Vt.: Middlebury College Press, 1969.

Andres, Glenn M. *A Walking History of Middlebury*. Middlebury, Vt.: The Sheldon Museum, 1997.

Bain, David H. *The College on the Hill.* Middlebury, Vt.: Middlebury College Press, 1999.

Graaf, Nancy. *At Home in Vermont: A Middlebury Album.* Middlebury, Vt.: Rainbow Books, 1977.

Petersen, James E. *Otter Creek: The Indian Road.* Salisbury, Vt.: Dunmore House, 1990.

Petersen, James and Max. *Lord Dunmore's Lake*. Salisbury, Vt.: Dunmore House, 1998.

Petersen, Max P. *Salisbury: From Birth to Bicentennial.* Salisbury, Vt.: Dunmore House, 1991.

Smith, H. P. *History of Addison County*. Syracuse, N.Y.: D. Mason Company, 1886.

Swift, Samuel. *History of the Town of Middlebury*. Rutland, Vt.: Charles E. Tuttle, 1971.

Town of Brandon, The. *Brandon, Vermont 1761–1961*. The Town of Brandon, 1961.

Vermont Division of Historic Preservation. *The Historic Architecture of Addison County.* State of Vermont, 1992.

INDEX